90 0275441 5

KW-255-024

INDONESIA

ASSESSMENT 1995

Development in Eastern Indonesia

The **Institute of Southeast Asian Studies (ISEAS)** was established as an autonomous organisation in 1968. It is a regional research centre for scholars and other specialists concerned with modern Southeast Asia, particularly the many-faceted problems of stability and security, economic development, and political and social change.

The Institute is governed by a twenty-two-member Board of Trustees comprising nominees from the Singapore Government, the National University of Singapore, the various Chambers of Commerce, and professional and civic organisations. A ten-man Executive Committee oversees day-to-day operations; it is chaired by the Director, the Institute's chief academic and administrative officer.

The Research School of Pacific and Asian Studies (RSPAS) at the Australian National University is home to the Indonesia Project and the Department of Political and Social Change, which were the joint organisers of the Indonesia Update Conference in 1995. The annual Update offers an overview of recent economic and political developments, and also devotes attention to a theme of particular importance in Indonesia's development. Financial support for the conference series is provided by the Australian Agency for International Development and this was supplemented in 1995 by a generous grant from the Ford Foundation. The *Indonesia Assessment* series contains papers presented at these conferences, and also sometimes includes other specially commissioned pieces.

The **Indonesia Project** is a major international centre of research and graduate training on the economy of Indonesia. Established in 1965, it is well known and respected in Indonesia and in other places where Indonesia attracts serious scholarly and official interest. The Project obtains its core funding from the Australian National University; in addition, the Australian Department of Foreign Affairs and Trade has provided an annual grant since 1980. A major activity is producing and distributing three times a year an internationally recognised journal on the Indonesian economy, the *Bulletin of Indonesian Economic Studies*, each issue of which contains a Survey of Recent Economic Developments. The **Department of Political and Social Change** focuses on research in domestic politics, social processes and state-society relations in Asia and the Pacific. It has a long established interest in Indonesian affairs.

INDONESIA

ASSESSMENT 1995

Development in Eastern Indonesia

Edited by Colin Barlow and Joan Hardjono

WITHDRAWN
FROM
UNIVERSITY OF PLYMOUTH
LIBRARY SERVICES

Research School of Pacific and Asian Studies
AUSTRALIAN NATIONAL UNIVERSITY
Canberra

 INSTITUTE OF SOUTHEAST ASIAN STUDIES
Singapore

UNIVERSITY OF PLYMOUTH

Item No. 9002754415

Date 1 5 JUL 1996 S

Class No. 338.9598 IND

Contl. No. 9813055189

LIBRARY SERVICES

Published jointly by

Institute of Southeast Asian Studies
Heng Mui Keng Terrace
Pasir Panjang
Singapore 119596

Research School of Pacific and Asian Studies
Australian National University
Canberra ACT 9299
Australia

All rights reserved. No part of this publication may be reproduced, stored in a retrieval system, or transmitted in any form or by any means, electronic, mechanical, photocopying, recording or otherwise, without the prior permission of the Institute of Southeast Asian Studies.

© 1996 Institute of Southeast Asian Studies, Singapore

The responsibility for facts and opinions in this publication rests exclusively with the authors and their interpretations do not necessarily reflect the views or the policy of ISEAS or the RSPAS.

Cataloguing in Publication Data

Indonesia Assessment 1995; development in eastern Indonesia/edited by Colin Barlow and Joan Hardjono.
1. Indonesia—Economic policy.
2. Indonesia—Economic conditions—1945–
3. Indonesia—Social conditions.
4. Rural development—Indonesia.
5. Indonesia—Politics and government—1966–
I. Barlow, Colin.
II. Hardjono, Joan.
III. Title: Development in eastern Indonesia.
DS644.4   I41 1995   1996   sls 95–105583

ISBN 981–3055–18–9

Printed and bound in Singapore by Prime Packaging Industries Pte Ltd

Contents

Tables and Figures

Figures

Glossary

abangan	nominal Muslim
ABRI	(Angkatan Bersenjata Republik Indonesia) Indonesian Armed Forces
adat	custom or tradition
AFTA	Asean Free Trade Association
AJI	(Aliansi Jurnalis Independen) Association of Independent Journalists
aliran	a school of thought or beliefs
aliran kepercayaan	traditional beliefs
ANU	Australian National University
APBN	(Anggaran Pendapatan dan Belanja Nasional) Routine and Development Budget
APEC	Asia Pacific Economic Cooperation
aparatur	administrative apparatus
ASEAN	Association of South East Asian Nations
AusAID	Australian Agency for International Development
bahasa Indonesia	the Indonesian language
BAKIN	(Badan Koordinasi Inteligen) Intelligence Coordinating Body
BAKORSTANAS	(Badan Koordinasi Stabilitas Nasional) National Stability Coordinating Body

Bangu Udu	head of clan [Savu]
BAPEPAM	(Badan Pengembangan Pasar Modal) Capital Markets Regulatory Agency
BAPPEDA	(Badan Perencanaan Pembangunan Daerah) Provincial/District Level Planning Body
BAPPENAS	(Badan Perencanaan Pembangunan Nasional National Development Planning Body
BI	Bank of Indonesia
Bimas	(*Bimbingan Massal*) Agricultural extension program (now finished)
BKPM	(Badan Koordinasi Penanaman Modal) Capital Investment Coordinating Board
BPIS	(Badan Pengelola Industri Strategis) Agency for the Development of Strategic Industries
BPPC	(Badan Penyangga dan Pemasaran Cengkeh) The Cloves Marketing Board
BPR	(Bank Perkreditan Rakyat) People's Credit Bank
BPS	(Biro Pusat Statistik) Central Bureau of Statistics
BULOG	(Badan Urusan Logistik) Food Procurement Agency
BUMN	(Badan Usaha Milik Negara) State enterprise
bupati	administrative head of a *kabupaten* (district)
CAP	Development Budget Reserves
CBS	Central Bureau of Statistics
CCO	crude coconut oil
CEPT	Common Effective Preferential Tariff
CGI	Consultative Group on Indonesia
CIDA	Canadian International Development Agency
CPO	crude palm oil

CMR	child mortality rate
CPI	consumer price index
CSIS	Centre for Strategic and International Studies
CUSO	Canadian University Service Overseas
dalang	puppet master in a shadow play
DDI	(Dewan Dakwah Islam) Moslem Missionary Council
DDI	Direct Domestic Investment
daerah	region
daerah percontohan	a *kabupaten* selected for the Local Autonomy Pilot Project
Delsos	a Catholic Church NGO working on local development
desa	village
Dinas Tk.I	provincial-level service in the provincial government administrative structure
DIP	(Daftar Isian Proyek) Project Budget Allocation
DPR	(Dewan Perwakilan Rakyat) The People's Representative Council
DPRD	(Dewan Perwakilan Rakyat Daerah) The People's Representative Body at provincial and district levels
DRC	domestic resource cost
Eastern Indonesia	The provinces of North, Central, South and South East Sulawesi, West and East Nusa Tenggara, Maluku, East Timor and Irian Jaya
Eastern Indonesia-Plus	The nine provinces of Eastern Indonesia together with the four provinces of Kalimantan
ERP	Effective Rate of Protection
ESCAP	Economic and Social Commission for Asia and the Pacific

FDI	Foreign Direct Investment
FWI	(Forum Wartawan Independen) Independent Journalists Forum
GATT	General Agreement on Tariffs and Trade
GBHN	(Garis-Garis Besar Haluan Negara) Broad Outline of State Policy
GDFCF	Gross domestic fixed capital formation
GDP	gross domestic product
Gersatera	(Gerakan Desa Sejahtera) Prosperous Rural Movement
GMIT	(Gereja Majlis Injili Timor) Protestant Church in Timor
GNP	Gross National Product
Golkar	(Golongan Karya) government political party
GRDP	Gross Regional Domestic Product
GRP	Gross Regional Product
GUPPI	(Gabungan Usaha Pengembangan Pendidikan Islam) The Islamic Organisation of Golkar
gula sabu	Syrup from the *Borassus* palm [Savu]
HYV	high-yielding varieties of crops
IBT	(Indonesia Bagian Timur) Eastern Indonesia
ICMI	(Ikatan Cendekiawan Muslim Indonesia) Association of Indonesian Muslim Intellectuals
ICOR	incremental capital-output ratio
IDT	(*Inpres Desa Tertinggal*) Presidental Instruction for Assistance to Backward Villages
IGGI	Inter-Governmental Group on Indonesia
ijon	the sale of crops before harvest
ikat	a type of hand-weaving in Eastern Indonesia

IMR	Infant Mortality Rate
INKUD	primary cooperative
Inmas	*(Intensifikasi Massal)* Rice intensification program without financial assistance
Inpres	*(Instruksi Presiden)* Presidential Instruction for Special Grants Programs
IPTN	Indonesian aircraft industry production plant
IRR	internal rate of return
IRSAM	Interregional Social Accounting Matrix
ISEAS	Institute of Southeast Asian Studies
ISIC	International Standard Industrial Classification
jilbab	female headgear that covers head and ears but not the face
kabupaten	district (administrative unit below province)
kanwil	*(kantor wilayah)* provincial-level office of a sectoral Department
Kebatinan	mysticism movement
Kecamatan	sub-district (administrative unit below *kabupaten*)
Kerogo	sub-clan
KNIL	(Koninkliik Nederlands Indisch Leger) Dutch colonial army
KONI	(Konite Olahraga Nasional Indonesia) Indonesian National Sports Committee
KOPKAMTIB	(Komando Operasi Pemulihan Keamanan dan Ketertiban) Law and Order Restoration Command
kretek	traditional cigarette containing cloves
KUD	(Koperasi Unit Desa) village cooperative
KUHP	Penal Law

labuhan	marine fishing area
Lamtoro	the *Leucaena leucocephala* shrub
LIPI	(Lembaga Ilmu Pengetahuan Indonesia) Indonesian Institute of Sciences
LNG	liquified natural gas
M1	narrow money
M2	broad money
MDI	(Majelis Dakwah Islamiyah) Islamic Council
MMR	maternal mortality rate
Mone Ama	Board of priests [Savu]
MPR	(Majelis Perwakilan Rakyat) The People's Consultative Assembly
NGO	non-government organisation
NIT	(Negara Indonesia Timur) Federal State of East Indonesia
NU	(Nahdatul Ulama) Muslim Scholars' Organisation
ODA	overseas development assistance
OPEC	Organisation of Petroleum Exporting Countries
OPM	(Organisasi Papua Merdeka) Free Papua Organisation
PCPP	(Persatuan Cendekiawan Pembangunan Pancasila) Union of Intellectuals for the Development of *Pancasila*
PDI	(Partai Demokrasi Indonesia) Indonesian Democratic Party
pegawai negeri	public servant
PEM	protein energy malnutrition
Permesta	regional rebellion in North Sulawesi in 1958

Pertamina	the state-owned oil company
pencekalan	prohibition on speaking in public
Perda	(Peraturan Daerah) Provincial Regulation
PERTI	Islamic Political Party (no longer exists)
pesantren	Islamic school
petuanan	traditional marine tenure system
PJP I	(*Pembangunan Jangka Panjang I*) First Period of Long-term Development (1969-94)
PJP II	(*Pembangunan Jangka Panjang II*) Second Period of Long-term Development (1994-2019)
PKK	Family Welfare Movement
PKPLN	Foreign Commercial Borrowing Team
PLN	State Electricity Company
PMA	(*Penanaman Modal Asing*) foreign investment
PMDA	(*Penanaman Modal Dalam Negeri*) domestic investment
PKPLN	Foreign Commercial Borrowing Coordinating Team
Posyandu	primary health care post
PP	(*Peraturan Pemerintah*) Government Regulation
PRRI	(*Pemerintah Revolusioner Republik Indonesia*) regional rebellion in Sumatra during the late 1950s
prahu or *perahu*	non-motorised sailing vessel
Puskesmas	(Pusat Kesehatan Masyarakat) community health centre
PUSKUD	Primary Cooperative
PWI	(Persatuan Wartawan Indonesia) Association of Indonesian Journalists
Repelita	(*Rencana Pembangunan Lima Tahun*) Five-Year Development Plan

RSPAS	Research School of Pacific and Asian Studies
SAM	Social Accounting Matrix
sasi	customary regulation of access to marine resources
SBI	(*Sertifikat Bank Indonesia*) Bank of Indonesia Certificate
SBPU	(*Surat Berharga Pasar Uang*) Money Market Securities
sero	permanent fish trap
SITC	Standard International Trade Clasification
SOKSI	(Sentral Organisasi Karyawan Sosialis Indonesia) Indonesian Socialist Workers' Organisation
SPSI	(Serikat Pekerja Seluruh Indonesia) All-Indonesia Workers' Union
SRC	(Sumbangan Rehabilitasi Cengkeh) Cloves Rehabilitation Fund
SUCOFINDO	PT Superintending Company of Indonesia
SWKP	(Sumbangan Wajib Khusus Petani) Farmers' Obligatory Contribution
TBA	traditional birth attendant
tripang or *teripang*	sea cucumber
uda	clan [Savu]
ulama	Moslem scholar
UNSRAT	University of Sam Ratulangi, Manado
VA/O	value-added to output ratio
WALHI	(Wahana Lingkungan Hidup Indonesia) Indonesian Environmental Forum
wawasan nusantara	archipelago concept
wini	subdivision in a matrilineal line [Savu]

WHO	World Health Organization
WN	World Neighbors
WTO	World Trade Organisation
YAO	Yayasan Alpha Omega
yayasan	foundation
YGM	(Yayasan Geo Meno) Geo Meno Foundation
YTN	(Yayasan Tana Nua) Tana Nua Foundation

Contributors

Professor Heinz Arndt founded the Indonesia Project in the Department of Economics, Research School of Pacific Studies, Australian National University, in 1964. He also founded the *Bulletin of Indonesian Economic Studies*, the leading international journal on the Indonesian economy which he edited from 1965-82. He has written extensively on Indonesian affairs, and contributed in major ways to understanding the Indonesian economy. He has been one of Australia's foremost economists, working in monetary and international economics as well as in development studies. He now edits the influential *Australia Pacific Economic Literature*.

Professor Iwan Azis has been Chairperson of the Department of Economics at the University of Indonesia, and is currently a Visiting Professor at Cornell University. He specialises in planning economics, regional and environmental economies and international trade, and has written many papers in these spheres. He has worked in research institutions in Japan, Europe and North America, and is a member of several editorial boards including that of the *Bulletin of Indonesian Economic Studies*.

Dr Colin Barlow is a Senior Fellow in Economics at the Research School of Pacific Studies, Australian National University. He has worked much on regional development, doing this recently in East Nusa Tenggara. He is President of the Nusatenggara Association, an NGO assisting small developments in West Timor. His latest book (with Sisira Jayasuriya and Suan Tan) is the *World Rubber Industry* (Routledge, 1994).

Dr Richard Chauvel is a Senior Research Fellow of the Peter Hastings Memorial Fellowship and a Senior Lecturer, Department of Asian Studies and Languages at the Victoria University of Technology, Melbourne. He teaches South East Asian History and Politics at the Victoria University of Technology. He has research interests in the 19th and 20th century political history of Maluku and Irian Jaya. He is currently working on a history of the West New Guinea dispute under the Peter Hastings Memorial Fellowship.

Ir A.P.Y. Djogo is Director of Agriculture at the Kupang Polytechnic, East Nusa Tenggara, and a Lecturer at the University of Nusa Cendana. He is Chairperson of the NGO *Yayasan Geo Meno*, and collaborates with the Indonesian Department of Agriculture and Ford Foundation on ecosystem research. He is also an expert on soils, and has worked in several World Bank and other development projects.

Professor James Fox did his first fieldwork on the island of Rote in 1965, and has continued to return to Eastern Indonesia regularly over the past thirty years. He visited Rote and Timor most recently in July of this year, where he accompanied a *60 Minutes* TV team who was preparing a program on the problems of traditional Eastern Indonesian fishermen. He has written books and papers on a diversity of subjects ranging from kinship and ritual changes to palm ecology and seaworm ceremonies.

Dr Afan Gaffar is Chairperson of the Department of Government at Gadjah Mada University, Yogyakarta. He is active in political discussions in Indonesia, and has written many papers contributing to these. He is the author of *Javanese Voters* (Gadjah Mada Press, Yogyakarta, 1992), and is the Co-chairperson for Training of the Political Science Association of Indonesia.

Dr Joan Hardjono has a PhD in Geography from the University of New England, Armidale, and teaches at Padjadjaran State University, Bandung. She has lived in Indonesia since the late 1950s, and has carried out extensive research in rural areas. She has covered topics including transmigration, education, rural development and environmental change in Indonesia. Her major publications include *Transmigration in Indonesia* (Oxford University Press, Singapore, 1977) and *Land, Labour and Livelihood in a West Java Village* (Gadjah Mada University Press, Yogyakarta, 1987).

Dr Hadi Soesastro is Executive Director of the Centre for Strategic and International Studies in Jakarta, and a Lecturer at the University of Indonesia. He is a macroeconomist with special interests in trade, technology and international political economy. He is also Chairperson of the Pacific Economic Community Cooperating Group. He has written many papers on the Indonesian economy, and is well known for his book (with

Mari Pangestu) on *Technological Challenge in the Asia-Pacific Economy* (Allen and Unwin, 1990).

Mr Cliff Marlessy is the Executive Secretary of the Irian Jaya NGO Forum, and has been working on community development in both Irian Jaya and Maluku for many years. He has recently been involved in Seram (Central Maluku) with researchers from the Biodiversity Convention Network.

Dr Ben Mboi is a member of the Supreme Advisory Council of Indonesia. He served two successive terms as governor of his home province of East Nusa Tenggara, and prior to this had a distinguished career in public health. He was a member of the People's Consultative Assembly (MPR) for fifteen years. Dr Mboi has written extensively on Indonesian political development and history, and in 1986 he and his wife, Ibu Nafsiah, jointly received the Magsaysay Award.

Dr Nafsiah Mboi is an Indonesian paediatrician and Member of Parliament. She is also a member of the Global Commission on Women's Health and the Indonesian National Working Group for AIDS. For thirty years before being elected to Parliament in 1992 she was a civil servant with the Health Department, working in key posts at regional level. For ten years she led the Family Welfare Movement (PKK) in East Nusa Tenggara. She has been active in HIV/AIDS work, and has concentrated on NGO capacity-building in this respect. She and her husband received the Magsaysay Award in 1986.

Professor Lucky Sondakh is Dean of the Faculty of Agricultural Economics and Animal Husbandry at the University of Sam Ratulangi, Manado, North Sulawesi. He is also a member of the Committee on Society, Politics, Culture and Philosophy under the Indonesian National Research Council. He is a specialist in agricultural economics, and has written widely in this area.

Dr Frans Radja Haba is the founder and Director of the Ie Rai Foundation, an NGO working for community development on Savu Island since 1981. He worked for many years as a medical doctor, finishing in 1984 as head of the District Health Service in Kupang, East Nusa Tenggara. He has recently been a consultant to the Australian-Indonesian Integrated Area Development Project in East Nusa Tenggara, and has also collaborated with the World Bank in various projects. He is chairperson of two private companies in Kupang.

Dr Riwanto Tirtosudarmo is a Research Associate at the Centre for Population and Manpower Studies, Indonesian Institute of Sciences (LIPI), Jakarta. He is currently working on child labour and educational planning in East and West Nusa Tenggara, and is a member of the LIPI-ANU Eastern Indonesian Population and Development Research Project. He has worked in the past on transmigration problems.

Acknowledgments

Colin Barlow and Joan Hardjono

Three organisations contributed major resources to the running of the August 1995 *Indonesia Update* conference and the preparation for publication of this *Indonesia Assessment, 1995*. The Ford Foundation, the Australian Agency for International Development (AusAID) and the Australian Department of Foreign Affairs and Trade all provided generous grants, and the Research School of Pacific and Asian Studies (RSPAS) of the Australian National University furnished vital help in kind including services of staff and use of facilities. The organisers and editors wish to thank these groups for their help, which further allowed the Update to be run without a registration fee and hence attract a wide range of participants.

As well, the Institute of Southeast Asian Studies (ISEAS) in Singapore agreed once more to publish *Indonesia Assessment, 1995*, giving access to its first class printing facilities and wide distribution network throughout South East Asia and elsewhere. This follows the successful and high quality publication by ISEAS of *Indonesia Assessment, 1994*, and is a huge advantage which the editors gratefully acknowledge.

Large numbers of people contributed to the 1995 Update. Special mention must be made of Professor Heinz Arndt, the doyen of Australian Indonesianists, who generously agreed to open the Update in his eightieth year. The speakers who delivered such excellent papers had a vital role, and the chairpersons and discussants not only strengthened sessions but also provided lively comments which boosted the tenor of the conference. Many people added to discussions from the floor.

The members of the small conference secretariat gave crucial assistance, and here special mention must be made of Winnie Pradela from the Indonesia Project in the Department of Economics, and Bev Fraser and Allison Ley from the Department of Political and Social Change. These three persons all spent long hours spent in checking applications, keeping accounts, organising conference dinners, looking after speakers, and making sure in so many ways that the conference itself proceeded smoothly. Shannon Smith of the Department of Political and Social Change coordinated contacts with the press. Members of the Association of Indonesian Students provided good advice, and likewise gave time as aides during the proceedings. Drs Daliyo of the Indonesian Institute of Sciences, Jakarta, helped in preparing background statistics.

Lulu Turner, Department of Political and Social Change, did major work in editing this volume and contributed the index, while Kerri Potter did most keyboard work. Triena Ong, Managing Editor of ISEAS, pleasantly and efficiently handled the transformation from photo-ready copy to published book.

Finally, Merle Ricklefs, Director of the RSPAS, Hal Hill, Head of the Indonesia Project, and Harold Crouch, Chris Manning and Ross McLeod, gave valuable advice. Warwick McKibbin, Head of the Economics Department, supplied direct support through allowing use of his departmental staff and equipment. Officials of the Indonesian Embassy in Canberra provided guidance, and also helped look after some speakers.

The efforts of all these persons are much appreciated, and they are gratefully thanked. It is hoped that this publication of proceedings by the Institute of South East Asian Studies will be seen as an appropriate testament to their efforts.

Opening Address

Heinz W. Arndt

This is the twelfth annual Indonesia Update. The series, which began after my formal departure from the Economics Department and the Indonesia Project, has been developed by Hal Hill and his colleagues into an immensely valuable, popular and influential event. Each conference covers recent developments in Indonesia and a special theme — education, politics, labour, or the financial system, for example. This year the special theme is Eastern Indonesia. Let me, in this Opening Address, give a little background to each part.

Recent developments

In a lecture I have written for next month's conference to celebrate the 40th anniversary of Gadjah Mada University, I have contrasted 'Then and Now', my impressions of Indonesia during my first visit in 1964 and what Indonesia looks like in 1995. The transformation that has occurred during these thirty years is almost incredible. Sustained economic growth at an average rate of more than 6 per cent has more than trebled per-capita income. From near the bottom of the World Bank listing of 'low-income' countries, Indonesia has become one of the booming, industrialising 'middle-income' countries. The proportion of the Indonesian people living in poverty has declined from over 70 to well under 20 per cent. There have been striking improvements in almost every sector of the economy. In place of the tiny, inefficient manufacturing industry of the 1960s, Indonesia now has a large, diversified and increasingly export-oriented manufacturing sector. Rapid rise in rice yields has made it possible to reconcile greatly improved nutrition standards with food self-sufficiency. The infrastructure of road and air transport, and of telecommunications, has undergone a virtual revolution. Remarkable improvements in the literacy and infant mortality rates reflect expansion in health and education services. Rising levels of income and education, reinforced by the effort that has gone into family planning, have yielded a significant decline in the birth rate. Rapid growth of industry and services has created enough jobs for a workforce increasing by more than two million a year without a serious rise in unemployment or underemployment. Television sets in almost every house, a superabundance of cars, newspapers and bookshops, all attest to the rise of a substantial middle class.

Indonesia in the early years of the New Order had two pieces of luck: the 'green revolution' of high-yielding varieties of rice and the OPEC oil boom. But overwhelmingly, Indonesia's outstanding economic performance is due to good economic management, prudent macroeconomic policies and, especially during the 1980s, major microeconomic reforms which in successive packages substantially deregulated the banking system and capital market, liberalised trade, facilitated direct foreign investment and reformed the tax system. Indonesia turned its back on the inward-looking strategy of industrial development based on import substitution by highly protected industries and opened its economy to international markets and competition. Most of the credit for this achievement is due to the remarkable group of technocrats led by Professor Widjojo and to the President, who listened to their advice, though the contribution of financial assistance by the IGGI consortium and technical assistance by World Bank and other foreign advisers was not negligible.

In recent years, there has, in the view of many observers, been some falling off in performance. The good record of macroeconomic policy is marred by an uncomfortably large foreign debt (although most of the capital inflow finances productive investment) and by weaknesses and troubles in the deregulated banking system, by a tendency to erode the principle of budget balance through off-budget expenditures and, partly in consequence of this, by too high a rate of growth of money supply and therefore an inflation rate nearly double the *Repelita* VI target. No less worrying is the impression that the impetus to microeconomic reform has stalled. The President's splendid support for the APEC principles of 'open regionalism' at Bogor notwithstanding, Indonesia's tariffs remain high, giving some industries absurdly high rates of effective protection. Cement, sugar, plywood and many other industries are controlled by lucrative, well-connected monopolies. Little progress, indeed some retrogression, is evident in reform of the taxation and legal systems. One cannot help wondering whether these signs of drift reflect a loss of influence on economic policy of the team that guided it so successfully in the first quarter century of the New Order. No doubt the 'succession' issue, with the political uncertainties it is generating, is also casting its shadow forward. I look forward to hearing more about all this from Dr Hadi Soesastro.

On political developments, which Dr Afan Gaffar will discuss, I can claim no expertise. I expect we shall hear from him about the succession

1

Introduction

Colin Barlow

Nineteen ninety five is a celebration year for the Republic of Indonesia, being the fiftieth anniversary of its independencefrom the Netherlands. On 17 August 1945, Sukarno read the declaration of independence outside his house in Jakarta, and the red and white flag was raised. Thus was born the biggest nation in South East Asia, which has grown today to over 190 million people living in 27 provinces across a great archipelago (Figure 1.1).

This volume, marking Indonesia's fiftieth year, is based on papers delivered at the annual *Indonesia Update* Conference, held at the Australian National University, Canberra, on 25 and 26 August 1995. Its format once more follows that of previous volumes and updates, with a first part devoted to reviews of current economic and political developments throughout Indonesia, and a second part covering a special topic. This time that topic is the key issue of *Development in Eastern Indonesia*.

This introductory chapter sets out to give general background on Indonesia as a whole, and more specific information about Eastern Indonesia. It is intended to inform the discussions of subsequent chapters, especially where readers are not familiar with the Indonesian scene. But it is also meant to put those discussions into the wider perspective helpful to appreciating major issues. Other general information on Eastern Indonesia is provided by Jones and Rahardjo (1995).

Changes

So much has altered in Indonesia since that flag-raising ceremony in 1945. In politics, the early turbulent years to the mid-1960s of finally expelling the Dutch, experimenting with various constitutional forms and dealing with regional dissidence all helped cement the idea of nationhood, and reinforced centralist tendencies that have persisted ever since.

Figure 1.1: *Indonesia and surrounding countries*

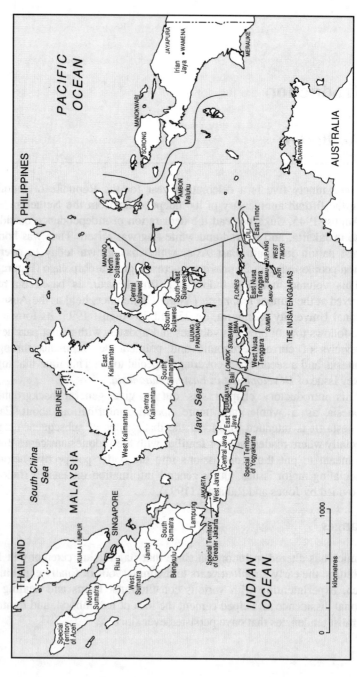

Then from the late 1960s there has been the long and relatively stable period of the New Order under President Soeharto, with its shifting power balances between army and *Golkar* and a continuation of authoritarian rule. But the huge accompanying economic changes and improvements in education have also seen the growth of a substantial middle class and the burgeoning of many national and regional non-government groups concerned with religious, cultural and other aspects including economic and social development. Such groups contribute much to the evolving social fabric and intellectual debate, and as growing elements have major long-run implications for the Indonesian polity.

Indonesia today enters middle age as a well-established nation with numerous good augurs for a the future. Yet it still faces enormous political difficulties, including the issues of succession to Soeharto dealt with in Chapter 3 and the challenges of continued regional disputes in Aceh, East Timor, and Irian Jaya. These disputes are at least partly associated with the problems of regional development addressed below in the context of Eastern Indonesia. The problems need to be tackled seriously in the course of securing the bright future suggested.

Economics

In economics, Professor Arndt has aptly described the transformation of Indonesia as 'incredible' (p.xxv), pinpointing great alterations that have occurred. As one indication of this shift, the average national gross domestic product per head of Rp1,336,000 or US$668 in 1992 (Table 1.1) had risen from well below US$100 (at 1992 prices) at the time of independence, and had indeed reached almost US$800 by 1995.

Meanwhile, the earlier dominant share of agriculture in the economy had given way to industry, which in a rapid recent advance had become the chief sector in 1990. By 1992, the latter occupied 21.8 per cent of GDP (gross domestic product), compared to 19.5 per cent for agriculture (Table 1.2) which had now come to occupy only 54 per cent of the Indonesian workforce (Table 1.3). The biggest components of manufacturing involved apparel, textiles and footwear, as well as plywood and oil and natural-gas processing. But the sector was now moving towards larger shares of products with heavy export orientation, including electronic equipment, chemicals and processed agricultural items. Manufacturing was undertaken by firms ranging in size from small family concerns of a few persons to huge companies including conglomerates. These conglomerates were spearheading growth in more capital-intensive spheres, which especially involved petroleum, steel and automobiles.

Table 1.1: *Major economic aspects, Indonesia and provinces, 1992*[a]

	GRDP[b] Rp billion at 1992 prices	GRDP per capita At 1992 prices, Rp '000	GRDP per capita % Annual real growth, 1983-92	Monthly expenditure > Rp.60,000 % of population
Sumatra	59,151	1,562	0.9	14.9
excluding oil	40,653	1,060	na	
Java-Bali	147,228	1,330	4.4	24.7
excluding oil	840,880	1,270	na	
Kalimantan	22,838	2,358	0.7	24.7
excluding oil	14,058	1,452	na	
Eastern Indonesia				
West Nusa Tenggara	1,870	535	4.9	7.0
East Nusa Tenggara	1,639	482	4.0	4.7
East Timor	386	489	5.4	9.4
North Sulawesi	1,962	769	4.6	14.4
Central Sulawesi	1,267	703	4.5	11.0
South Sulawesi	6,071	840	5.8	10.3
South East Sulawesi	1,063	733	4.6	7.8
Maluku	1,940	993	5.5	16.4
excluding oil	1,923	984	na	
Irian Jaya	3,059	1,733	1.7	22.3
excluding oil	2,814	1,594	na	
Total	19,257	788	4.6	na
excluding oil	18,995	777	na	
All Indonesia	248,583	1,336	2.5	na
excluding oil	214,395	1,152	na	

[a]For 1992 unless otherwise indicated. [b]GRDP=Gross regional domestic product   Sources: Biro Pusat Statistik, 1993b and 1989-94.

Table 1.2: *Composition of gross regional domestic product, Indonesia and provinces, 1992 (percentages)*[a]

	Agri-culture	Mining & quarrying	Manu-facturing	Electricity gas & water	Construct-ion	Trade, restaurants & hotels	Transport & communi-cations	Banks & finance	Rents	Govern-ment	Other
Sumatra	23.0	25.9	16.5	0.7	2.7	15.8	5.4	1.9	1.7	5.2	1.3
Java-Bali	19.5	2.7	23.7	2.0	6.1	21.0	6.6	2.3	1.9	6.7	4.7
Kalimantan	15.8	23.5	28.3	0.6	3.3	15.3	4.8	1.7	1.6	4.1	1.1
Eastern Indonesia											
West Nusa Tenggara	45.8	1.6	2.8	0.4	6.5	17.3	9.0	2.0	0.8	11.2	2.7
East Nusa Tenggara	47.1	0.6	2.0	0.8	3.6	12.1	9.5	1.6	1.7	19.1	2.0
East Timor	38.6	0.8	2.2	1.1	15.0	9.9	8.5	1.9	1.8	19.2	1.1
North Sulawesi	36.5	1.0	6.8	0.8	4.3	12.9	13.9	2.3	2.1	14.8	4.6
Central Sulawesi	40.2	2.8	5.4	0.7	7.5	13.7	8.5	2.1	3.2	14.2	1.7
South Sulawesi	43.4	4.2	8.8	1.0	3.4	18.4	7.5	1.2	3.2	8.2	0.8
South East Sulawesi	38.1	7.7	2.7	0.6	4.0	13.6	9.0	1.0	3.6	19.0	0.7
Maluku	31.7	6.0	17.3	0.5	5.7	19.9	4.2	2.3	1.1	9.8	1.5
Irian Jaya	16.4	55.6	2.1	0.4	4.3	5.3	4.1	0.9	0.6	9.2	1.0
Total	37.5	8.9	5.6	0.7	6.0	13.7	8.2	1.7	2.09	13.8	1.8
All Indonesia	19.5	11.5	21.8	0.8	5.9	16.4	6.6	4.8	2.5	6.7	3.5

[a]Of provincial or regional GRDP. Percentages for each area sum to 100.
Sources: Biro Pusat Statistik, 1993a and 1989-94.

Table 1.3: *Other economic aspects, Indonesia and provinces, 1992*[a]

| | Government activity | | | Agricultural employment | | Cash crops | Crop yields t/ha | |
| | Central Disbursements[b] as % of | | Public servants | % of workforce | % decline in share 1971-92 | % of value of agricultural output | Rice | Maize |
	'000 per head[c]	GRDP	Per '000 persons					
Sumatra	118.1	8.2	22.0	66.8	7.9	28.4	3,678	2,188
Java-Bali			19.6	45.9	23.4	12.9	5,168	2,108
Kalimantan	169.8	7.2	9.4	83.5	8.3	13.2	2,510	1,395
Eastern Indonesia								
West Nusa Tenggara	81.6	15.2	19.4	61.8	9.4	7.1	4,568	1,923
East Nusa Tenggara	120.5	25.0	23.3	77.1	5.9	10.8	2,551	1,775
East Timor	296.0	60.3	31.6	74.4	na	25.8	2,790	1,410
North Sulawesi	122.5	15.9	35.4	61.4	6.2	37.0	3,954	1,842
Central Sulawesi	171.4	24.4	28.7	67.9	9.5	21.7	3,154	1,847
South Sulawesi	96.8	11.5	26.7	63.5	4.2	12.5	4,336	1,785
South East Sulawesi	170.5	23.2	32.3	71.4	11.7	20.0	2,778	1,815
Maluku	174.7	17.6	30.1	67.7	4.2	18.9	2,151	1,218
Irian Jaya	336.0	19.4	37.5	72.9	na	3.2	2,620	1,247
Total	174.4	22.1	29.4	68.7	7.3	17.4	2,902	1,540
All Indonesia	103.7	7.8	21.5	53.7	16.3	na	4,376	2,203

[a]For 1992 unless otherwise indicated. [b]Through *Impres* and DIP, For more details see Chapter 5. [c]For 1994/95, and taken from Tables 5.15 and 5.17.

Sources: Biro Pusat Statistik, 1993b and 1995c.

Within agriculture, food crops were the biggest segment (Table 1.4), being increasingly sold for cash by what nonetheless persisted as predominantly small 0.5-1.0 ha. holdings. These little farms likewise produced most tree crops (including rubber, coffee and cloves) and livestock (including cattle, goats, pigs and poultry), often conducting several such enterprises together in a diversified system. Rice, which was mostly grown in wet paddies, was by far the biggest food crop (Table 1.5), although maize and root crops were also significant for subsistence especially. Yields of rice had been hugely enhanced through introducing high-yielding materials in a process of capital-intensive and labour-saving innovation paralleled to a lesser extent in other crops. Thus the average rice yield of 4.4 tonnes per ha in 1992 (Table 1.3) was now amongst the highest in Southeast Asia.

Government, which occupied 6.7 per cent of GDP in 1992 (Table 1.2), had from the late 1960s contributed much to economic changes, providing stability and direction underpinned by its coordinated and centralised administrative apparatus (*aparatur*). Its substantial disbursements from the centre (Table 1.3) had helped to greatly improve education, health, roads and other basic infrastructures across the archipelago, where this was well reflected in social statistics for 1992 (Tables 1.6 and 1.7). Such infrastructures, which had also been assisted by aid from foreign national and international agencies, vitally underpinned economic and social growth in many fields of endeavour.

Poverty and regional inequality

Despite this economic transformation, however, Indonesia remains a poor country on an international scale, and is still listed near the bottom of the World Bank's 'Lower Middle Income' range in terms of gross national product per capita (World Bank, 1995). In 1992 most infrastructures were still very inferior on a developed world standard, and required huge improvements. The country also contained wide regional disparities, with great divergences in GRDP (gross regional domestic product) per head and other welfare measures. Hence the mean GRDP per head of Kalimantan in 1992 was over three times that for Eastern Indonesia, while that of Java-Bali was 70 per cent more than the latter. Differences between the richest and poorest provinces were far greater, with East Kalimantan's Rp6,725,400 per head being almost fourteen times the figure of Rp482,000 for East Nusa Tenggara. And although the average growth in GRDP per head in Eastern Indonesia was faster than that of other regions in the ten years to 1992

Table 1.4: *Composition of agriculture's contributions to GRDP[a], Indonesia and provinces, 1992*

	Food crops %	Estate tree crops %	Smallholding tree crops %	Livestock %	Fisheries %	Forestry %	Total agric. contrib to GRDP Rp billion[b]
Sumatra	42.3	12.2	16.2	11.0	11.6	6.7	13,604
Java-Bali	67.1	2.9	10.0	12.0	6.3	1.7	28,709
Kalimantan	33.3	1.4	11.9	5.6	18.0	29.8	3,608
Eastern Indonesia							
West Nusa Tenggara	65.6	7.1	-	14.3	11.1	1.9	856
East Nusa Tenggara	56.3	0.1	10.7	23.0	8.6	1.3	772
East Timor[c]	47.4	-	25.8	14.5	1.6	0.8	191
North Sulawesi[c]	39.3	0.0	37.0	3.5	11.5	3.7	716
Central Sulawesi[c]	23.8	0.1	21.5	12.4	12.5	9.7	50
South Sulawesi	58.0	0.3	12.2	10.3	18.8	0.4	2,634
South East Sulawesi	49.4	-	20.0	10.3	17.5	2.8	405
Maluku	21.4	-	18.9	2.6	26.2	30.9	615
Irian Jaya	62.6	-	3.2	5.1	21.7	7.4	502
Total[c]	47.1	0.8	16.6	10.6	14.4	6.6	7,200
All Indonesia	56.8	4.9	12.3	11.2	9.7	5.1	53,121

[a]Percent of total GRDP from agriculture. Per cents for each area sum to 100 unless otherwise indicated.; [b]At 1992 prices.
[c]'Other activities' account for following shares of agricultural GRDP: East Timor, 9.9%; North Sulawesi, 5%; Central Sulawesi, 20%; and total Eastern Indonesia, 3.9%.
Sources: Biro Pusat Statistik, 1992 and 1995a and d.

Table 1.5: *Harvested areas and production of major food crops, 1992*

	Wet paddy		Dry paddy		Maize	Cassava	Sweet potatoes	Ground nuts
	Area '000 ha	Prod. '000 t	Area '000 ha	Prod. '000 t	Prod. '000 t	Prod. '000 t	Prod. '000 t	Prod. '000 t
Sumatra	2,393	9,595	483	1,056	966	3,672	413	91
Java-Bali	5,317	25,114	395	1,000	5,630	10,121	11,390	504
Kalimantan	696	2,,452	278	490	53	466	66	21
Eastern Indonesia								
West Nusa Tenggara	245	1,108	15	15	37	77	54	25
East Nusa Tenggara	80	249	64	64	376	840	91	7
East Timor	19	45			82	49	11	3
North Sulawesi	67	265	11	21	129	94	40	6
Central Sulawesi	126	421	16	16	17	88	20	4
South Sulawesi	786	3,437	16	16	591	560	78	61
South East Sulawesi	54	187	17	17	87	243	18	6
Maluku	1	2	2	2	17	247	59	3
Irian Jaya	9	25	4	4	4	31	179	2
Total	1,387	5,759	145	155	1,340	2,229	550	117
All Indonesia	9,799	42,413	1,304	2,826	7,995	16,515	2,171	739

Sources: Biro Pusat Statistik, 1995a.

Table 1.6: *Population and education, Indonesia and provinces, 1992*[a]

	Population			Education enrolment per '000 persons			Primary schools	
	Total '000	% Ann. growth 1971-92	Density per km²	Primary	Secondary	Tertiary	Total	per '000 persons
Sumatra	38,366	2.7	81	164	58	16	32,981	0.86
Java-Bali	110,720	1.7	824	129	49	13	77,772	0.70
Kalimantan	9,684	3.0	18	158	46	13	11,038	1.14
Eastern Indonesia								
West Nusa Tenggara	3,493	2.2	173	145	35	12	2,770	0.79
East Nusa Tenggara	3,403	1.8	72	171	41	10	3,850	1.13
East Timor	789	na	53	123	49	4	590	0.75
North Sulawesi	2,550	1.9	134	141	65	21	2,925	1.15
Central Sulawesi	1,803	3.2	25	168	49	12	2,320	1.29
South Sulawesi	7,229	1.6	99	147	58	18	7,193	1.00
South East Sulawesi	1,450	3.3	52	166	56	17	1,667	1.15
Maluku	1,954	2.7	26	182	68	20	2,516	1.29
Irian Jaya	1,765	na	4	145	52	14	2,061	1.17
Total	24,436	2.3	71	154	52	14	25,892	1.06
All Indonesia	186,042	2.1	97	141	51	14	147,683	0.8

[a] For 1992 unless otherwise indicated.
Sources: Biro Pusat Statistik, 1994a and b.

Table 1.7: *Health and roads, Indonesia and provinces, 1992*

| | Hospitals | | | Doctors | | Roads (km) | | | |
| | | No of beds | | | | Asphalt | | Others | |
	Total	Total	Per '00,000 persons	Total	Per '00,000 persons	Total	Per '000 persons	Total	Per '000 persons
Sumatra	257	24,890	64.9	3,148	8.2	43,676	1.1	56,674	1.5
Java-Bali	466	65,887	59.5	10,591	9.6	58,082	0.5	38,321	0.3
Kalimantan	63	6,224	64.3	858	8.9	11,365	1.2	23,618	2.4
Eastern Indonesia									
West Nusa Tenggara	12	898	25.9	177	5.1	3,082	0.9	2,435	2.7
East Nusa Tenggara	23	1,597	46.9	156	4.6	3,966	1.2	11,637	0.7
East Timor	22	568	72.0	106	13.4	1,905	2.4	3,036	4.6
North Sulawesi	24	2,588	100.3	373	14.6	3,931	1.5	3,659	1.4
Central Sulawesi	23	1,152	63.9	191	10.6	2,496	1.4	7,497	4.2
South Sulawesi	16	5,028	69.5	651	9.0	8,211	1.1	15,768	4.2
South East Sulawesi	57	675	46.6	105	7.2	2,609	1.8	3,580	2.5
Maluku	12	1,616	82.7	144	7.4	3,185	1.6	3,907	2.0
Irian Jaya	19	1,656	90.8	138	7.8	2,709	1.5	7,339	4.2
Total	208	15,778	64.6	2,041	8.4	32,094	1.3	60,582	2.5
All Indonesia	994	112,779	60.6	16,638	8.9	145,217	0.8	179,183	1.0

Sources:Biro Pusat Statistik, 1995c and d.

(Table 1.1), it could still take decades to rectify what might indeed be an unbridgeable difference.

These figures highlight the position of Eastern Indonesia as the poorest national region, with its poverty being a major issue for government and other concerned groups. The main features of the region are now examined.

Eastern Indonesia

This is defined for the present book as that part of Indonesia east of the Wallace Line (see Chapter 4). That line was first distinguished by the famous English naturalist, Alfred Russel Wallace, and is one passing east of Kalimantan and Bali on the map of Figure 1.1. It separates what Wallace saw as essentially 'South East Asian' 'flora' and 'fauna' to its west from 'Papua New Guinean and Australian' types to its east. Eastern Indonesia on this definition is a massive rectangle of 2,000 by 2,500 kms, comprising the islands of Sulawesi, the Nusa Tenggaras, Maluku and Irian Jaya. It is frequently referred to in Indonesia as *Indonesia Bagian Timur* (IBT) (the eastern division of Indonesia) or *Kawasan Timor Indonesia* (the eastern area of Indonesia), and in late Dutch colonial times was called the *Groote Oost* (Great East). Professor Azis in Chapter 5 introduces the somewhat enlarged region of 'Eastern Indonesia Plus', which also takes in Kalimantan.

The nine provinces of Eastern Indonesia (Table 1.1) are separated by huge stretches of sea, and Maluku especially is itself divided into scattered and far-flung islands. Irian Jaya, on the other hand, is chiefly inaccessible jungle interspersed by small settlements. The whole region of 24 million people in 1992 (Table 1.6) varies greatly in population density, ranging from high levels of 130-180 per km² in North Sulawesi and West Nusa Tenggara to only four persons in the jungles of Irian Jaya. The region is bounded not only by Indonesian provinces to its west, but also on other sides by Malaysia, the Philippines, Papua New Guinea and Australia (Figure 1.1).

The climate of the vast Eastern Indonesian region varies substantially, with a big contrast between the generally wet conditions and relatively high and well distributed rainfall of Sulawesi, Irian Jaya and Maluku on the one hand and the much drier Nusa Tenggaras and East Timor on the other. But there is nevertheless considerable microclimatic variation within given areas, where lands at higher altitudes in West Timor and Flores (Figure 1.1), for example, get much higher rainfall than lower territories of those places. Again, some mountainous stretches of Irian Jaya are so cold they are covered by snow all year round.

Economic divisions

Eastern Indonesia can be divided into four rather distinct zones of economic activity, basically coinciding with geographical and provincial location. All zones grow food crops for their still predominantly agricultural populations (Tables 1.3 and 1.4). Apart from this, however, the Sulawesis as one of the zones are distinguished by their cultivation of coconuts, cloves and coffee, and by important fisheries. There is also a very significant 'rice bowl' of wet paddy in South Sulawesi (Table 1.5), and nickel in the South East province (Table 1.2). In contrast, a further zone comprising West and East Nusa Tenggara and East Timor is an important producer of cattle and buffalo, while East Nusa Tenggara and East Timor are also prominent coffee producers and West Nusa Tenggara has some paddy. Maluku as another zone is very strong in forestry and fisheries (Table 1.4) with some tree crops, and further has considerable industry (Table 1.2) centred chiefly around timber and fish processing. The final zone of Irian Jaya is a major producer of copper, gold, oil and fish with some forestry. All products except food crops from these zones are largely exported elsewhere, and are major sources of external revenue for those concerned. Such exports mean that not only internal roads but also port facilities and ocean transportation are highly important, although as indicated they are frequently inferior by developed world standards. A large portion of exports from Eastern Indonesia goes through the port of Surabaya in East Java (Figure 1.1), which is a great centre of trade and important base for those organising and controlling this commerce.

The prosperity of residents as reflected by GRDP per head in these zones varies materially, and Irian Jaya with its high average of Rp1,733,000 per head (including oil) in 1992 (Table 1.1) appears as by far the most prosperous. Maluku with Rp932,000 comes second, while the Sulawesis range from Rp700,000 to Rp850,000. The poorest zone of the Nusa Tenggaras and East Timor is also the poorest part of Indonesia, with GRDP levels around Rp500,000. The implications of these estimated income levels for poverty are further drawn out by proportions of population with monthly expenditures over Rp60,000 (Table 1.1). These proportions are very low indeed for the Nusa Tenggaras and East Timor, as well as for South East

Sulawesi. Such implications are illustrated further by many figures presented in following chapters.[1]

But attention should also be drawn to high income enclaves existing in all zones, where Irian Jaya has them occurring around administrative and commercial centres including Jayapura, Merauke, and Sorong (Figure 1.1). These and several other enclaves in that province are characterised by relatively high income populations, served by reasonable infrastructures and living amongst a sea of isolated mainly subsistence farmers.

Again in the Sulawesis, North Sulawesi province as a whole stands out as better served in terms of infrastructures (Tables 1.6 and 1.7), while the provincial capital of Ujung Pandang and its environs are prominent in South Sulawesi. Ambon and its surrounding *kabupaten* is much the most economically advanced part of Maluku, and the same is true of Bima and Kupang respectively in West and East Nusa Tenggara. It should be mentioned that under current administrative systems most oil, mineral and timber revenues essentially flow to the centre in Jakarta, with little except direct spillovers being retained at local levels. This particularly reduces the apparent relative prosperity of Irian Jaya, with its major mineral and oil production.

As noted earlier, the government has greatly improved local infrastructures, and has managed through these measures to reduce isolation and improve the previously abysmal health and education levels which have been major causes of poverty. This important aspect is explored more fully in Chapters 5, 9 and 10.

Social and cultural elements

These exhibit huge diversity, with a rich and varied mosaic of ethnic groups and languages. The ethnic groups include, for example, such widely different peoples as the remote tribal communities in the Irian Jaya highlands, the seafaring and trading Buginese of South Sulawesi and the Rotinese from the island of Roti (Figure 1.1) with their penchant for government service. Religious affiliations, too, differ from place to place, with traditional beliefs in Irian Jaya and parts of the Nusa Tenggaras, Islam in South Sulawesi, North Maluku and West Lombok, and Christianity in

---

[1] They are also broadly confirmed by the more accurate figures of Bidani and Ravallion (1993), which allow for spatial price differences. These figures further highlight Maluku as another especially poor area.

most of the Sulawesis, the Nusa Tenggaras, East Timor, South Maluku and Irian Jaya.

Most societies likewise have strong traditional content, with *adat* leaders and customs governing crucial aspects of daily life including land use and cultural behaviour. Such arrangements exist parallel to the government structure of community administration, and are especially strong away from urban centres. Indeed, they often involve the same *adat* and government people in positions of leadership, and to that extent have less potential for conflict. Traditional structures are themselves highly diverse, with rather different customs often characterising adjacent village communities in the same area.

Social and cultural patterns have greatly affected migration, where peoples coming in from Asia and the Pacific over thousands of years have much influenced the features of society today. Some highly mobile groups such as the Buginese have impacted on societies around Eastern Indonesia, while the Dutch and Portuguese during several hundred years of colonialism stamped major characteristics on societies they controlled; the Indonesian government apparatus is having its own effects today. The Chinese in relatively small numbers have dominated trade for hundreds of years. More latterly, Irian Jaya, Maluku and East Timor have had big autonomous migrant intakes from other parts of Indonesia, and Irian Jaya and Maluku have additionally received Javanese transmigrants under the official program. On the other hand, there has been much out-migration to Java and Malaysia from the Nusa Tenggaras and Sulawesis. Both in- and out-migration leads to transfers of customs and ideas, which have been highly significant in the places mentioned.

The social and cultural differences of Eastern Indonesia cannot be neatly categorised like economic activity, although because of their mainly geographical basis the four economic zones mentioned do divide societies into clusters that are generally more similar to one another than to those associated with other provinces. Some social and cultural elements have major effects on individual and group behaviour and economic activity, and must be seriously addressed in economic and other analyses of development.

Classification

Hal Hill (1989:4) in his comprehensive study of Indonesian regional development since 1970 classified most of the nine eastern Indonesia provinces as either 'isolated' (the two Nusa Tenggaras and East Timor) or 'sparsely populated' (all but one of the Sulawesis and Maluku), the only exceptions being North Sulawesi ('settled') and Irian Jaya ('resource rich'). Yet the latter two provinces are also far from the centre in Java, and isolation actually characterises the whole region. This feature together with persisting poor infrastructures leads to lack of information, and helps explain pervasive market failure where market prices and opportunities are not well known to those concerned. Such failure reduces peoples' welfare, since they cannot realise what are in fact better potentials. This is an aspect underlying most issues treated through the pages of the book.

Arrangement of the volume

Following this Introduction, Hadi Soesastro in Chapter 2 reviews overall economic developments, looking especially at implications for the future of recent changes including modifications in official policies. Afan Gaffar in Chapter 3 considers major political questions surrounding the Soeharto succession, together with factors apparently determining this vital political transition. These two chapters plumb key economic and political issues in the Indonesia of 1995, giving interesting and informative perspectives on what is happening.

Next on the special topic of Eastern Indonesia, Richard Chauvel in Chapter 4 looks at immediate historical antecedents surrounding the concept of this region, scrutinising ways in which the concept came into being. Iwan Azis in Chapter 5 thoroughly examines the Eastern Indonesian economic picture, especially checking relative levels of growth and development, financial transfers from the centre and possible impacts of liberalisation.

Later chapters explore selected Eastern Indonesian issues in depth. Ben Mboi in Chapter 6 assesses the role of government in social and economic development, while Lucky Sondakh in Chapter 7 addresses the position of agriculture and ways in which government has both encouraged and discouraged its improvement. James Fox in Chapter 8 reviews the situation of fisheries, drawing attention to ecological pressures stemming from introduction of new technologies and complications surrounding marine tenure. Nafsiah Mboi in Chapter 9 treats the health status of Eastern Indonesian peoples and communities, exploring ways of improving their poor current situations. Riwanto Tirtosudarmo in Chapter 10 tackles human resource development, appraising education and health situations and factors impinging on these.

Then in the section of the book on community development, Frans Radja Haba describes the cultural circumstances of Savu Island, and ways in which his local NGO has worked to improve local conditions. Tonny Djogo checks lessons from past rural development projects, and canvasses approaches through which NGOs can assist future initiatives. Cliff Marlessy discusses the problems of government development policy in Irian Jaya, pinpointing useful roles for NGOs in development.

Finally, Colin Barlow in Chapter 14 draws together main thrusts of previous chapters, highlighting what he considers to be the chief development issues of Eastern Indonesia.

PART I: RECENT DEVELOPMENTS

2

The Economy: A General Review

Hadi Soesastro

Introduction

At the beginning of the year the government pledged to keep inflation at a maximum of 5 per cent in order to help maintain the competitiveness of Indonesia's non-oil exports. Today the government is trying hard to keep inflation below 10 per cent. It has taken an essentially tight monetary policy stance and has adopted a conservative fiscal policy. And yet more needs to be done: there is a suggestion for the need to create a larger budget surplus than last year's and to appreciate the rupiah in order to prevent an overheating of the economy.

Interest rates have gone up, but the efficacy of policies addressing the demand side is being questioned. Supply constraints and supply shocks have been responsible for the inflation as well, and the government may need to overhaul its policies with regard to its management of so-called 'strategic' commodities such as rice and cement.

The signs of an overheating economy are already evident. The current account balance has deteriorated as imports increase at the rate of about 27 per cent, although non-oil exports have performed much better than last year. Under a worst-case scenario, however, the 1995 current account deficit will amount to about 3 per cent of the gross domestic product (GDP), higher than the government's new target of 2 per cent of GDP, but still manageable.

There is the question of how to finance the current account deficit in a sustainable fashion, in view of the country's increased debt burden that has accumulated rapidly both as a result of the yen appreciations over the past ten years and the rise in private sector external debt. Enhancing the country's debt servicing capacity requires full commitment to promoting non-oil manufactured exports.

There are signs that unskilled labour intensive sectors are beginning to lose competitiveness, and new manufactured exports will need to be developed. The new pattern of approved investment, both foreign and domestic, seems to support this. If these planned investments are realised, then Indonesia's export capacity will be greatly enhanced. Their realisation, however, will depend on an improvement of the policy environment, which seems to be deteriorating as a result of the proliferation of non-market and non-transparent arrangements in the promotion of industrial development.

The 1995 State Address

Indonesia celebrates the golden anniversary of its independence with some sense of accomplishment, particularly with regard to its economic development. It has graduated into a middle-income country with a per-capita income today of close to US$1,000, up from less than US$100 about 25 years ago. In real terms, per-capita income has tripled during that period, which is now referred to as the First Long-Term Plan (or *Pembangunan Jang-ka Panjang I*).

In his State Address delivered on 16 August 1995 President Soeharto devoted a large section of his speech to an assessment of Indonesia's economic progress during the past twenty-five years. The next twenty-five years, he postulated, will see per-capita income in Indonesia increase four-fold in real terms. This is believed to be well within reach since the economy has been able to grow much faster than previously estimated. The new 1993 and 1994 GDP estimates are reproduced in Table 2.1. It is rather unusual that in a state address the President would go to some length in referring to the revised national accounts statistics.

As already explained by the Biro Pusat Statistik (BPS or Central Bureau of Statistics) at the beginning of the year, the revised national accounts statistics have involved three significant changes: (a) a rebasing of the constant price series from 1983 prices to 1993 prices; (b) an upward revision in the estimates of nominal GDP as a result of improved estimates of production; and (c) an improved sectoral classification that is more detailed and involves a reclassification of some subsectors. The practical implications of these revisions are, among other things: (a) higher real growth rates in 1994 and for the entire *Repelita* V period (1989/90-1993/94) (7.3 per cent and an average of 8.3 per cent per annum, respectively) than previous estimates (6.8 per cent and an average of 6.9 per cent per annum, respectively) due to the revised sectoral weights derived from 1993 prices; (b) higher nominal and per-capita income by about 9 per cent than previously estimated; and (c) higher weight given to consumption in the classification by expenditure category than previously.

Table 2.1: *Gross domestic product by industrial origin 1993-94*
(Rp billion, current market prices)

	1983 base	1993 base	
	1993	1993	1994
1. Agriculture, livestock, forestry and fishery	55,745.5	58.963.4	65,821.1
a. Farm food crops	31,403.5	32,093.4	34,739.9
b. Non-food crops	9,422.0	9,014.8	10,135.4
c. Livestock products	7,025.9	6,202.7	7,210.5
d. Forestry	2,541.4	6,267.6	7,451.6
e. Fishery	5,352.7	5,384.9	6,283.7
2. Mining & quarrying	30,749.6	31,479.3	31,381.0
a. Oil & natural gas	23,168.6	23,120.8	21,223.0
b. Other mining and quarrying	7,581.0	8,376.5	10,158.0
3. Manufacturing	67,441.4	73,556.3	90,206.8
a. Refinery oil	5,210.7	5,540.5	5,742.7
b. LNG	4,253.3	4,253.3	4,483.9
c. Non-oil & gas mfg.	57,977.4	63,762.5	79,980.2
4. Electricity, gas & water	2,714.3	3,290.2	3,912.8
5. Construction	18,139.9	22,512.9	27,942.2
6. Trade, hotels & restaurants	49,789.4	55,297.6	62,581.5
a. Retail & wholesale trade	41,496.1	44,604.8	49,751.5
b. Hotels & restaurants	8,293.3	10,692.8	12,810.0
7. Transport & communications	20,728.2	23,248.9	26,927.0
a. Transport	18,183.1	20,101.2	23,018.7
b. Communications	2,545.1	3,147.7	3,908.3
8. Banks & finance	15,256.6	14,005.3	16,871.2
9. Ownership of dwellings/real estate	7,610.6	9,695.1	11,239.0
10. Other services	33,842.4	37,708.9	40,491.7
a. Public	22,458.0	22,458.1	22,817.7
b. Other private & service	11,384.4	15,250.8	17,674.0
Gross domestic product	302,017.9	329,775.9	377,354.3

Source: Biro Pusat Statistik, 1989-94.

Perhaps more interesting and important are the implications for policy which can be drawn from the President's address. First is the suggestion for an upward revision of the targets of development, namely, a revision of *Repelita* VI's (1994/95-1998/99) growth targets from an average of 6.2 per cent per annum to an average of 7.1 per cent per annum as well as the aim of achieving a larger share of manufacturing in GDP to above 25 per cent by the end of this century. By then, according to the President, Indonesia should already have become a newly industrialising country. Secondly, as manufacturing activities are seen as the engine of growth in the future, it is suggested that there is a need to 'target' the development of certain industries to achieve a set of specific objectives. Five such categories of industries have been identified.

First are industries that are strategic in terms of meeting domestic needs and that are affecting the livelihood of the population at large; these include land, sea and air transport industries and agriculture-supporting industries such as fertiliser and agricultural implements, as well as industries that meet the needs of the population at large such as the food processing, cement, paper, and yarn and textile industries.

The second category consists of industries which already have or potentially can develop export markets, and in which Indonesia has static or dynamic comparative advantage. The third is of industries which process Indonesia's own natural resources, namely, agriculture, fisheries, animal husbandry, plantations and forestry as well as those which are based on the large pool of human resources. The fourth takes in industries that are strategic in terms of the development and mastery of technology as well as those with strong linkages to other industries; these include engineering industries, machinery industries, parts and components industries, and biotechnology-based industries, as well as the strategic industries under the supervision of the Badan Pengelola Industri Strategis (BPIS, or Agency for the Development of Strategic Industries), which are spearheading the development of high technology, namely, the land, sea and air transport industries already mentioned and the steel and electronic industries. The fifth category includes industries that can stimulate economic activities in regions outside Java, particularly Eastern Indonesia.

This 'new' industrial policy will give high priority to the development of industries that meet many of the above objectives. President Soeharto explicitly stated in his address that government support will not be given in the form of protection. On other occasions, following the Bogor APEC leaders' meeting, he reiterated the view that sooner rather than later Indonesia will have to open up its markets and that tariff protection or import restrictions could no longer be used as a means to develop domestic industries. Indonesia's active participation in the GATT/WTO, APEC and AFTA rests on the belief that Indonesia would gain much more from participating in an open global economy than from focusing its activities on the domestic market. Nonetheless, President Soeharto also pointed to the huge size of the Indonesian market by the end of this century, and warned that this market should not be lost to foreign producers. In his view, this can be achieved only if Indonesian consumers consciously prefer to use Indonesian products.

It is not clear how far this proposition will work as it assumes that local products will be preferred, even though they are more expensive than imported ones. Can export-oriented industries afford to rely on more costly local inputs? Concerns have been expressed with regard to the development of inefficient upstream industries, often involving 'mark-ups', which are seen as a major source of the high cost economy (Nasution 1995a). There appears to be some contradiction in the state address when in one part of the speech the domestic market is identified as providing the main engine for industrialisation,while in another part it is the export market which is seen as the main source of industrial growth, both now and in the future. It is also unclear what instruments can and will be used to implement industrial targetting as described above.

A preview of what may be in store may have already been given by the Chandra Asri case. When this petrochemical project was originally given approval, tariff protection appears to have been granted in principle by the government. This was before the Indonesian government was caught on the wave of trade liberalisation, particularly in the context of APEC of which it was the chair in 1994. Using the yen appreciation as an argument, Chandra Asri later pressed the government to grant a 35 to 40 per cent tariff protection. However, the Bogor Declaration makes it look ridiculous for the government to do so. Initially, the possibility of granting tariff protection for a definite period of about eight years was seriously considered, and was thought to be justified on the grounds that this would not entail a violation of any of Indonesia's regional or global commitments. Nonetheless, this was still seen as a violation of the Bogor Declaration in spirit, although not in letter. The Minister of Finance also opposed the granting of protection on other grounds, and his opposition appears to have led to his removal as chair of the Tariff Team.

In the end Chandra Asri was not given the tariff protection it sought, but it has not been left empty-handed and may end up receiving a much better deal. It is unfortunate, however, that the kind of support that was devised is of a non-market and non-transparent nature, namely, through a pricing formula jointly agreed upon by the government, Chandra Asri and the domestic users of its products. The essence of this non-market arrangement is for domestic users to agree to purchase a certain percentage of their needs from Chandra Asri under the agreed pricing formula: if the domestic producers' price exceeds or is below the international price, the price to domestic users is to be somewhere in between those two prices.

Other non-market arrangements may also be introduced in relation to the development of the aircraft industry. IPTN, Indonesia's aircraft manufacturer, successfully launched its N-250 on its maiden flight on 10 August 1995. However, questions have been raised as to whether and how soon these planes will actually be manufactured in Alabama in the United States, since the financing of the enterprise remains unresolved. The ability of IPTN to draw American or European investors into the enterprise will provide the ultimate market test for the commercial viability of the N-250, but thus far this has not been proven to be the case. Yet already there is talk of developing the N-2130 jet-engine airplanes. President Soeharto supports this plan, but has stated that the financing of N-2130's development will not come from the government's budget. Instead, Indonesian state enterprises Badan Usaha Milik Negara (or BUMN) will be requested to participate in its financing through the purchase of IPTN shares. No market test will be required as it would be difficult for state enterprises to refuse to accept this request.

If non-market measures of the types described above proliferate and become the main instrument for industrial development (and targetting), in its 50th year Indonesia may indeed be entering an exciting phase in its industrialisation. This development is a cause of great concern, but thus far appears to be overshadowed by other concerns that have arisen lately in Indonesia's macroeconomic picture: persistent inflation, deterioration of the current account balance in the balance of payments, an increased debt-servicing burden, the declining competitiveness of non-oil exports, and the sustainability of foreign direct investment flows.

Controlling inflation

Up to the end of July 1995 inflation, as measured by the change in the CPI (Consumer Price Index), reached 6.09 per cent on a cumulative basis, already exceeding the official target of 5 per cent for the entire year. At the beginning of the year, the government was concerned over the high rate of inflation in the previous year (9.24 per cent on a cumulative basis), and pledged to make concerted efforts to keep the inflation rate at a maximum of 5 per cent in order to improve the competitiveness of Indonesia's exports (*The Jakarta Post*, 28 January 1995).

As in 1994, inflation in the first quarter of 1995 was already above 3 per cent. The increase in inflation was mainly due to food prices going up because of the shortage of rice. Foodstuffs comprise 35 per cent of the CPI basket. The pressure on rice prices came about due to lower production and less than anticipated imports, combined with a period of seasonal high demand due to the fasting month in February and the Moslem New Year in early March. In addition, the Badan Urusan Logistik, BULOG, the food procurement agency in charge of ensuring sufficient stocks of rice, did not import adequate amounts in anticipation of the shortage.

In the second quarter of 1995, inflation was lower at 2.34 per cent, reaching only 0.16 per cent in June, although the figure had surged to its highest level of 1.6 per cent in April. The main factors causing inflation in the second quarter would appear to be the rise in minimum wages, which was effective from April, and the rise in the housing component, which was in turn caused by the rise in cement prices. The daily minimum wage in Jakarta and West Java was raised from Rp3,800 to Rp4,600, following an increase of Rp800 a year earlier. A rise in cement prices usually also leads to an increase in the price of other construction materials, with a lag effect on the price of houses and housing rentals. Furthermore, there is still the possibility that the price of cement will increase again later in the year, since the price will now be reviewed every six months and it would appear that increased demands for infrastructure needs will outstrip supply. Past experience has shown that underestimation of the demand for infrastructure has been partly responsible for the rapid overheating of the economy. It is of interest from a political economy perspective that the President sought to address the problems of inflation by ordering his cabinet to improve coordination (*The Jakarta Post*, 4 May 1995).

The rate of increase of inflation subsided in May and June but was up again in July by 0.71 per cent, again due to food prices. Inflation for the entire year 1995 can be expected to be below 10 per cent, because in the final analysis the government will do whatever it needs to do (and at any cost) to maintain a one-digit inflation rate. However, this will not be easy. Supply-side and cost push factors are expected to continue to put pressure on inflation; these include the prices of paper, sugar and electricity.

The appreciation of the yen could also lead to imported inflation due to higher input prices from Japan. The depreciation of the rupiah against foreign currencies always adds a component of imported inflation. A study undertaken at the Faculty of Economics, University of Indonesia, has estimated that for every 1 per cent depreciation there is a 0.32 per cent effect on inflation (Indrawati *et al.* 1995). Therefore, a 4 per cent depreciation of the rupiah against the US dollar would contribute about 1.3 per cent to the inflation rate. The growth of consumer demand and investment, estimated at 9 per cent in 1994, is also expected to continue to be strong, adding to demand side pressures.

The government's efforts to control inflation have been largely focused on addressing the demand side through a tight monetary policy and conservative fiscal policy. These are far from adequate, since the real problem appears to lie in the supply side. Addressing the supply side means not only a continuation of deregulation to reduce supply constraints, but also a more coordinated and sensible policy on the supply and price controls of so-called 'strategic' commodities such as rice and cement.

The Bank of Indonesia (BI) has been running a relatively tight monetary policy since the last quarter of 1994. Growth of narrow money (M1) has slowed down to 16 per cent for the twelve months up to May 1995 from about 23 per cent during 1994. The growth of broad money (M2) has remained relatively stable and was about 22 per cent for the twelve months up to May 1995. These developments have been due to a combination of the relatively tight monetary policy in response to inflationary concerns, problems in the banking sector and the increase in interest rates. The government target of growth rates for M1 and M2 of 19 per cent and 20 per cent respectively in 1995 will probably be reached, as BI is expected to continue with the tight monetary policy for the remainder of the year.

For a short period at the beginning of 1995, BI has had to take an expansionary stance due to external pressures. By the first week of February BI had twice raised SBPU (Money Market Securities) and SBI (Bank of Indonesia Certificates) rates by 0.5 per cent each time, first because of the rush to buy dollars which was precipitated by the Mexican crisis, and second in response to the increase in the Federal Funds rate. To offset the capital outflows that occurred in the post-Mexican crisis period, BI also sold SBI to an amount close to Rp5 trillion (US$2.4 billion). BI succeeded in restoring confidence in the rupiah, and in the last week of March it reverted back to a contractionary stance.

In April and May there were renewed concerns about the balance of payments due to the effect of the yen appreciation on debt servicing, about growth in imports, and about non-oil export growth, which have led to some capital outflow. BI again had to adopt a slightly expansionary stance which was, however, only short-lived because of continued inflationary pressures.

Up to June 1995, SBI rates had risen by close to 2.5 per cent from the end of 1994. As banks compete for deposits in the tight liquidity situation, average three months deposit rates have gone up by more than 2 per cent. It is expected that interest rates will remain unchanged for the time being.

Credit from the banking sector continues to show strong growth. Up to May 1995 growth of bank credits remained above 20 per cent for the previous twelve-month period. BI is targetting credit growth to the private sector at 19 per cent. Besides higher interest rates, BI has provided various signals that it will tighten its supervision and strengthen the enforcement of the legal lending limit. BI has also introduced administrative guidelines to influence credit given by private banks. At the beginning of the year, BI introduced several administrative regulations such as requirements for banks to submit their business plans and detailed credit programs to BI. Banks that have problem debts of more than 7.5 per cent of their total credit also have to provide a plan to BI, detailing how they will resolve problem loans. Of particular concern to BI is the phenomenal increase in credit to the property sector. The growth rate of lending to this sector is believed to be in the order of 40 per cent per annum. An overexposure to this sector could lead to an increase in problem loans. It has also raised concerns about a further increase in inflationary pressures (Nasution 1995b).

Since June 1995 there seems to be a renewed wave of capital inflow, driven in part by the fall in US interest rates. During the month of June the foreign assets of the banking system increased by about US$3 billion. This trend, if it continues, could lead to an overheating of the economy. The efficacy of monetary policy in controlling inflation has been questioned for some time now. In view of the country's open capital account, raising interest rates as a means to curb inflation would increase the inflow of capital which counteracts the tight monetary policy and creates problems of sterilisation that can be costly (Nasution 1995a). What then can be expected from a more active use of fiscal policy and exchange rate policy?

The state budget for 1995/96, which was approved by the Parliament in March 1995, is essentially a conservative budget. The planned budget increase of less than 12 per cent over last year's planned budget would not amount to much real growth, given that inflation is expected to be close to 10 per cent. A simple calculation of the domestic impact of the budget, namely the amount of revenues entering the domestic economy minus the amount of money going out, indicates that the budget is slightly contractionary.

The conservative fiscal policy complements the tight monetary policy in the attempt to control inflation. It is estimated that at the end of the 1994/95 budget year, the government had run a small surplus. This has been achieved primarily through careful disbursement of development expenditure funds by the budget-conscious Ministry of Finance. The 1995/96 budget is also aimed at creating a small surplus to enable the government to retire its external debt early and to build up the Development Budget Reserves (CAP). However, in view of the possible danger of an overheating of the economy, perhaps the government should aim at an even larger budget surplus.

The other option is to allow an appreciation of the rupiah for the purpose of slowing down the inflow of short-term capital. This would certainly require a major change in the government's exchange rate policy. At the beginning of the year the Minister of Finance 'pre-announced' a depreciation rate of 4 per cent for the entire year. Up to the end of June 1995 the rupiah had depreciated by 2.1 per cent against the dollar. Appreciation of the rupiah is not regarded as a favourable option, because this may reduce the international competitiveness of Indonesia's non-oil exports. Another option, aimed in particular at reducing the volatility of short-term capital flows, would be for the government to increase the cost of switching from rupiah to foreign currencies and vice versa. This policy is apparently being adopted through a widening of the band between the buying and selling rates. By late July 1995 the difference between the two rates was already 50 per cent larger than in late May 1995.

The balance of payments

The current account balance worsened in 1994, with the deficit increasing by US$0.9 billion from US$2.3 billion to US$3.2 billion. The trade balance declined by about US$0.4 billion while the balance on the services account declined by about US$0.5 billion.

The main reasons for the worsening of the trade balance were the slight decline in oil exports due to lower prices, the sluggish growth in non-oil exports, and a pick-up in import growth. Non-oil exports grew by only 12 per cent in 1994, compared with 16 per cent in 1993 and 27 per cent in 1992. Import growth picked up significantly in 1994 to reach 11.6 per cent after falling to very low growth rates below 5 per cent in the previous two years. The increase in imports was due to the rise in investment realisation.

The deficit on the services account increased as a result of the rise in interest rates and the 12 per cent appreciation of the yen in 1994. The appreciation of the yen has had a significant effect on the debt stock and debt service payments of Indonesia since 40 per cent of the government debt is denominated in yen. For every 1 per cent appreciation of the yen against the dollar, Indonesia's debt stock has increased by US$ 350million and interest payments have gone up by around US$20 million.

The worsening of the current account balance in 1994 was not seen as a cause for alarm as the current account deficit remained below 2.5 per cent of GDP. The picture for 1995 could look different. Preliminary estimates for the first quarter of 1995 indicate a further worsening of the current account balance with the deficit already amounting to US$1.7 billion (Table 2.2).

Table 2.2: *Balance of payments 1993-95 (First quarter) (US$ million)*

	1993	1994	1995 (Q1)
A. Current Account	-2,298	-3,178	-1,728
1. Merchandise	8,231	7,804	1,436
a. Exports, fob	36,607	40,126	10,143
- non-oil	26,994	30,290	7,739
- oil/gas	9,613	9,836	2,404
b. Imports, fob	-28,376	-32,322	-8,707
- non-oil	-24,576	-28,697	-7,786
- oil/gas	-3,800	-3,625	-921
2. Services, net	-10,529	-10,982	-3,164
- non-oil	-7,351	-8,094	-2,342
- oil/gas	-3,178	-2,888	-822
B. Capital Account	5,962	3,233	1,427
1. Official cap., net	743	257	656
a. Inflows	6,005	5,647	1,953
- CGI	(5,786)	(5,303)	(1,542)
- non-CGI	(219)	(344)	(411)
b. Debt repayments	-5,262	-5,390	-1,297
2. Private cap., net	5,219	2,976	771
- Direct investments	(2,003)	(2,108)	(956)
- Others	(3,216)	(868)	(-185)
C. Total (A+B)	3,664	54	-301
D. Errors and omissions, net	-2,923	752	467
E. Reserves[a]	-741	-806	-166

Note: [a]Negative indicates increase.
Source: Bank Indonesia, 1995.

Compared with the first quarter of the previous year, exports increased by 14.3 per cent, which indicates an improvement particularly in regard to non-oil exports, which increased by close to 17 per cent. However, imports continued to pick up and even grew by over 15 per cent. The services account worsened by 22 per cent largely as a result of the further appreciation of the yen.

The government's projection for the 1995/96 budget predicted a deterioration in the current account balance, with the current account deficit expected to increase by US$400 million to about US$4 billion. Non-oil exports were projected to grow by 16.5 per cent, whereas imports were projected to increase by 13 per cent.

Preliminary trade figures up to May 1995 show that exports had increased by about 17 per cent, but that imports were growing at a phenomenal rate of close to 28 per cent. The non-oil trade balance for January-May 1995 experienced a deficit of US$1.3 billion from a small surplus of US$18 million for the period January-May 1994. This strong import growth is reminiscent of 1991 when imports grew at 30 per cent. The expected boom in investment in 1995 will put pressure on import growth. Detailed import figures up to April 1995 show, however, that the increase in import growth was also accounted for by a dramatic increase in consumer goods imports of almost 100 per cent. Attempts by the government to control overexpansion in the economy through relatively tight monetary policy and to control credit growth could ease the pressures on imports. It should be noted that these imports have also increased by about 50 per cent but oil imports cannot easily be suppressed.

On the export side, the strong growth in oil exports helped somewhat although it is not certain whether prices will remain strong. The deficit on the services account is likely to widen in 1995, from US$11 billion to between US$11.9 billion and US$12.6 billion depending on the yen movements.

Under favourable conditions, namely, an export growth of 17 per cent, an import growth of 22 per cent, and an increase in the deficit on the services account of only 8 per cent, the current account deficit would be about US$4.4 billion. However, if imports grow by 25 per cent or exports increase by only 15 per cent, while the deficit on the services account increases by 15 per cent, the deficit in the current account could jump to US$6.1 billion. This still amounts to about 3 per cent of GDP, but is about US$2 billion larger than projected by the government. How can this larger deficit be financed? The Governor of BI recently announced that the government's policy is to aim at a current account deficit of 2 per cent of GDP.

In 1994 total net flows of capital were 46 per cent lower than in the previous year, because of a much smaller net borrowing by the public sector from US$740 million to US$250 million and much reduced inflows of private long- and short-term capital from US$3.2 billion to less than US$900 million. Net foreign direct investment flows stood at about the same level at US$2 billion.

Capital inflows in 1995 are expected to be higher than in 1994 for several reasons: increased foreign investment flows following the June 1994 deregulation in foreign investment, a new wave of relocation of Japanese firms, and large infrastructure projects involving private foreign firms as well as higher portfolio flows as interest rates in the US fall and the perception of increased risk post-Mexican crisis subsides.

The outlook for attracting portfolio flows remains good. Indonesia's sovereign credit rating has been upgraded recently by Standard & Poor from BBB- to BBB. This is good news for Indonesia since it was announced in the midst of a scrutiny of Indonesia's higher debt burden and its ability to offset the yen appreciation, as well as in the wake of the Mexican crisis. However, given that the rating remains below Indonesia's neighbours, Malaysia (AA+) and Thailand (A-), the government needs to consider the steps required to continue to improve the rating. Another encouraging change in capital market developments is the recent automation of transactions on the Jakarta Stock Exchange, as well as the expected passing of the Capital Market Law, which will enhance the investigative powers of the capital markets regulatory agency (BAPEPAM) and allow open-ended mutual funds.

Developments in the capital account during the first quarter of 1995 show an increased share of net official capital inflow; this may be due to increased dollar disbursement of yen-denominated government loans caused by the yen appreciation. However, increased official capital inflow during the first quarter of the calendar year, which is the last quarter of the budget year, has been the pattern of official capital disbursements. There definitely has been an increase in foreign direct investment inflow but, as mentioned earlier, there also was a major outflow of short-term capital at the beginning of the year.

Debt servicing capacity

The concern over Indonesia's external debt was heightened by the Mexican crisis, which led to a brief run on the rupiah in January 1995. Data on Indonesia's external debt vary by source. According to BI, at the end of December 1994 disbursed debt outstanding stood at US$87.6 billion, consisting of central government debt of US$58.6 billion, state enterprise debt of US$5 billion and private sector debt of US$24.0 billion (*Kompas*, 18

February 1995). Morgan Stanley (1995) estimates Indonesia's total external debt at year-end to be US$103.8 billion.

World Bank data, considered to be of greater reliability, show that by the end of 1993, Indonesia's total external debt outstanding (excluding undisbursed) already amounted to US$89.5 billion, consisting of public debt of US$52.5 billion and private debt of US$37.1 billion, of which about US$20 billion was short-term.

Indonesia's external debt almost doubled from 1981 to 1986, rising from US$23 billion to US$43 billion, and it has again doubled from 1986 to 1993 to close to US$90 billion (Table 2.3). From 1981 to 1986 public external debt grew by an average of 15.5 per cent per annum whereas private foreign debt increased by about 8.1 per cent per annum. Since 1986 the role has been reversed, with public external debt growing more slowly (7 per cent per annum) than private debt (over 20 per cent per annum).

Table 2.3: *External debt outstanding and disbursed 1981, 1986, 1993 (US$ billion)*

	1981	1986	1993
Outstanding debt (excl. undisbursed)	22.8	42.9	89.5
a. Public and publicly guaranteed	15.9	32.7	52.5
- Multilateral	2.3	7.0	17.8
- Bilateral	7.8	11.5	26.5
- Other (including commercial)	5.8	14.2	8.1
b. Private	6.9	10.2	37.1
- Long term	3.6	3.8	16.4
- Short term	3.3	6.5	20.7
Memorandum items:			
Total debt/GNP (%)	25	56	66
Public sector debt/GNP (%)	18	43	39
Total debt/exports (%)	91	268	219
Debt service/exports (%)	14	37	33
Public debt service/exports (%)	8	29	20

Source: World Bank, 1995c.

This reversal is reflected in the shift in the financing of the current account deficit. Nasution (1995a) has argued that the government's strategy to maximise borrowing of soft loans (ODA) cannot be sustained as such resources will no longer be forthcoming to a country that has already graduated. In its editorial, *The Far Eastern Economic Review* (17 August 1995) even suggested that Indonesia should no longer rely on foreign aid at all, and that Indonesia should send back the modest increase in new aid that the Consultative Group on Indonesia (CGI) pledged in its June meeting in Paris. The editorial argues that Indonesia's huge infrastructure development programs would be better undertaken by the private sector '... in a way that is typically less expensive than foreign aid, better attuned to real needs, and far more likely to correct than confirm the many inefficiencies and distortions that plague the Indonesian economy'. Popular Indonesian perceptions today would not necessarily agree with this assessment, as many people believe that private groups currently involved in a number of infrastructure projects are essentially rent-seekers and untouchable.

It is evident that the investment boom in the latter half of the 1980s has led to a surge in foreign borrowing by the private sector. Over a period of only four years, from 1989 to 1993, the foreign debt of the private sector increased by US$22.6 billion. The tight monetary policy that was adopted by the government in the early 1990s to cope with the overheating of the economy had led to increased foreign borrowing by the private sector (Soesastro and Drysdale 1990). For those who have access to offshore loans, this is an attractive source of financing because of lower interest rates, while the availability of BI's swap facility virtually eliminates the foreign exchange risk. The concern with the dramatic rise in private sector foreign borrowing is that some of this debt carries an implicit government guarantee, at least in the creditors' eyes.

The currency realignments of the mid-1980s were a major cause for the build-up of public sector debt. During the period 1985-87, the dollar value of public debt increased by about US$8 billion, when the yen appreciated from 201 yen to the dollar to 124 yen to the dollar. An appeal to the Japanese government to reduce the debt service burden met with no success, but instead the Japanese government provided more yen loans which are of a fast disbursing nature. The total yen exposure of public debt rapidly increased from 30 per cent in 1984 to 46 per cent in 1990. Concern over debt servicing led to the establishment of the Foreign Commercial Borrowing Coordinating Team (PKPLN) to monitor foreign loans from commercial sectors and to set the annual ceilings of new commitments at US$2.5 billion.

In 1993-94, with a further appreciation of the yen, public sector debt increased by about US$6 billion. A renewed appeal to the Japanese to reduce the debt service on Japanese loans was again answered by increased loans carrying lower interest rates, as announced at the last CGI meeting. In fact, by the end of 1993 total yen exposure (including from multiple-currency loans) had already increased to 51 per cent. BI has announced that it holds

35 per cent of its official reserves in yen. This should help somewhat to cushion the effects of yen appreciation.

The government also looks set to continue listing the shares of its state enterprises in the capital markets, both domestically and internationally. Following PT Indosat, the next company to go public later this year, is PT Telkom, the state-owned telecommunications company which is expected to be three times the size of the Indosat listing. The government has clearly indicated that some of the proceeds will be used to retire its debt early. This is a wise strategy to reduce Indonesia's debt burden as well as to prevent expansionary effects from spending the proceeds.

Indonesia has managed to avoid a debt crisis in the past, and so long as it continues to follow sound macroeconomic policies it can avoid a debt crisis in the future. In comparison with other highly indebted countries such as Mexico, Indonesia's current account deficits are at a much more sustainable level and the government has relied much less on short-term debt, including portfolio capital flows. But perhaps more importantly, Indonesia has been consciously promoting exports to enhance its debt servicing capability.

Concerns have arisen about the possible debt implications of the new government policy to promote industrial development as discussed earlier, especially if the government takes a much more active role in promoting and investing in certain industries. Continued rapid growth in private sector borrowing is also a source of concern if the funds are being used to finance other than the production of tradables. This can be avoided if the deregulation process continues. Increased foreign borrowing by private sector projects that carry implicit government guarantees or have a strong government affiliation would rapidly lead to a deterioration in the country's debt servicing capability.

Trade deregulation and non-oil export performance

Until the issuance of the 23 May 1995 deregulation package, no significant deregulation was made in the area of trade. Tariff reductions are the core of this package. Removal of some non-tariff barriers was also announced, but on this score the package has been rather disappointing. In addition, provisions were made to improve the management of export processing units and preshipment inspection, as well as some changes in investment regulations. A detailed description of the package can be found in Nasution (1995b).

The most positive development is the tariff reduction schedule. This answers the criticism that has often been put forth with regard to the need to have an announced schedule rather than piecemeal announcements. The schedule proposes that tariffs be reduced to between 0-5 per cent or 0-10 per cent by 2003, depending on the present level of tariffs. Tariffs which are now greater than 20 per cent have to be reduced to 20 per cent or less by 1998 and to 10 per cent or less by 2003. Some tariffs were immediately reduced, such as those on news print, cooking oil, and certain components and capital goods. Tariffs that are now 20 per cent or less will reach 5 per cent or less by 2000. Having a schedule is important, as it indicates the direction of protection reduction and reduces uncertainty. However, to 'lock in' the deregulation, it will be important to ensure that the exceptions are limited; to the extent possible the tariffs should be bound (at the WTO) at those lower levels to prevent future increases (Soesastro and Pangestu 1995).

The reductions for the automotive, chemical and metal industries are regulated separately. Even though it was stated that for some products the tariffs will reach 10 per cent by 2003, the automotive schedule shows that for sedans, jeeps and minibuses as well as components, the tariffs by 2003 could still be around 60 per cent.

To some extent, the 23 May 1995 trade deregulation will have more far-reaching effects than AFTA, in the sense that if by 2003 all tariffs affected by the deregulation have been reduced to 5 per cent or less, then in practical terms Indonesia will have multilateralised all of its AFTA preferences. In fact, it will even have gone beyond this, as around 2000 tariff items not included in the AFTA CEPT (Common Effective Preferential Tariff) scheme will also be reduced to between 0 and 10 per cent. In ASEAN, there is now talk of accelerating the AFTA implementation to the year 2000. Another proposal to be decided upon at the next ASEAN Summit in Bangkok in December 1995 is reduction of all CEPT items to 0 per cent tariffs by 2003. This is likely to have an influence on Indonesia's unilateral trade liberalisation in the future. There is some kind of dynamics at play that has the effect of accelerating unilateral and regional trade liberalisation efforts.

The big question that is continuously being asked is whether Indonesian industries are ready to meet this challenge. The government's response is that industries must make themselves ready, and the scheduled gradual reduction or elimination of tariffs should sufficiently prepare them to be able to compete globally, including in their home market. Critics, however, point to the fact that the domestic environment for fair competition has not improved, but instead has tended to deteriorate since some upstream industries remain protected through their monopolistic position. The 23 May 1995 package has resulted in these protected sectors being left totally exposed.

The perceived decline in the competitiveness of Indonesian manufactured exports has lately been blamed on the protection of industries that have a strong connection to the government. This contention rests on the argument that they are the main cause of the persistently high rates of inflation. There is also concern about the increased cost of electricity and other infrastructure services resulting from mark-ups in the cost of privately developed projects of this kind. They will all contribute to a decline in the competitiveness of Indonesian manufactures.

The decline in non-oil export growth in 1994 appears to have begun in mid-1993. There are sector-specific reasons for the decline, but two factors stand out, namely, the decline in the realisation of export-oriented investments (since 1992) and increased competition from China, India, Sri Lanka, Bangladesh and Vietnam for labour-intensive exports such as garments. The high growth of manufactured exports in 1992 of almost to 30 per cent was driven by the boom in export-oriented investments in the 1989-91 period.

In 1994 there was a substantial slow-down in growth in two product groups that dominate manufactured exports, namely, plywood and textiles and garments. Plywood exports, which account for over 20 per cent of manufactured exports, experienced negative growth in 1994. The slow-down is mostly due to the fall in plywood prices and some decline in demand due both to the recession in Japan and to the slow-down in China's growth in 1994 as it struggles to keep a rein on overheating. There has also been some discussion that the slow-down was partially caused by the problems that importers faced due to the cartelised system of plywood exports, whereby exporters are required to go through the plywood association and imports by Japan and Korea are to be undertaken through a designated distributor assigned by the association. As a result some importers have switched to Malaysia and Papua New Guinea as alternative suppliers.

Textile and garment exports also experienced negative growth in 1994. Textiles and garments combined account for 27 per cent of total manufactured exports. The cause of the decline in textiles has been partly due to a shortage of the raw input and an increase in its prices, whereas the decline in garments may relate to increased competition. Even emerging exports such as footwear experienced a decline in growth from 26 per cent in 1993 to 14 per cent in 1994. However, other manufactured exports such as audio-visual equipment, furniture and vegetable oils continue to experience robust growth.

Preliminary data for January-April 1995 show a further decline in plywood exports by 16 per cent compared with the same period of the previous year. Both textile and garment exports have recovered. Overall, however, the shares of these three dominant export items in total manufactured exports continue to decline. A meticulous analysis by James (1995) shows that sectors relying on unskilled labour performed poorly in 1994, and provided indications that these sectors are losing competitiveness. This being the case, James has suggested that Indonesia should begin to look for new emerging non-oil manufactured exports that do not rely purely on unskilled labour or natural resource-based comparative advantage, and that have strong growth potential in terms of favourable income and price elasticities of demand.

The shares of human capital intensive and technology-intensive manufactured products in Indonesia's total manufactured exports have increased from 7.5 per cent and 4.8 per cent respectively in 1988 to 15.7 per cent and 10.5 per cent respectively in 1995 (January-April), amounting to a doubling of the shares (Table 2.4). This is an encouraging trend.

The new pattern of investment may indeed support this trend. Based on investment approval figures, both foreign and domestic investments appear to be experiencing a shift in the direction of those products (Tables 2.5 and 2.6). However, this trend appears to be spearheaded by foreign investors. Cumulative approvals of foreign investments from 1993 to 1995 in manufacturing increased by 176 per cent compared with cumulative investments for the 1990-92 period. About 83 to 84 per cent of all investment projects were export-oriented. Estimated values of annual exports resulting from these investments are also expected to increase by 160 per cent from US$10.2 billion to US$26.8 billion.

Of total foreign investments in manufacturing, the share of those in non-metallic minerals, basic metals, metal goods, chemicals, and other manufactures, or the more human capital- and technology-intensive sectors, increased from 62 per cent in the former period to 77 per cent in the latter period. Their share of annual export values increased more significantly from 44 per cent to 78 per cent.

The picture is slightly different with regard to domestic investments, but the same trend can be detected. Domestic investments in manufacturing have tended to become less export-oriented than foreign direct investments. Estimated values of annual exports declined from US$26.5 billion for approved projects in the 1990-92 period to US$17.5 billion for approved projects in the 1993-95 period. Although the share of investments in the more human capital- and technology-intensive sectors increased from 29 per cent to 56 per cent, the share of estimated values of annual exports increased only from 31 per cent to 35 per cent, indicating that domestic investors in these sectors are less export-oriented than foreign investors. In other words, they are eyeing the domestic market. Nevertheless, if these approved investments are realised, Indonesia's manufactured export capacity as a whole will be greatly enhanced and its prospects will be bright.

The key to the realisation of these investments is the creation of an economic policy environment that promotes transparency and stays away from the use of non-market and non-transparent arrangements in promoting industrial development in particular and economic development in general.

Table 2.4: *Manufactured exports by intensities 1988-95 (January-April)*

Intensity[a] (Selected SITC)	1988	1998	1994	1995 (Jan-Apr)
Total manufactures	5,910	19,788	21,140	6,914
Natural resource	3,101	5,714	5,507	1,734
- (63 Wood)	2,297	5,129	4,833	1,461
Unskilled labour	1,807	9,416	9,263	3,106
- (65 Textiles)	681	2,537	2,498	831
- (84 Garments)	797	3,502	3,206	947
- (85 Footwear)	82	1,661	1,888	626
Physical capital	362	766	971	349
- (51-2 Chemicals)	76	360	396	132
- (672-9 Steel)	269	281	274	93
Human capital	445	2,508	3,544	1,086
- (69 Metal mfg.)	40	318	328	102
- (761-3 Television, radio & recorders)	9	706	1,073	320
- (78 Road vehicles)	21	334	314	92
- (897 Jewellery)	78	240	736	161
Technology	285	1,385	1,856	728
- (56 Fertiliser)	134	152	178	64
- (764 Telecomm. eqp.)	11	257	400	121
- (77 Electric Mach., excl. 775)	41	403	579	229

Note: [a] Intensities are indicated by SITC numbers as follows:
        Natural Resource Intensive: SITC 61, 63, 661-3, 667, 671, 68.
        Unskilled Labour Intensive: SITC 65, 664-6, 793, 81-85, 893-95, 899.
        Physical Capital Intensive: SITC 51-52, 71-74, 751.
        Human Capital Intensive: SITC 53, 55, 62, 64, 69, 761-3, 775, 78, 791, 885, 892, 896-8.
        Technology Intensive: 54, 56-59, 752-9, 764, 771-4, 776-8, 87, 881-4.
Source: Calculated from Biro Pusat Statistik, *Buletin Ringkas BPS* (various issues).

Table 2.5: *Approved foreign direct investments in manufacturing, 1990-95[a]*

	1990-92				1993-95			
	Invest-ments[b]	Projects[c]		Exports[d]	Invest-ments[b]	Projects[c]		Exports[d]
	US$b	A	B	US$b	US$b	A	B	US$b
Total Manufacturing	15.3	779	644	10.2	42.2	753	631	26.8
- Food	0.7	45	39	0.7	2.0	71	51	1.2
- Textiles	2.2	188	172	2.8	1.1	91	85	1.9
- Wood	0.3	52	47	0.6	0.3	44	42	0.4
- Paper	2.5	16	13	0.9	6.1	33	27	2.3
- Pharmaceuticals	0.0	-	-	0.0	0.9	1	0	0.0
- Chemicals	5.0	154	119	1.2	2.5	173	143	15.1
- Non metall. minerals	1.1	29	19	0.3	0.9	38	29	0.3
- Basic metals	1.1	22	22	0.6	2.5	40	34	0.8
- Metal goods	2.2	222	168	2.0	3.8	238	197	4.7
- Other	0.2	51	45	0.4	0.1	24	23	0.2

Note: [a]Cumulative approvals at 15 July, 1995. [b]Value of investments in US$ billion.
[c]Number of projects; (A): Total number of projects; (B): Number of investment oriented projects.
[d]Estimated value of annual exports in US$ billion.
Source: Calculated from Badan Koordinasi Penanaman Modal, 1990-95.

42

Table 2.6: *Approved domestic investments in manufacturing, 1990-95[a]*

| | 1990-92 | | | | 1993-95 | | | |
| | Invest-ments[b] | Projects[c] | | Exports[d] | Invest-ments[b] | Projects[c] | | Exports[d] |
	US$b	A	B	US$b	US$b	A	B	US$b
Total manufacturing	68.9	1629	1355	26.5	74.4	896	650	17.5
- Food	4.0	201	155	2.5	8.4	137	100	2.4
- Textiles	18.8	440	414	9.5	12.4	120	107	5.5
- Wood	4.4	188	183	3.3	3.8	67	65	1.8
- Paper	21.9	120	71	3.4	8.2	66	39	1.6
- Pharmaceuticals	0.2	7	4	0.0	0.6	10	2	0.0
- Chemicals	2.0	294	237	3.5	15.7	231	171	2.4
- Non metal. minerals	11.3	100	77	1.2	18.8	85	63	2.0
- Basic metals	3.2	54	40	1.5	2.4	26	17	0.5
- Metal goods	3.0	177	129	1.3	4.0	145	79	1.0
- Other	0.3	48	45	0.3	0.2	9	7	0.3

Note: [a]Cumulative approvals at 15 July, 1995. [b]Value of investments in Rp.billion.
[c]Number of projects; (A): Total number of projects; (B): Number of export oriented projects. [d]Estimated value of annual exports in US$ billion.
Source: Same as Table 2.5.

3

Indonesia 1995: Setting the tone for transition towards the post-Soeharto era?[1]

Afan Gaffar

R. William Liddle, a well-known Indonesian specialist, writing in 1992 about President Soeharto and his administration, said that Soeharto is 'a dying king, or at least a ruler whose authority has begun slowly to ebb away'. What has been revealed by Liddle (1992) is a typical misperception of social scientists concerning the strength and longevity of the Soeharto regime. Liddle's perception is not really new because in 1978 another well-known Indonesian specialist, Benedict Anderson, was already writing about 'the last days of Soeharto'. Soeharto has proven to many observers and academics that they were wrong. In fact, his government is still very strong since no one really has the courage to challenge his authority.

Nevertheless, 1995 is a very interesting year in which to watch Indonesian politics because many things have happened that could lead to the probability of a coming to terms for Indonesians towards political transitions. First of all, there is much discussion among Indonesians that Soeharto has to face the fact that at one time or another he will have to relinquish power because he is getting older, since this is a law of nature that no one can avoid. Observers have raised questions concerning the actual time when Indonesia will have a new President. Does President Soeharto want to continue his regime until the year 2003 or is he going to step down in 1998?

Secondly, Suhardiman, a retired army general and one of the most outspoken political analysts, has predicted that there will be a political upheaval in 1995 that will lead to the instability of the country and that

[1] I would like to thank Dr Riswandha Imawan for various comments and suggestions. Mr Harry Tjan Silalahi of the CSIS provided financial support for preparation of the paper, for which I am grateful. They do not share responsibility, however, for any mistakes in the argument presented in this paper.

there will be a strong chance for political succession in 1998. He has even offered to cut off one of his fingers if he is wrong. Even if he proves wrong, Suhardiman represents a group that no longer has influence in government. No one can take him lightly, however, because he is the chairman of Swadiri Organisasi Karya Sosialis Indonesia (SOKSI), one of the cornerstones of the government party Golongan Karya (Golkar), and therefore the debate over whether there will be a succession in 1998 still continues.

Thirdly, the government faces a challenge from the pro-democratic movement originating from several groups in the country, such as the former Sukarnoist and nationalist elements of the Indonesian Democratic Party (PDI) led by Megawati Sukarnoputri, some elements of Nadhatul Ulama (NU) under the leadership of Abdurrahman Wahid, members of NGOs, campus activists and intellectuals.

Therefore, if the President wants to renew his regime in 1998, I am convinced that he will face very strong opposition from many other elements of the pro-democratic movement, even though he may have no problem in convincing the Majelis Perwakilan Rakyat (MPR)[2] to re-elect him for the next five-year term. Increasing political opposition in the country can be discerned in all political affairs during 1995, which from my point of view will set the tone concerning the transition towards the post-Soeharto era.

Human rights and political tribunals

There is no doubt that politics in Indonesia under the New Order regime are tightly controlled through a combination of the elements of cooptation and repressive means.[3] The space for political opposition to manoeuvre is very small because the government will apply various efforts to ensure the

---

[2] Six hundred out of 1,000 members of the national assembly (MPR) are appointed by the President while 400 are elected through general election. The election itself is arranged in such a way as to ensure that the government party of Golkar wins with an absolute majority.

[3] There are several institutions involved in the repression process such as BAKIN (State Intelligence Coordinating Body), local military offices, and the Directorate General of Social and Political Affairs (Department of Home Affairs) with all its local offices. In the early period of the New Order government, the role of KOPKAMTIB was very significant. KOPKAMTIB has been replaced by BAKORSTANAS, the National Coordinating Body for Stability. For further analysis of the intelligence organisations in Indonesia, see Tanter (1990).

stability and order of the country.[4] This has been the case in 1995 because one of the most conspicuous problems concerns human rights. In an attempt to control all political activities, the government has attempted to use certain political instruments that were used under the colonial government as well as under the Old Order regime.

First of all, the New Order government requires all gatherings of more than five persons to have a permit in accordance with Indonesian law. Otherwise the government apparatus such as the local police officers will break up the gatherings.[5] There are many instances in which the police have broken up gatherings such as seminars and discussions conducted by non-government organisations, students, intellectuals and even political parties in a number of cities, such as Jakarta, Yogyakarta, and Surabaya.[6] Permits in Indonesian politics are among the most significant and effective instruments used by the government in controlling political activities critical of the regime.[7] The government also requires that permits be obtained for all survey research conducted by students and teaching staff from universities. The local bureaucrats under the Office of Social and Political Affairs scrutinise research proposals and questionnaires to find out whether they contain political elements or not.[8]

---

[4] The nature of the regime of the New Order government has been the subject of debates among students of Indonesian politics. Basically it is an authoritarian regime within which the presidency is the most dominant political institution because of its ability to control enormous political as well as economic resources. For further analysis, see Anderson and Kahin (1992).

[5] The government argues that as long as the laws have not been invalidated by new laws, the old laws can be implemented. Concerning permits for all gatherings, social as well as political, the police apparatus applies Penal Law (KUHP) article 510 in addition to Presidential Decision Number 13, 1961, and the 1963 Law Number 5.

[6] In Jakarta the police broke up a discussion conducted by the Legal Aid Institution concerning 'Pluralism in Indonesian Agrarian Laws' because it did not have a permit. Participants in the discussions were members òf parliament (DPR), prominent intellectuals from the University of Indonesia and Gadjah Mada University, and political activists. For the same reason the police also broke up a gathering sponsored by WALHI at Bulungan Youth Centre, Jakarta, when the impact of Chernobyl was being discussed. The latest incident was when the police broke up a discussion conducted by Yayasan Indonesia Baru (Foundation for the New Indonesia). The principal speaker, Robert Hefner, an Indonesian specialist in Islam, was interrogated by the police for several hours (*Forum Keadilan*, 3 July 1995).

[7] See my article '*Politik Perijinan*' [The Politics of Permits] in *Forum Keadilan*, 3 July 1995, concerning the modes and procedures applied by the government.

[8] Each local office, the Kantor Sosial dan Politik (The Office of Social and Political Affairs) is under the Directorate General of Social and Political Affairs, Department

Secondly, the Indonesian government is very active in preventing and prohibiting certain people from speaking as well as conducting gatherings (*pencekalan*) Nobody is able to trace accurately when this type of policy began in Indonesia. It is under the New Order government, however, that prevention of people from travelling abroad and being active in seminars and discussions on political affairs has been widely used, especially after the so-called *Petisi 50* became the principal opposition to the regime. In 1994/95 the application of this kind of political instrument to control opposition has become common; from January to June 1995 the government has used it about sixteen times.

Usually the most outspoken human rights activists are the principal targets of *pencekalan*, such as Adnan Buyang Nasution. A member of the National Human Rights Committee, Rumini Soedjono, has even been prevented from attending a seminar in Surabaya. The cases of Abdurrahman Wahid, Emha Ainun Najib, and Megawati Sukarnoputri, I believe, are the most significant and warrant discussion in this analysis.

Emha Ainun Najib is a poet and a prolific writer as well as a very attractive performer. He has been prohibited from talking as well as performing in Central Java, in Ujung Pandang and in Bandar Lampung. Concerning this kind of policy, he has protested to government officials. 'Even God does not prohibit people from talking. Why do you prohibit people from talking? ... The prophet teaches us wisdom, you teach us brutality', he protested openly.[9]

Megawati Sukarnoputri is also a principal target of *pencekalan*. Since she was elected President of the PDI she has had to face the fact that it is very difficult in Indonesia to reach out to one's constituents. In several cities in East Java the local government has prohibited her from conducting meetings with local activists of the PDI. Even in the city of Blitar, the place her ancestors came from and the place where Sukarno is buried, local police officers broke up a meeting. They argued that local party activities did not mention in the permit application that Megawati was to be one of the principal speakers. However, the logic behind the policy was the fact that the PDI had been able to increase its share to more than 10 per cent of the popular vote in the 1992 general election. One of the most effective means of

---

of Home Affairs, in Jakarta. It keeps an eye on all political activities in the country, including seminars and religious activities. This office usually gives a recommendation to local police officers whether to issue a permit for a seminar or political gathering.

[9] See *Forum Keadilan*, 3 July 1995, for a complete interview with Emha Ainun Najib concerning prevention of people speaking recently.

controlling the PDI in its efforts to increase its support for the 1997 elections is by prohibiting its activists from conducting an early campaign such as the government party, Golkar, is at present doing intensively. Furthermore, Megawati has become one of the symbols of political opposition in the country since early 1994.

The case of Abdurrahman Wahid is the most interesting in the context of *pencekalan*. Abdurrahman Wahid is also a symbol of political opposition in Indonesia since he established the so-called Forum Demokrasi with many other prominent Indonesian intellectuals and activists. His problems increased after the publication of Adam Schwartz's book, *A Nation in Waiting: Indonesia in the 1990s*. His political opponents were able to convince the President that he had made a comment that was an insult to the President. Since then, Wahid has had problems in meeting with his constituents because local officials have broken up the meetings for the same reason, that is, they did not have permits. This happened in East Java, the province in which his organisation, Nahdlatul Ulama, was established. In several municipalities such as Lamongan, Jember and even his home town of Jombang in East Java, the police have broken up meetings without any specific reason.

The third instrument in controlling political opposition is to put people on trial, and political tribunals have also been among the most significant affairs in 1995. At least three political activists have been put on trial since June 1995, and two others may soon be on trial, namely, Sri Bintang Pamungkas and Abdurrahman Wahid.[10]

Permadi is a prominent leader of the mysticism movement or *kebatinan* in Java. He claims that he is a follower of Sukarno's teachings. Nevertheless he is very critical of the government because he is disappointed with the fact that the New Order, from his point of view, is much worse than the Old Order regime under Sukarno. He has openly criticised almost all government policies, especially those related to the business activities of the children of the President and officials in Jakarta. The government as well as military officials have long been irritated by Permadi's activities. When a group of journalists asked his opinion about General Suyono's comment on Megawati Sukarnoputri, he said 'Don't trust PANGDAM'.[11]   His words

---

[10] In Abdurrahman Wahid's case his political opponent, Abu Hasan, is suing him in the civil court. The case carries a lot of political weight because Abdurrahman Wahid is very critical of the regime.

[11] Suyono was then Regional Commander of the Diponegoro Division. He is now the General Chief of Staff of the Armed Forces of Indonesia (ABRI) in Cilangkap,

were put on air by a private radio station in Yogyakarta,[12] and Permadi's
comment was taken as an insult to Suyono. Then Dien Syamsuddin entered
the arena. As chairman of the division of research and development of
Golkar and with the support of Harmoko, he traced all of Permadi's
comments. When he found that Permadi had made a comment that was very
sensitive to Islam, he accused the latter of insulting Islam when he said that
the prophet Muhammad was a dictator. This created strong support from
some elements of Islamic groups who actually did not know the true context
of Permadi's comment at a seminar conducted by students of Gadjah Mada
University. Finally the government developed a case against Permadi.[13]

The second political tribunal is under way in Jakarta now. A group of
independent journalists published a weekly magazine called *Forum
Wartawan Independen*.[14] They are members of Asosiasi Journalis
Independen (AJI) or the Association of Independent Journalists. This
association was created on 9 August 1994, following the banning of *Detik
Editor*, and *Tempo* in June 1994, as a symbol of protest against the
government-sponsored group, namely, Persatuan Wartawan Indonesia
(PWI) or the Association of Indonesian Journalists. The government
perceived this group to be an unlawful organisation, and therefore when they
conducted a meeting in a hotel in Jakarta the police arrested Ahmad Taufik
bin Abubakar, Danang Kukuh Wardoyo and Liston Siregar. Nevertheless,
only Ahmad Taufik, Eko Maryadi, and Danang Kukuh Wardoyo are being
put on trial. They are accused of spreading and printing hatred, hostility and
degrading news about the government.[15]

Jakarta. He is also the son-in-law of Mrs Mien Sugandhi, Minister of Women
Affairs, in the sixth Soeharto cabinet.
[12] The radio station, Radio UNISI, belongs to the Islamic University of Indonesia in
Yogyakarta. This radio station has a special program on political affairs that invites
comments from political scientists about daily affairs in Indonesia. It is interesting to
note that the Islamic University of Indonesia sponsored a national seminar at which
George Adicondro made comments that are critical of the regime. The government
plans to put Adicondro on trial because of his comments, but it has so far failed since
Adicondro is in Australia.
[13] Permadi is still on trial at the local court in Yogyakarta. He will be sentenced
sometime in September 1995.
[14] The acronym of this magazine is FWI. The government and most of the pro-
government journalists perceive it as a rival to the government-sponsored
association, the PWI.
[15] *Forum Wartawan Independen* has a circulation of about 10,000 but it does not
have the permit required by Indonesian law. It has the courage to reveal things that
the regular newspapers and magazines find impossible to discuss. The tenth issue,

At present there are four other political activists waiting for their cases to go to court, namely, Abdurrahman Wahid, Sri Bintang Pamungkas, George Adicondro, and the director of the Yayasan Indonesia Baru (The New Indonesian Foundation). The rivalry between Abdurrahman Wahid and Abu Hasan is about the leadership of NU and the matter will be settled before the civil court, but it carries political weight since Wahid is one of the most outspoken critics of the regime. Sri Bintang Pamungkas has been accused of involvement in the demonstration against Soeharto in West Germany; George Adicondro is accused of speaking degradingly of the President; and Sugeng Suprawoto is accused of the unlawful activity of conducting a seminar without a permit.

All of these phenomena indicate that even though Indonesians are enjoying the 'golden year' of independence, the question of freedom and liberty for those who question the government is still blurred.

Islam and the regime

Islam is a very important element in Indonesian politics, because it has become a political commodity for both those who are within the bureaucratic circle and those outside the ruling elite. Since the early 1990s, there has been a new mode of relationship between Islam and the state, involving a shift from an antagonistic type of relationship to one of mutual accommodation (Gaffar 1992).

At the beginning of the New Order the Islamic community had expected to play a dominant role because the New Order appeared to be a kind of panacea that would eventually bring about democracy. For Islam in Indonesia, democracy was important because with democracy the Islamic political cause would be shaped. It did not take long for Islam to realise that the Soeharto government was in favour of economic development rather than democracy. Islam therefore became part of the opposition and very critical of the regime. There have been many instances in which conflict between Islam and the regime could not be avoided. The sources of the problems were various, ranging from whether or not the government should implement democracy to specific policies that were considered unfavourable

---

for example, revealed that Minister of Information Harmoko controls shares in 32 newspapers and magazines, while the twelfth issue appeared with the title 'The President Is Ill? Political Elites Are Struggling'.

to Islam.[16] This went on until the mid-1980s, when the Islamic political
community accepted *Pancasila* as the only ideology of the community, and
the government gradually changed its policies towards Islam.[17]

The relationship between Islam and the state has become much better
since 1990, especially since the government recognised the fact that Islam is
inevitable in Indonesian politics. A high point in this mutual
accommodation occurred when the Association of Indonesian Muslim
Intellectuals (ICMI) was established in December 1990. The question arose
as to why the state had become so accommodating to Islam. There are at
least two answers to this question: first, the government believed that Islam
was no longer a threat to the state as in the past; and second, the presence of
people around the President who have a very strong empathy towards Islam,
in particular, B.J. Habibie. From the Muslim community political
perspective, the tendency towards accommodation is strong because of the
existence of a new element of Islamic leaders in Indonesia who are more
pragmatic and realistic in working with the state, compared to the old
generation. New Islamic leaders such as Nurcholis Madjid, Amien Rais,
Dawam Rahardjo, Amin Azis and many others are a product of the New
Order. They believe that Islam and politics can be reconciled within a non-
zero sum game. Working together with the government is not sinful
behaviour, but it is a way of promoting the Islamic political cause in
Indonesia.

It is also interesting to note that every political association in Indonesia
has the inclination to claim that it represents Islam. This is different from
the past, when the Islamic parties such as Partai Muslimin Indonesia, Partai
Nahdlatul Ulama, Syarikat Islam, and PERTI had almost exclusive rights to
the claim that they represented Islam. Nowadays Golkar and the other two
political parties are inclined to claim that they too represent Islam.
Especially within the Golkar leadership, an element of Islam is quite strong.

---

[16] For example, policies in the 1970s and concerning national holidays during the
fasting month of Ramadhan whether high school students were to be allowed to wear
jilbab (female headgear that covers head and ears, but not the face).

[17] Those policies are as follows: (1) allowing Muslim high school girls to wear
jilbab; (2) sending 1,000 Islamic missionaries to the transmigration and isolated
areas with the sponsorship of the government; (3) financing the construction of
hundreds of mosques throughout the country; (4) establishing the Muamalat Bank;
(5) passing of both Islamic court laws; (6) passing of National Educational Systems
laws; (7) recruiting a number of Islamic figures for the bureaucracy as well as the
parliament and finally (8) erasing of permits to become preacher for Islamic leaders.

Another interesting element we can discern is the fact that the government has shown different treatment to the two largest Islamic organisations, NU and Muhammadyah. The government even now still does not want to recognise the leadership of Abdurrahman Wahid in NU because of his degrading statement about the President quoted in *A Nation in Waiting*.[18] The President, however, was in favour of Muhammadyah. When Muhammadyah conducted a national congress in Banda Aceh in early July 1995, he openly said that in his blood there was a seed of Muhammadyah.[19] It is interesting to note that Soeharto accepted the leadership of Amien Rais, even though the latter had offended Soeharto when in 1993 he talked about the succession of national leadership. The reason why he accepted Amien Rais as chairman of Muhammadyah was that he did not want to add another front of conflict with another Islamic leader, and Minister Habibie was able to convince him that Amien Rais was fully supported by members of Muhammadyah.

The implication of this mutually accommodating relationship between Islam and the state is that the regime can rely on Islam in mobilising political support, while from the Moslem perspective they will be able to promote their own interests, especially in economic terms, in a way that was impossible in the past. They will have access to power and their role will no longer be peripheral when it comes to shaping national policy. 'It is our turn', a Moslem activist recently asserted.[20]

The politics of succession

The discussion of succession was brought up for the first time by Amien Rais in Surabaya in 1993 before the preliminary congress (*Tanwir*) of the Muhammadyah movement. According to Amien Rais at that time,

---

[18] Usually after conducting a congress to elect new leaders, every social and political organisation visits the President. Abdurrahman Wahid was humiliated at the NU congress in Cipasung, West Java, because the President did not want to share the stage with him. It is a symbol of rejection of Wahid's leadership, but he nevertheless survived with a very small margin of support. Up to the present, Wahid has not been able to see the President.

[19] When Muhammadyah held its national congress in addition to the President and Vice President there were thirteen members of the cabinet who presented papers. It was a show of support for Muhammadyah.

[20] This was the assertion of Adi Sasono quoted in 1994 in *Hidayatullah*, a magazine published by a *pesantren* in East Kalimantan but widely distributed in Central and East Java.

succession was a must for several reasons: (a) the regime had been in power for more than thirty years and corruption was continuing without any systematic effort to wipe it out; (b) there was a tendency within the political community to adopt 'the cult of the individual'; (c) succession, rotation or whatever is a must within a democratic political framework; (d) the presidential elites in power had been there too long and therefore they had lost vision and creativity; and (e) the inclination to perceive office as a personal domain is very strong if the elite stays in power for a long time (Rais 1995).

Certainly not many people shared Amien Rais's point of view, especially when he put forward some criteria for the next president. The next president, according to Rais, has to (a) be loyal to *Pancasila* and the national constitution; (b) have personal integrity in the sense that he is not corrupt, has never been involved in a sex scandal, and is a true role model; (c) be a just leader and also fully committed to the people; (d) be highly acceptable to the people; and (e) have a strong vision of science and technology (*ibid*). He seemed to be promoting Habibie because of the reference to a strong vision of science and technology. The real reason, however, why people did not discuss the matter openly was that they did not have the nerve to do so because they did not want to offend Soeharto. 'It is unethical to talk about succession while the President is still in office', they said.

The discussion of succession disappeared for quite some time but it appeared again last June when Habibie was interviewed by a magazine in Jakarta. Habibie asserted that the chance for succession taking place in 1998 is very slim because no one has the leadership qualities of Soeharto. 'It is impossible, no one is able to replace Soeharto', he asserted to *Forum Keadilan* (22 June 1995). However, retired General Suhardiman had a different point of view. He said that the possibility for succession in 1998 is great because the President has revealed some indications of his own opinion about succession. Those indications are: (a) when the President met Ambassador Lopez da Cruz, he asserted that if he is no longer in office he will still have a commitment to helping solve the East Timor affair; (b) Minister Susilo Sudarman said that the dedication of the 1945 generation will finish in 1998; and finally (c) the President asked a *dalang* (puppet master) to perform a special program that suggests succession.[21]

Of course the principal question still remains whether there will be political succession in Indonesia in 1998. In explaining this issue, I attempt

---

[21] The title of the program was *Semar Mbabar Jati Diri* (Semar Revealing His Image) (*Kompas*, 21 June 1995).

to look at the possibility of several political scenarios in the near future or at least in 1998.

The first scenario would be that the President will leave office in 1998 but will try to groom a person able to replace him. This is a 'crown prince' type of scenario in the political system of monarchy. As a great and senior statesman and a person with great influence, he has no difficulty in attempting to find a way for a peaceful transition. The question then is the kind of person to replace him and the kind of political mechanism that can guarantee a peaceful transition. Soeharto would obviously try to find a person whom he can really trust to continue his economic policies. As president he has the authority to summon Golkar leaders and as the supreme commander of the armed forces he has the authority to influence the army to support him for a peaceful transition. Therefore the most important thing is that Golkar has to be able to make a very strong showing and to win with an absolute majority in the 1997 general election. If this is the case, I am convinced that a great majority of the people in the country will support him.

The second scenario would be that the President would leave office in 1998 and let the political community find a way to elect a person who could replace him in a more democratic manner. He would not attempt to promote any individual as the next president. Assuming that the general election in 1997 is the same as in 1992 or in the 1970s and the 1980s, it is up to Golkar and army leaders to decide who the next president would be. We can imagine the possibility of conflict among the elites simply because Indonesia does not have experience in dealing with succession. Suhardiman has said that if that is the case, it will be a 'bloody' conflict. There are many groups adopting a stance right now and waiting for the right moment to take action. 'They have the same tactical as well as strategic interest, that is, anti-establishment and anti-New Order', he said (*Forum Keadilan*, 22 June 1995).

The third scenario would be that the President will stay in office in 1998, which means that there will be no succession until the year 2003, unless he were to become incapacitated before that time. Assuming that he remains in good health, there is no reason for Soeharto to step down; he still wants to see a new and modernising Indonesia enter the next millennium.

The question then is which scenario seems to be the most likely. From my point of view, the chance for the first scenario is very slim because Soeharto would have to face a lot of pressure from several groups of political elites, despite his wide influence. It would be very difficult to find a person who is highly acceptable across the line, and one he could really trust to protect his own interests after he left office. Once he finds a person to be groomed, Soeharto has to take the initiative and call on all strategic political groups around him to reach a national consensus in accepting a new candidate. This would be a very difficult scenario to implement, because pressure would be mounting before consensus was reached and the chance for conflict would also be great.

The second political option is not a good scenario in terms of protecting Soeharto's own interests, because there is no guarantee that the person who replaces him will have similar commitments when he is in office. We also have to take into account the fact that in most countries of the Third World, accountability takes place when the leader is no longer in office because the competing elites then have the opportunity to scrutinise all the policies of the leader who leaves office. Hence I do not see much chance of this scenario eventuating because it would not be good for Soeharto, even if it was preferable for democracy in Indonesia.

The third scenario, I believe, has the best chance of emerging in 1998. The reasons are as follows. First, no one in the country has the courage to tell the President that it is about time for him to leave office and to give a chance to the new generation since he has been there for such a long time. Secondly, the people around him, especially his immediate family members and the conglomerates as well as politicians such as Habibie and Harmoko, have great stakes in maintaining the continuity of the regime in terms of their business as well as political interests. Therefore it is hard for Soeharto to reject the pressure to stay in power, even though he may want to retire. Thirdly, most of the political community do not want to take any risks in the sense that there is no guarantee that the new leader will have the same capacity and commitment as the present incumbent does. This is the case especially for Indonesian Moslems.[22] Finally, the President does not show any kind of weariness when he meets people, which means that, although he is getting old, he still has a very good mind in leading the country. Almost every week he meets people and talks for hours about almost every aspect of economic development. He seems to enjoy meeting people and shows no signs of fatigue, which indicates that there is no reason for leaving office.

---

[22] Recently a number of Moslem *ulamas* made a pledge to support Soeharto again in 1998. They came from Jombang (East Java) and Serant (West Java). About 75 *ulamas* from Aceh also met the President in Jakarta. These are indications that the political community, especially the Islamic community, does not want to take the risk of replacing Soeharto.

From the above analysis one can discern that the possibility of succession in 1998 is very unlikely and that Soeharto will stay in office until 2003, assuming that he remains in good health.

Preparing for political transition?

Although succession is not going to take place in the near future, a lot of things occurred in 1995 that I believe will eventually lead in setting the tone for political transition. The changing of military elites that shaped a new political alliance and faction and the emergence of new ruling elites dominated by Moslems are cases in point.

Soeharto is a political genius when it comes to choosing people whom he can really count on. In January 1995 he replaced the flamboyant General Wismoyo Arismunandar with General Raden Hartono, a Moslem officer from East Java, as chief of staff of the army.[23] Following the removal of Wismoyo Arismunandar, we also observed the removal of several army leaders from important positions within the army, such as Hendropriyono (Commander of the Jakarta Division), Agum Gumelar (Commander of the Red Berets), and Harris Sudarno (Commander of the Brawijaya Division). Those generals were associated with Wismoyo. Many people considered that the change within the army will determine the kind of succession that occurs in 1998 (*Gatra*, 4 September 1995).

In fact, Soeharto's action was intended to create a 'new and stronger political alignment' with the Islamic political community in preparing for political transition in the near future. The popular belief in Indonesia today is that there is a strong alliance between B.J. Habibie, Minister of Research and Technology and Chairman of ICMI (plus at least thirty other strategic positions), and Raden Hartono, Chief of Staff of the Army. They are supported by Harmoko, Minister of Information and Chairman of Golkar. These three individuals have such great access to the President that they have the opportunity to shape government policy. It is interesting to note that this alliance is also supported by the children of the President, especially Mrs Hardianti Rukmana and Bambang Trihatmojo. Both of them are at present leaders of Golkar, being Vice Chairman and Treasurer respectively.

---

[23] Wismoyo Arismunandar is a brother-in-law of Mrs Soeharto and therefore may people expected him to become the Joint Chief of the Armed Forces of Indonesia in place of General Faisal Tanjung. The president did not renew his term, and in fact appointed Wismoyo Arismunandar as chairman of the Indonesian Olympic Committee.

Certainly the Islamic political community has the same perspective and therefore they fully support the above alliance. What I mean by the 'Islamic political community' here are those who belong to ICMI, most of the Muhammadyah activists, an element of the Dewan Dakwah Islam (DDI) or the Moslem Missionary Council and of course all Islamic organisations that belong to Golkar such as Majelis Dakwah Islamiyah (MDI) and GUPPI, and members of the NU who are not in line with the pro-democratic or reformist group led by Khalik Mawardi and Slamet Effendi Yusef.

These are the groups that will play a dominant role in the next general election, which will eventually decide the future of Indonesian politics. I mention these groups in the political community as the alliance of the 'pro-establishment' groups.

In 1995 we are also able to identify another political alignment of the elites led by senior army officers such as Moerdiono, Minister of the Office of the President, and Edi Sudradjat of the Department of Defence. General Edi Sudradjat has voiced some critical opinions about the present development of the country. It was Edi Sudradjat who openly criticised the role of bureaucratic offspring in Indonesian business (*Forum Keadilan*, 31 July 1994). His latest controversial comments were about members of the armed forces who had become guardians of the conglomerates.

This alignment certainly has its own following who share the same perceptions and commitments, that is, they want to see changes towards a more democratic Indonesia. This is what I called the alliance of the 'pro-democratic' groups.[24] Supporters of the pro-democratic alliance are as follows: (a) members of non-government organisations (NGOs); (b) intellectuals who do not belong to ICMI, such as the Forum Demokrasi group; (c) human rights activists; (d) a number of the nationalists or Sukarnoists as well as the *abangan* political community; (5) a number of the reformists of the NU led by Abdurrahman Wahid; and certainly (e) most of the Protestant and Catholic political communities. The pro-democratic alliance no longer plays a significant role in influencing the President. The motive of this group is that they want to limit the role of Islam in Indonesian politics, especially within the bureaucracy.

The first indicator of the difference between these groups was their perception of ICMI. From the beginning of its existence, the reception of ICMI was marked by pro and contra arguments. The people who do not

[24] To avoid misunderstandings I want to make it clear that the effort for democracy does not only belong to these groups; the 'pro-establishment' groups also have democratic aspirations but they have difficulties in articulating them because they are very close to the regime.

accept ICMI believe that the creation of an intellectual organisation of this kind takes Indonesia back to the old political cleavages of the 1950s based on *aliran*. It was General Edi Sudradjat who was in favour of creating a different intellectual organisation, namely Ikatan Cendekiawan Nasional Indonesia, while Hartono, Habibie and Harmoko were in favour of ICMI.[25]

The difference between the two groups could be discerned also when the Nahdlatul Ulama held a national congress last year in Cipasung, West Java. The pro-establishment element by implication did not accept the leadership of Abdurrahman Wahid because the latter was very critical of the regime as well as of Islamic activists, especially members of ICMI. Abdurrahman Wahid on the other hand bluntly complained that it was General Raden Hartono who had attempted to influence NU activists to reject him becoming chairman of NU. Nevertheless, Wahid survived by mobilising a number of NGOs and with the support of senior army officers, namely, Edi Sudradjat and Moerdiono.

Certainly there are several other indicators concerning the difference between these two alliances and I believe that politics in Indonesia for the years to come will be characterised by a tug-of-war between the 'pro-establishment' on the one hand and the 'pro-democratic' groups on the other hand. They are now preparing their stances in preparation for political transition towards the post-Soeharto era in Indonesia. The type of political transition very much depends on which group prevails.

---

[25] Edi Sudradjat's efforts to create such an intellectual organisation did not come into existence because of the timing, when it created an impression of limiting the movement of ICMI. Another group of people sponsored by Alamsyah Ratuprawiranegara, former Minister of Religious Affairs, attempted to establish Ikatan Cendekiawan Kebangsaan Indonesia but failed. The latest development was that a group of people in Purwokerto, Central Java, with the support of Susilo Sudarman, established Persatuan Cendekiawan Pembangunan Pancasila (PCPP) or United Intellectuals for the Development of *Pancasila*.

PART II: EASTERN INDONESIA

4

Beyond the Wallace Line

Richard Chauvel

Eastern Indonesia — Indonesia 'goes east'

The references in President Soeharto's Budget Speech of January 1990 to the importance of developing the eastern region of the archipelago represented an important departure in post-Independence Indonesian thinking about the nature and composition of the state.[1] The republican tradition dating from the Revolution had sought to emphasise the unity of the state and disparage the Netherlands' federal policies, with their emphasis on the differences and diversities among the societies of the archipelago. The Netherlands policy, its obvious political motives aside, counterposed that Indonesian societies' complexities and variation should be reflected in the structure of government. The regional challenges to Jakarta's authority during the 1950s served to strengthen the felt need for strong centralised control from the centre. Among the New Order government's achievements has been the extension and consolidation of the central government's authority throughout the archipelago. The old republican ideal has been to a large extent realised during President Soeharto's long tenure. Indonesia's diversity is recognised in the national motto, but its representation is more evident in Taman Mini than in effective regional autonomy.

The President's speech was made at a time when concerns about growing inequalities of wealth were being expressed publicly and his remarks seem to have legitimised discussion of regional differences. The media discussion which followed was protracted and lively. It was the first time a region had been singled out as a development problem. Commentators spoke of the

---

[1] The term *Indonesia Bagian Timur* (Eastern Indonesia) was first coined in 1980 at a meeting organised by the East Nusa Tenggara Provincial Government in Kupang. It did not gain much currency until the President used it. I am indebted to Dr Ben Mboi for this information.

government's new found 'political will' to develop Eastern Indonesia.[2] The recognition of Eastern Indonesia's particular problems was welcomed, not least by leaders from the region itself. They were keen to identify the complexities of the problems to be confronted, but the government's recognition was greatly appreciated.[3] Without wanting to draw too close a parallel, the response was not dissimilar to that of the East Indonesian delegates at the Malino and Denpasar conferences, when van Mook unveiled the State of East Indonesia. In 1946 the region's leaders accepted the State, not as an expression of their support for van Mook's anti-republican strategy, but rather as an indication that the colonial authorities were intent on redressing decades of neglect, which had left them with the impression that the government only had eyes for Java and Sumatra and that the eastern archipelago was forever being left behind (Groen 1979:13).[4]

The participants in the media discussions and the inevitable seminars which followed the President's speech were aware that regional imbalances had long been a feature of Indonesian economic development. The old colonial saying *De Molukken het verleden, Java het heden en Sumatra de toekomst* (Maluku is the past, Java the present and Sumatra the future), was transformed and used as a statement of optimism. Professor Sumitro Djojohardikusumo proclaimed that Eastern Indonesia would become the source of hope for future generations of Indonesians. The position of Java, as the economic power house, had passed to Sumatra and Kalimantan. 'From an economic standpoint Java only remains as the past and Eastern Indonesia represents Indonesia's future.[5]

The President's remarks and much of the discussion which followed were directed to the problems of economic development in Eastern Indonesia. There were few dissenters from the proposition that Eastern Indonesia had been left behind in the country's impressive economic growth over the previous decade. Issues of poor communication infrastructures, small isolated communities, low and declining levels of domestic and foreign investment and access to markets were all canvassed. The great potential of the region's maritime, forestry and mineral resources was also noted. How

[2] F.Seda, *Pemerintah Indonesia "Goes East"*: *Diperlukan Kerangkah Konseptual'* [The Indonesian Govenrment 'Goes East', The Need for a Conceptual Framework].
[3] See for example ibid; Nikolaas, HE, *'Mengurangi Kemiskinan Dan Isolasi Sasaran Pembangalan Indonesia Timur'*.
[4] Petra Groen, *'Oprichting, Functioneren en Opheffing van de Deelstaat Oost-Indonesie: 1946-1950'*,. Doctoraal scriptie, University of Utrecht, 1979, p.13.
[5] Prof. Sumitro, *'Jawa Masa Lalu Indonesia Timur Masa Depan'*, Suara Pembaruan, 16-1-90.

could the perceived imbalance in Indonesia's economic development be remedied? As Hadi Soesastro (1990) pointed out, the obstacles to development were easier to identify than the solutions. However, there were those who thought of Eastern Indonesia in a broader context, and realised that the government's recognition of Eastern Indonesia's economic backwardness had far-reaching implications.

The development of Eastern Indonesia opened a grand vista for some commentators. It would mean the realisation of the *wawasan nusantara* (archipelago concept). Indonesia would be transformed from being a mere political power to an economic and cultural one as well.[6] Frans Seda put the proposition another way. He considered that the imbalance in development between Western and Eastern Indonesia posed a danger to national unity and the *wawasan nusantara*. Minimising the imbalance would combat the emergence of regional jealousies which are increasing by being concocted.[7] Professor Sumitro anticipated that in the 21st century Eastern Indonesia would be at the crossroads of Asia-Pacific trade.[8] The region would be Indonesia's doorway into the world of Australia and the South Pacific. The development of Eastern Indonesia was seen to have a role in the solution of present-day threats to national unity. Attention was drawn to the areas of political discontent — Irian Jaya and Timor Timur (East Timor) — where there were 'those who did not agree with or did not understand our policies'. Even the revolts of the Republic of the South Moluccas and Permesta occasionally resurfaced in the discussion.[9] Retired General Soemitro argued that developing Eastern Indonesia would extinguish the fires of separatism, which had done so much to discredit Indonesia internationally..[10]

There were also cautionary notes in the public discussion. The former Governor of East Nussa Tenggara, Ben Mboi, warned that Eastern Indonesia should not be seen merely as a macro problem. The region did not present one set of problems but many. The complexity of economic problems reflected the structure of a region composed of many relatively small and

---

[6] Soemitro, '*Alternatif Pemikiran Pembangunan Indonsia Bagian Timur*'.

[7] Frans Seda, '*Pemerintah Indonesia* "Goes East": *Diperlukan Kerangkah Konseptual*', *Kompas*, 21-3-90.

[8] Prof. Sumitro, '*Jawa Masa Lalu Indonesia Timur Masa Depan*', *Suara Pembaruan*, 16-1-90.

[9] Ben Mboi, '*Indonesia Bagian Timur Isu Arah Pembangunan Desawarsa 90-an*', *Suara Pembaruan*, 26-2-90.

[10] '*Soemitro: IBT Jangan Iri Hati*', *Suara Karya*, 3-5-90.

often isolated communities.[11] This approach opened the way for others to argue the case for development strategies appropriate to local economic structures and cultures. Irian Jaya was the most often cited case, where the development strategy should be entirely different from other areas.[12] There was some broader recognition that a decentralised approach to planning should replace the highly centralised policy formulation and implementation which had characterised economic planning under the New Order.[13] Given the vast distances within Eastern Indonesia and its constituent provinces, effective local autonomy should be an important ingredient in development strategies in the region.

The Wallace line

One feature of the Indonesian discussion of Eastern Indonesia was the frequent references made to the Wallace line as a means of delineating the region. The references to Wallace's century-old observations remind us that the idea that Eastern Indonesia is somehow different has a long history. Wallace argued that the Indonesian archipelago had always been treated as 'one compact geographic whole', but his more careful and detailed study revealed the unexpected fact that it was divisible into two portions of nearly equal size and formed parts of two primary divisions of the earth. Java, Sumatra and Borneo resemble in their 'natural production' the adjacent areas of mainland South-East Asia, while the islands from Sulawesi and Lombok eastwards exhibit almost as great a similarity to Australia and New Guinea as the western islands do to the mainland. Wallace went beyond observing the differences in flora and fauna. He divided the inhabitants of the archipelago into two 'radically distinct races'. Wallace felt able to classify the peoples of the archipelago as either 'Malays' or 'Papuans', who 'differed radically in every physical, mental and moral character'. He contended that the racial dividing line lay further to the east, running through Maluku and between Sumba and Sumbawa (Figure 1.1), than that which distinguished the archipelago's flora and fauna. He explained the difference between the two Wallace lines in terms of the Malays' maritime enterprise and higher civilisation enabling them to inhabit a portion of the

---

[11] Ben Mboi, 'Indonesia Bagian Timur Isu Arah Pembangunan Desawarsa 90-an', Suara Pembaruan, 26-2-90.

[12] Prof Dr Hendra.Esmara, 'Pendekatan Pembangunan Irian Jaya Berbeda Dengan Daerah Lain', Suara Pembaruan, 3-2-90.

[13] 'Soemitro: IBT Jangan Iri Hati', Suara Karya, 3-5-90.

adjacent region (Wallace 1962:2, 10, 11, 15). Given the strength, clarity and racist overtones of Wallace's views, it is perhaps surprising that his division of the archipelago still has some currency in contemporary Indonesian discourse.

Wallace's division of the archipelago found greater resonance in colonial Netherlands attitudes to the nature and composition of the archipelago. The dominant Netherlands conception saw the archipelago more as a mosaic of cultures and societies, almost accidentally brought under one colonial administration, rather than in terms of Wallace's clear division. However, among some officials who served in the eastern archipelago, Wallace's delineation was adopted as seemingly relevant to their administrative tasks. One retiring Resident of the Moluccas advised his successor in these terms:

> As you come out of the west, you feel that to the east
> of Buton you have stepped into another world. You
> have crossed the threshold of the Australian Pacific,
> the world of the South Seas ... Jack London's stories,
> Hawaiian girls, beachcombers and pearl divers take
> shape, crotouquirlandes and hula-hula dances become
> reality.

It was first necessary for a newly appointed official to transform himself. In this extraordinary world other standards had to be established and an official had to feel things differently. The inevitable consequence was the possibility of persistent misunderstandings between Batavia and the local administration. Unlike Wallace, some colonial officials emphasised the great diversity to be found in the eastern archipelago and the administrative problems this posed. It was a meeting place of the most modern and the least developed peoples of the archipelago. Living side by side were the education-rich Christian Ambonese, with their highly Westernised culture, and Irianese head-hunters, with their erotic dances.[14]

The structure of the colonial administration in the eastern archipelago was the product of three centuries of gradual but haphazard Netherlands administrative encroachment. The result was a patchwork quilt of administrative arrangements. Until the creation of the government of the *Groote Oost* (Great East) in 1938, the region was administered in five governments or residencies: Menado, Sulawesi and dependencies, the Moluccas including Irian Jaya, Timor and dependencies, Bali and Lombok. Within these entities the administration was divided between directly ruled areas and 115 indirectly-ruled 'self-governing' territories. The latter

---

[14] B.J. Haga, *Mcmorie van Overgave van Bestuur van den Aftreden Resident der Molukken*, 1937.

constituted some 70 per cent of Eastern Indonesia's territory. The indigenous political structures were preserved to a degree, and the territories enjoyed some notional local autonomy. The relatively smaller size of ethnic groups in Eastern Indonesia, compared with Sumatra, meant that rarely was a single ethnic group of sufficient size to constitute a residency. Given the *ad hoc* growth of the administrative system, some ethnic groups were administered in different districts and under direct and indirect styles of administration.[15]

The Groote Oost

The Netherlands Indies State, as it was consolidated at the turn of the century, was governed through a highly centralised administrative structure. The general thrust of administrative reform during the last half century of Netherland's rule was directed at breaking down Batavia's iron grip. 'Decentralisation' became the label of a variety of administrative reforms, which included the establishment of autonomous or self-governing entities. Principal among the objectives of 'decentralisation' was the promotion of administrative efficiency, in order to support the expansion and penetration of commercial enterprise (Furnivall 1976: 261-63).

The focus of administrative reform, as with most other matters, was in Java then Sumatra. It was important to make the administration more efficient so as to facilitate development. In 1930 the government submitted proposals to the *Volksraad* for the creation of three new 'governments' in the outer islands: Sumatra, Borneo and the *Groote Oost*. The proposals were approved in 1932, after protracted and at times heated discussion, but it was not until 1938 that the new governments were established. The rationale for Sumatra and Borneo seemed clear in the government's mind, but the *Groote Oost* was a residual category where the remainder of the archipelago was grouped together as much for administrative convenience as out of the belief that the region formed a cultural, political or economic entity. It was the government's intention to make Sumatra into a 'province', but there were doubts whether there was sufficient community of interest in the *Groote Oost*. Ironically, the proposal to establish the *Groote Oost* was supported by the region's representatives in the *Volksraad*. Indeed they defeated an attempt to transfer the administration of Bali to Java. It was the Sumatran

---

[15] 'N', *'De Regeeringsplannen voor de Bustuurs-hervorming in de Buitengewesten in den Volksraad'*, *Koloniaal Tijschrift*, jg 21, 1931. pp.395-6.

representatives who opposed the creation of one government for their island out of fear of inter-ethnic conflict.[16]

The colonial government's objective in creating the large administrative units of Sumatra, Borneo and the *Groote Oost* was to bring great uniformity and continuity to bureaucratic reform. It was felt that the rapid economic and political change in the outer islands had brought the previously closed and isolated communities into greater contact with each other as well as exposing them to massive influence from outside. The resulting administrative problems were no longer local in character. The rationale for creating a huge administrative entity encompassing the eastern archipelago was the belief that effective reform and decentralisation could only take place where the administrative entity was sufficiently large to possess a wide range of technical and managerial skills to assume significant government responsibilities.[17] In the eastern archipelago the dilemma was that such an expansive entity had no indigenous roots. No sense of common identity underpinned it.

Eastern Indonesia came to form an administrative unit on the eve of the Pacific War. Although it had the support of the region's representatives in the *Volksraad*, the *Groote Oost* was a central government policy-makers' solution to a set of administrative and economic development problems. The outbreak of the war meant that the *Groote Oost*'s historical importance was as a precedent for the creation of the postwar Federal State of East Indonesia (*Negara Indonesia Timur*, NIT). Its life span was insufficient to suggest whether it would have developed as a vehicle for territorial decentralisation. As it was, the Netherlands Indies ended as a unity state with a small measure of autonomy at the local level.

The Japanese separation of the eastern archipelago as an area of naval administration represents a sharper break in the administration of the area than anything the Dutch contemplated. It would seem that the Japanese envisaged that after the successful completion of the war eastern Indonesia would remain part of the empire, while the western archipelago would be granted self-government (Chauvel 1990:174-75). The Allied division of responsibility between Australian and British forces for the reoccupation of Indonesia perpetuated an administrative distinction between Eastern

---

[16] Simon van der Harst, *Overzicht van de bestuurshervorming in de Buitengewesten van Nederlansch-Jndie, in het bijzonder op Sumatra*, NV A, Oosthock, Utrecht, 1945. pp.57-8; 'N', '*De Regeeringsplannen voor de Bustuurs-hervorming in de Buitengewesten in den Volksraad*', *Koloniaal Tijschrift*, jg 21, 1931. Pp.402, 404-5.

[17] 'N', '*De Regeeringsplannen voor de Bustuurs-hervorming in de Buitengewesten in den Volksraad.*' *Koloniaal Tijschrift*, jg 21, 1931. pp.397.

Indonesia and the remainder of the archipelago. Agung (1985:119-121) has argued that Australian policies contributed to the weakness of nationalist forces in the region, and when the Dutch established the Federal State of East Indonesia the nationalists had little option but to cooperate.

Negara Indonesia Timur

This is not the place to re-examine van Mook's attempt to contain and combat the republic through the creation of federal states. However, the NIT experience provides a unique opportunity to examine the social, cultural and political dynamics of the region. The NIT was the most significant political institution to encompass the region now referred to as Eastern Indonesia. Bali was an important part of the NIT, but Irian Jaya and East Timor lay outside its boundaries. The NIT was not merely a continuation of the pre-war government of the *Groote Oost*. In the very different political circumstances created by the defeat of Japan and the proclamation of Indonesian independence, the regional political elites played a not insignificant role in the creation and governance of the NIT. To what extent did the Indonesian participants consider that NIT constituted a political or cultural entity distinct from Indonesia as a whole? What were the forces and factors which bound the region together?

Before the war the creation of the *Groote Oost* was something of an afterthought in the priorities of Batavia's policy-makers. In 1945 and 1946 the region became a cornerstone of Dutch strategy against the republic. The eastern archipelago was a region where the Dutch had been able, with Australian assistance, to re-establish their control. It was somewhere the Dutch could construct their alternative to the republic. It hardly needs restating that the initiative to establish the NIT was Dutch. It was the first and most substantial of the federal states. What emerged out of the formation phase of the NIT were two distinct conceptions of the region: the Batavia policy-makers gazing out beyond the Wallace line, and the regional elites looking inward and upward to Makassar (now Ujung Pandang).

Van Mook's overriding objective in constructing a system of federal states was to contain the power and influence of the republicans in Java and Sumatra.[18] Since before the war a federal structure of government had been advocated as a means of preventing the domination of one ethnic group over the archipelago. Among the delegates at the Malino and Denpasar

---

[18] *Nota van* ...(van Mook?), 25-11-45, S.L. van der Wal (ed). *Nederlands-Indonesische Betrekkingen* (hereafter *NIB)* II, p.172

conferences of 1946 the Dutch hoped that this aspect of a federal system would have an appeal. Even among the delegates the Dutch themselves had appointed the strength of feeling for Indonesian national unity was dominant. The Dutch hoped that a system of federal states would offer an acceptable compromise between fulfilment of Indonesian national aspirations, on the one side, and the preservation of a full measure of local autonomy and protection from the unwanted influence of outsiders, on the other.[19]

Van Mook anticipated that the principal danger to be confronted at the Malino and Denpasar conferences was 'local patriotism' and demands for the creation of smaller states. He would be open to suggestions from the delegates, but he would not compromise on this point. He feared that if the outer islands were split up into small states, they would not be able to exercise sufficient influence to balance Java. He wanted to devolve as much as possible of the central government's responsibilities to the federal states. This would only be practical if the states were large.[20] Apart from the promise of constitutional balance and protection, van Mook appealed to the east Indonesians' sense of having been neglected. He acknowledged that before the war the highly centralised government's care and attention had not extended to the more distant territories in the east. Since the defeat of Japan the colonial authorities had been preoccupied with negotiations with the Republic and re-establishing their control. The NIT was the concrete embodiment of a commitment to change old priorities.[21]

As previously noted, the delegates from the eastern archipelago who gathered at Malino and Denpasar in general welcomed the establishment of the NIT. Seemingly they saw no contradiction between their support of Indonesian independence and the acceptance of a federal structure. Indeed one of the main themes of the Indonesian contributions to the discussions was a concern that the NIT would be sufficiently strong to be considered an equal to the Republic. The delegates did not want the NIT to be seen as a colonial creation. It should have the same constitutional and international status as the republic. Reflecting the old sense of neglect, one of the most frequent complaints directed towards the colonial authorities was that the Dutch had negotiated with the Republic and not with them. There were

---

[19] *Rapport van de regeringsvoorlichtingdienst voor Lt. Gouverneur-generaal*, 14-7-46, *NIB*, IV.p.653.

[20] *Kort verslag vergadering van departementshoofden te Batavia*, 10-7-46. NIB, IV, p.647.

[21] *De Conferentie te Denpasar*, deel 1, G. Kollf & Co. Batavia, 1947, pp.13, 15.

insistent demands that when the NIT was established there should be an agreement equivalent to Linggadjati.[22]

Below the level of general acceptance of the federal proposal, however, there were doubts expressed about the composition and nature of the proposed state. These contributions revealed the strength of the 'local patriotisms' and the absence of any more inclusive identity other than that of being Indonesian. As the Dutch had feared, there were demands for the creation of smaller states. There were those, particularly Balinese, who argued that there was no cultural bond between the component parts of the NIT. A separate state bringing together Bali, West Nusa Tenggara and East Nusa Tenggara would be more appropriate. This concern was also expressed in terms of the demand to preserve the local autonomy. Sukawati, the future 'President' of the NIT, feared that the new state would impinge on the responsibilities previously exercised by local administrations. Given the preponderance of indirectly-ruled 'self-governing' territories in the NIT, the insistence on local autonomy was closely related to the desire of the traditional elites from these territories to preserve their authority. The representatives of the small, more distant islands doubted the benefits of the creation of such an extensive state. They feared that their voice would carry little weight in Makassar.[23]

At Denpasar a representative from Flores noted that there was no ethos of citizenship among the diverse peoples of Eastern Indonesia. There was no identification with or affection for the community represented by the State. In these circumstances, the new state had to be as democratic and as open as possible, supporting individuals and communities to develop themselves.[24]

Another dimension of the fragmented character of the region at the time of the NIT's formation was the local rivalries. The colonial authorities saw these as an obstacle to the development of a more inclusive regional identity. Ambon and the Ambonese seemed to pose particular problems. The behaviour of Ambonese KNIL (Dutch colonial army) soldiers during the first year of the Revolution had done much to antagonise fellow Indonesians. In terms of the structure of administration in the new state, neither the local elites in North Maluku nor South East Maluku wanted to be under the same local administration as the Ambonese or to have Ambon as the administrative centre. In Irian Jaya local leaders were highly critical of the

---

[22] ibid, pp.34, 47.
[23] *Verslag van de bijeenkornst van de Malino-conferentie met de vertegenwoordigers van Bali, Lombok en Timor op 20 juli 1946, NIB* V, pp.41-43.
[24] Pastoor P.J. Raats, in *De Conferentie te Denpasar,* deel 1, G. Kolff & Co, Batavia, 1947, p.55.

dominant role that Ambonese officials, missionaries and teachers played. They wanted the Ambonese expatriated.[25] The issue of local dominance was as pertinent for the region's leaders as the broader balance of power within the archipelago was for the colonial authorities.

The Dutch concluded that support for the NIT in large measure would be dependent on appropriate regulation guaranteeing local autonomy. The Malino delegates were reassured that local autonomy would in no way be diminished. The responsibilities of the NIT would not be those previously exercised at the local level, but rather those undertaken by Batavia. Within the region, all the component parts carried equal weight. One area could not be outvoted by another.[26] As the *daerah* administration developed during the following years, the NIT became a federal system within a federal state, with the *daerah* administrations exercising wide authority independently of the government in Makassar.

The NIT might have been the most substantial and viable of the federal states established by the Netherlands, but it was a precariously balanced structure. South Sulawesi was the demographic centre of the state and Makassar was its political and administrative capital. The Netherlands only managed to re-establish its authority after Westerling's suppression of republican resistance. The suppression left a legacy of bitterness and hatred in the South Sulawesi heartland against the Dutch and those Indonesians who cooperated with the NIT administration. 'Outsiders' — Christian Menadonese and Ambonese together with Balinese aristocrats — were prominent in the NIT leadership. The overriding cleavage in NIT politics was between pro-Republic groups, centred in South Sulawesi but scattered throughout the region, and those who, to varying degrees, supported the Dutch or at least the federal states. However, there was a second layer of 'primordial' conflict which was much more reflective of the highly heterogenous composition of the region. At Malino and Denpasar the demands for local autonomy emanated mostly from Bali, East Nusa Tenggara and West Nusa Tenggara. By 1947 separatism in Menado, Ambon and West Timor posed a much greater threat to the integrity of the NIT. Support for separatism in these three areas was associated with some of the more conservative groups, traditional elites and KNIL soldiers and veterans, groups which would normally have been expected to support the Dutch.

---

[25] *Rapport van de regeringsvoorlichtingdienst voor Lt. Gouverneur-generaal*, 14-7-46, *NIB*. IV. p.655.

[26] *Verslag van de bijeenkornst van de Malino-conferentie met de vertegenwoordigers van Bali, Lombok en Timor op 20 juli 1946*; *Kort verslag van de ochtendvergadering van de Malino-conferentie op 20 juli 1946*, *NIB* V, pp.38, 41-43.

However, the separatist groups saw little community of interest with other peoples in the NIT and feared domination from Makassar nearly as much as domination from Java. They sought to use the self-determination articles (3 and 4) in the Linggadjati Agreement to disassociate their areas from the NIT and resume their rightful place as part of the Kingdom of the Netherlands.

Netherland's policy-makers appreciated the fragile nature of the NIT. They depicted three political groups in the state: republicans, ideologically nationalist but fearful of Javanese domination, the pro-Dutch federalists gathered around the Ambonese KNIL officer Julius Tahya, and the pro-Dutch federalists. Only the small Tahya group had any confidence in the NIT. The viability of the NIT would depend, first, on persuading the republicans that their nationalist aspirations could be satisfied in the NIT, and secondly, on making the separatists realise that their desire for local autonomy could only be found in the NIT.[27] Some of the political leaders who assumed positions in the NIT's institutions established careers which they might have felt would have been denied them in a unitary state.

When, in 1950, the crunch came for the NIT, the two levels of conflict — unitarists versus federalists and 'local patriotisms' — combined to hasten the state's collapse. President Sukawati and Soumokil's attempt to defend the NIT and, if necessary, proclaim the NIT as an independent state rested on some of the 'outsider' (ie non-South Sulawesi) leaders of the government together with the support of KNIL soldiers, mainly Menadonese and Ambonese. It failed because of the near total absence of support from the South Sulawesi heartland, and in the last analysis even the outlying Christian areas such as Menado and Ambon were deeply divided in their support for the NIT. The factors which gave the NIT some cohesion — fear of domination from outside, the preservation of local autonomy and the prospect of overcoming economic neglect — proved insufficient to overcome the conflicts and rivalries between the ethnic and religious groups within the state. No broader regional identity emerged to compete with Indonesian nationalism.

The pattern of post-1950 politics in Eastern Indonesia would suggest that the factors which undermined the NIT persist. The collapse of the NIT was the immediate catalyst for the proclamation of the Republic of the South Moluccas (the Moluccas are now called Maluku). At the same time in South Sulawesi Kahar Muzakar started his decade-long struggle with Jakarta. In 1958 the Permesta rebellion broke out in North Sulawesi, led by former Republican Army officers. Almost immediately following Indonesia's

[27] Ministry of Overseas Territories. VB 16-6-47, Q.37. no.169. ARA. The Hague.

successful struggle against the Dutch to (re)acquire Irian Jaya, Irianese started their resistance and in a sporadic, ill-organised and low-level way have sustained it under the OPM banner until now. Since Indonesia's annexation of East Timor, resistance has been developed, with varying degrees of international support, at a much higher level than in Irian Jaya. As is befitting the highly heterogenous character and composition of the eastern archipelago, each of these resistance movements emerged in particular historical circumstances and has been sustained by factors peculiar to each region. Nevertheless, some of the features of political conflict which characterised the NIT experience are still evident. Each of these movements is the product of what van Mook referred to as 'local patriotisms'. Each of them exhibits the desire to preserve local autonomy or establish independence, yet their appeal is restricted to the local ethnic group. The Republic of the South Moluccas was a Christian Ambonese affair. It was unable to mobilise significant support in South East Maluku because of the long-established local resentment of the domination of Ambon. The struggle of the East Timorese seemingly has not evoked any response from across the border in West Timor. Only Kahar Muzakar and Permesta had links to other resistance movements, Darul Islam and PRRI (the Sumatran rebel movement) respectively. Neither of them was able to broaden support within Eastern Indonesia.

The *Groote Oost, Negara Indonesia Timur and* Eastern Indonesia have one thing in common, apart from geography. They are all formulations of central government policy-makers. Although the objectives and political circumstances of each differed markedly, they do represent how the eastern archipelago appears from Batavia-Jakarta. The views of the region about itself have tended to be less straight forward. It is not the intention of this paper to suggest that there are not broad and useful distinctions between the eastern and western parts of the archipelago, but the difficulty emerges because the dominant characteristic of Eastern Indonesia is its very diversity, composed as it is of a large number of relatively small and often isolated communities. The historical experience of Eastern Indonesia's societies has not facilitated the development of a community of interest. These societies include some with as long and intense experience of colonialism as any in the archipelago, and yet others which had been barely touched by the Indies administration by the time of independence. The NIT experience and the post-independence pattern of regional resistance to Jakarta's authority would suggest that many societies in Eastern Indonesia share a desire for local autonomy and a longing to overcome their economic backwardness and isolation. Yet the sense of identification and definition of

interest has been such as to preclude much cooperation with neighbouring
societies.

5

Eastern Indonesia in the current policy environment

Iwan J. Azis

Introduction

Relatively speaking, Indonesia has a better record than many other countries in overcoming the adverse epiphenomena that generally accompany rapid economic growth and economic reform in developing countries. The incidence of poverty continues to decline, and a number of social indicators (including the school enrolment ratio, literacy rate, infant mortality and nutritional status) have also shown persistent improvement over the last decade.

In spite of the trend, however, a desirable level of regional balance has not yet been achieved. Often quoted illustrations in this context would traditionally be Java versus non-Java and, more recently, the imbalances between Eastern Indonesia and the western regions. Eastern Indonesia is, in general, less developed in terms of output and almost all production factors except its vast area and richness in natural resources. The insufficiency of infrastructure and the lack of a critical pool of skilled labour are frequently identified as important factors hindering further growth of the region[1].

The economic structure of Eastern Indonesia is also very different from that of Western Indonesia. In 1993, more than half of GRDP in Eastern Indonesia still originated in the agricultural sector, compared to a mere 18

---

[1] The non-physical catalysts are no less crucial. Numerous regulations and unnecessary bureaucracies still persist in the region, and their removal would have considerable impact on the revitalisation of the region's economy.

Table 5.1: *Shares of agriculture and manufacturing in GRDP of Western and Eastern Indonesia, 1993 (percentages)*

	Agri-culture	Small-holdings	Large estates	Live-stock	Fish-eries	Manu-facturing	Large & medium	Small & home	Non-oil mfg	GRDP[a]
Western Indonesia	17.81	2.38	0.85	1.97	1.41	22.39	18.15	2.86	21.00	100
Eastern Indonesia										
West Nusa Tenggara	45.99	3.33	0.00	6.76	4.81	2.73	1.15	2.20	3.35	100
East Nusa Tenggara	45.68	4.76	0.05	10.90	4.11	2.24	0.65	2.17	2.82	100
East Timor	35.04	6.91	0.00	6.58	0.64	1.65	0.73	1.45	2.18	100
North Sulawesi	38.43	12.63	0.00	3.77	3.63	5.64	4.06	3.30	7.36	100
Central Sulawesi	45.18	14.36	0.10	4.94	5.95	6.12	3.75	4.10	7.84	100
South Sulawesi	40.86	5.96	0.14	3.90	8.19	9.19	8.11	3.58	11.69	100
South East Sulawesi	43.62	17.06	0.00	4.47	5.25	2.27	1.41	1.40	2.81	100
Maluku	32.15	8.48	0.00	1.27	5.97	16.69	18.98	0.76	19.74	100
Irian Jaya	21.91	0.82	0.00	1.12	5.30	2.10	2.07	0.72	2.79	100
Total	56.68	10.61	0.09	4.27	5.94	9.70	6.79	2.91	9.70	100
All Indonesia	19.43	2.75	0.79	2.15	1.76	21.15	17.22	2.83	20.05	100

[a] Not all items in GRDP are included (see Table 1.2 for complete coverage), and thus constituent shares do not sum to 100.
Source: Biro Pusat Statistick, 198-94.,

Table 5.2: *Western and Eastern Indonesia's contributions to Indonesian agriculture and manufacturing GRDP, 1993*
(percentages)

	Agri-culture	Small-holdings	Large estates	Live-stock	Fish-eries	Manu-facturing	Large & medium	Small & home	Non-oil mfg	GRDP
Western Indonesia	84.46	79.47	99.42	84.44	73.56	97.56	97.45	93.34	96.87	92.14
Eastern Indonesia										
West Nusa Tenggara	1.74	0.89	0.00	2.31	2.00	0.09	0.05	0.57	0.12	0.74
East Nusa Tenggara	1.55	1.14	0.04	3.33	1.53	0.07	0.02	0.49	0.09	0.66
East Timor	0.24	0.34	0.00	0.41	0.05	0.01	0.01	0.06	0.01	0.14
North Sulawesi	1.81	4.19	0.00	1.60	1.88	0.24	0.20	0.99	0.31	0.91
Central Sulawesi	1.26	2.82	0.07	1.24	1.82	0.16	0.11	0.74	0.20	0.54
South Sulawesi	5.45	5.60	0.47	4.69	12.02	1.13	1.17	3.13	1.44	2.59
South East Sulawesi	1.07	2.95	0.00	0.99	1.42	0.05	0.04	0.23	0.07	0.48
Maluku	1.23	2.28	0.00	0.44	2.51	0.59	0.84	0.20	0.75	0.74
Irian Jaya	1.20	0.32	0.00	0.55	3.20	0.11	0.12	0.25	0.14	1.06
Total	15.54	20.53	0.58	15.56	26.44	2.44	2.55	6.66	3.13	7.86
All Indonesia	100.00	100.00	100.00	100.00	100.00	100.00	100.00	100.00	100.00	100.00

Source: Biro Pusat Statistik, 1989-94.

Table 5.3: *Annual growth rates of agriculture and manufacturing GRDP in Eastern Indonesia, 1988-93*
(percentages)

	Agri-culture	Small-holdings	Large estates	Live-stock	Fisher-ies	Manu-facturing	Large & medium	Small & home	Non-oil mfg	GRDP
Western Indonesia	4.42	5.62	6.63	5.99	7.17	9.95	11.12	7.20	10.53	6.95
Eastern Indonesia	7.19	11.70	8.74	5.91	8.66	12.19	14.36	7.93	12.19	8.08
West Nusa Tenggara	5.29	5.31		5.66	5.71	8.15	7.19	8.68	8.15	7.82
East Nusa Tenggara	4.74	7.16	1.76	5.12	5.82	9.66	13.48	8.66	9.66	7.28
East Timor	7.45	-2.02		8.70	26.76	11.30	12.51	10.71	11.30	9.60
North Sulawesi	10.44	13.63		6.31	11.09	11.92	18.01	6.42	11.92	8.64
Central Sulawesi	10.81	7.93	2.65	19.64	22.09	5.46	3.60	7.36	5.46	8.68
South Sulawesi	6.86	12.75	11.19	4.96	7.98	12.75	14.83	8.74	12.75	7.64
South East Sulawesi	9.69	25.72	-100.00	0.03	8.01	13.64	21.13	8.23	13.64	9.14
Maluku	3.49	7.46		8.20	7.44	15.70	16.39	3.61	15.70	6.67
Irian Jaya	9.32	9.96		6.22	9.05	7.15	7.56	6.04	7.15	9.52
All Indonesia	4.82	6.71	6.64	5.98	7.55	10.00	11.19	7.25	10.58	7.04

Source: Processed from PBS, *Gross Regional Domestic Product of Provinces in Indonesia By Industrial Origin, 1988-93*, February 1995.

per cent in Western Indonesia (Table 5.1).[2] In terms of the labour force, lmost 70 per cent of labour in Eastern Indonesia works in the farm sector. Manufacture's share in Eastern Indonesia is less than 10 per cent in terms of value-added and 5.7 per cent for the labour force, compared to 22.4 and 11.1 per cent in Western Indonesia. Within each sector there are also significant differences. In 1993, the production value of smallholder tree crops in Eastern Indonesia was larger than that of the large estates. Eastern Indonesia's contribution of smallholdings to the national total (21 per cent) is much larger than its contribution of large estates (a mere 0.6 per cent) (Table 5.2). A similar picture is found in the non-oil manufacturing sector. Eastern Indonesia's contribution to the national total is larger in small and home manufacturing (6.7 per cent) than in large and medium industries (2.6 per cent). Fisheries and livestock are two other Eastern Indonesia-specific subsectors. While the share of these sectors combined in GRDP is only 3.4 per cent in Western Indonesia, it is more than 10 per cent in Eastern Indonesia (Table 5.1). Recent growth rates of agricultural and manufacturing GRDP in Western and Eastern Indonesia are compared in Table 5.3.

Is the disparity between Eastern Indonesia and Western Indonesia really a reason for concern? The neoclassical theorists would emphasise the forces of convergence exerted by the allocative forces of relative prices. The proponents of Kuznets' hypothesis, on the other hand, will postulate that disparities between Eastern Indonesia and Western Indonesia are seen to be widening by necessity during the initial phases of development, while at some point in the future endogenous forces will bring about a reversal of this trend.

Although the focus of this chapter is on the development of Eastern Indonesia, some discussion is also presented of the dynamic trend in the gap between the two regions. As the title suggests, however, the bulk of the chapter concerns the trend in the national and regional policy environment and its repercussions on Eastern Indonesia's development.

---

[2] Some figures in tables of this chapter do not match as expected with those in Chapter 1.This is due partly to different sources, and partly to divergent reference periods. But since the general thrust of data in both chapters is very similar, it was not judged worth attempting the task of complete reconciliation (editors).

Table 5.4: *Per-capita consumption of Eastern Indonesia, 1987-93 (Rp)*

	1987			1990			1993		
	Urban	Rural	Total	Urban	Rural	Total	Urban	Rural	Total
Western Indonesia	3423.7	18513	23038	44623	24615	31031	65719	33915	45160
Eastern Indonesia									
West Nusa Tenggara	21423	15264	16523	34619	20805	23146	46736	28506	31753
East Nusa Tenggara	31320	14514	16144	36320	18547	20560	51003	25643	28749
East Timor	-	15041	15041	45414	24914	26582	67993	28539	31611
North Sulawesi	31694.	2198	23168	40248	27403	30143	60463	35032	41304
Central Sulawesi	32067	18326	19631	40291	22344	25038	55005	32439	36530
South Sulawesi	26135	15182	17268	37771	22751.	26397	47573	31233	35389
South East Sulawesi	29095	13369	14983	36845	20498	23236	25715	29166	33834
Maluku	35912	17938	20573	41239	25437	28486	64498	34042	41120
Irian Jaya	38479	15987	22109	47051	23937	29949	67607	37203	45695
Total	28700	16164	18209	38826	22481	25617	53664	30767	35552
All Indonesia	33824	181770	22437	44159	24300	30342	64756	33436	43929

Source: Biro Pusat Statistik, 1989-94; Susanas, 1995.

Table 5.5: Selected Development Indicators I in Eastern Indonesia

	Pop below poverty line 1990 (%)	Share of the poor 1990 (%)	Poor villages in provinces 1993 (%)	Share of poor villages 1993 (%)	Gini Index	Life expectancy at birth 1990 (years)	Infant mortality rate 1990 /1000LB[a]	Rural moderate & severe PEM[a] 1990 (%)	Illiteracy Rate of >1 year old 1990 (%)	Prevalence of anaemia of PW[a] 1992 (%)
West Nusa Tenggara	27.60	2.60	21	0.6	0.27	46	145	17	30.3	71.3
East Nusa Tenggara	45.60	4.20	27	2.3	0.25	58.6	77	16.2	21.9	59.7
East Timor	na	na	71	1.5	0.34	57	85	20	54.9	48
North Sulawesi	18.80	1.30	27	1.8	0.29	61.6	63	3.6	4.6	48.7
Central Sulawesi	24.90	12.0	41	2.9	0.29	55.4	92	6	10.9	45.5
South Sulawesi	23.10	4.60	26	3.2	0.27	60	70	11.6	22.2	50.5
South East Sulawesi	28.80	1.10	41	1.6	0.27	58.5	77	11.4	17.6	71.2
Maluku	29.00	1.50	56	3.4	0.3	58.7	76	14.7	7.4	69.8
Irian Jaya	na	na	79	8.4	0.37	57.9	80	8	31.3	71.4
All Indonesia	19.6	100	33	100	0.34	59.8	71	10.8	15.9	63.1

[a] PEM = Protein Energy Malnutrition; PW = Pregnant Women; LB = Live Births.
Source: Miscellaneous unpublished documents

Table 5.6: *Selected Development Indicators II in Eastern Indonesia*

	HH with electricity 1990 (%)	Dependency Ratio 1990	Per-capita HH expenditures 1993 (Rp/Mo)	Urbanisation rate 1990 (%)	Education:>10 with 9 years BE[a] male 1990 (%)	Education: >10 with 9 years BE Female 1990 (%)	Investment share[a] 1993 (%)
West Nusa Tenggara	40.8	82.3	31753	17.6	19.5	11.9	0.77
East Nusa Tenggara	14.8	79.4	28749	11.4	17	10.7	0.47
East Timor	16.6	77.1	31611	7.8	17.4	9.7	0.18
North Sulawesi	56.2	60.4	41304	22.8	28.8	28.6	0.53
Central Sulawesi	26.5	73.4	36530	16.4	25.1	18.7	0.56
South Sulawesi	40.7	70.8	35389	24.2	26.7	20.2	1.91
South East Sulawesi	19.5	87.6	33834	17	27.1	17.5	0.39
Maluku	37.8	81.3	41120	19.1	28.7	21.4	0.55
Irian Jaya	23.7	78.7	45695	24.2	25.2	15	0.32
All Indonesia	43.9	67.8	43929	30.9	25.8	18.1	100.00

[a] HH = Household; BE = Basic Education.
[b] Of private investment.
Source: Miscellaneous unpublished documents.

Why Eastern Indonesia?

Regions in the eastern part of Indonesia have only recently been receiving greater attention from central policy makers, particularly following the remarks made by the President in his annual budget speech in 1990. Basically, these regions are considered 'late-comers' and less developed, compared to most regions in the western part of Indonesia.

Indeed, in 1993 the Eastern Indonesia's share of GRDP and investment in the national total were recorded at less than 8 and 6 per cent respectively. The per-capita GRDP of Eastern Indonesia on average was about 56 per cent (total) or 83.4 per cent (non-oil) of the per-capita GRDP of Western Indonesia. The proportion in terms of per-capita consumption was roughly 79 per cent (Table 5.4). Such a level of development is consistent with the production structure noted earlier. With a low level of industrialisation, virtually all provinces in Eastern Indonesia have a low rate of urbanisation. Furthermore, with Irian Jaya the only exception, the intra-regional income disparity of these low income regions is better than in the rest of the country. As shown in Table 5.5, the 1993 Gini index in eight provinces of Eastern Indonesia was lower than the national average.

Other social indicators further clarify the relative position of Eastern Indonesia. Although only 16.5 per cent of the nation's poor live in Eastern Indonesia (the region's share in total population is a mere 13.2 per cent), the provincial proportions of population below the poverty line are generally greater than the national figure (Table 5.5). The only exception is North Sulawesi. At the extreme, in East Nusa Tenggara almost half of the province's population are poor. In terms of the number of poor villages, notable cases are Maluku, South East Sulawesi, Central Sulawesi, Irian Jaya and East Timor, where the share of poor villages is 56, 41, 41, 79 and 71 per cent respectively. In many cases, particularly in Irian Jaya, the isolation and difficult geographic conditions have left most villages untouched by adequate transport, communication and other services, placing them in even greater isolation, and causing the province to have the largest number of poor villages.

It is interesting to note that the poverty level in some parts of Eastern Indonesia, notably in East Nusa Tenggara, has the opposite relation with female labour force participation; this poor province has recorded the highest rate of female participation[3]. This indicates that most likely it is a

---

[3]As in East Timor, in this province women are more likely than men to be involved in certain industries, mostly cottage industry oriented to local markets.

matter of necessity for women to work. Those families who live just above the poverty line may actually not live much better than the poor.

Life expectancy in Eastern Indonesia is also lower than the national average, except for North and South Sulawesi. A similar figure is observed in the infant mortality rate. In four provinces the prevalence of anaemia among pregnant women is higher than the national average. The provinces' shares of moderate and severe rural protein energy malnutrition (PEM) in most of Eastern Indonesia are higher than the national figure, with the highest incidence in East Nusa Tenggara. Data on illiteracy rates clarify further the 'backwardness' of the Eastern Indonesia region. The 1990 Census shows that about one third and more than half of the population aged one year or older in East Timor and West Nusa Tenggara are illiterate. What about the educational level of the region's labour force? Five out of nine provinces in Eastern Indonesia have a lower percentage than the national average in terms of labour force with nine years'basic education (Table 5.6). This indicator shows that the provinces of East Nusa Tenggara, West Nusa Tenggara and East Timor lag seriously behind the national average. The percentage of households with electricity is generally lower than the national average, with the exception of North Sulawesi.

All these indicators support the general view that, compared to most areas in Western Indonesia, human resource endowment in Eastern Indonesia could indeed form a major constraint on improved regional development and growth acceleration. On the basis of the above social indicators, North Sulawesi is ranked the best among the Eastern Indonesia's provinces. Life expectancy, child mortality, nutritional conditions, the dependency ratio and the number of households with electricity all point to the superiority of North Sulawesi. The province's relative position is even better than some of Western Indonesia's provinces.

Nevertheless, it is clear that in general the eastern provinces are less developed than provinces in Western Indonesia. While the imbalance between Western Indonesia and Eastern Indonesia has been recognised for some time, it was not until 1990 that most government departments, particularly those responsible for the allocation of regional funds, began to assign priority to Eastern Indonesia. The 1993 GBHN (Garis-Garis Besar Haluan Negara [Broad Outline of State Policy]) also stresses the need to accelerate development in less developed areas, notably the provinces of Eastern Indonesia.

The next important question is that of trends. Here, some unexpectedly encouraging drifts can be observed; at worst, one would obtain few mixed results. The decline of child mortality rates in some provinces in Eastern

Table 5.7: Changes of Selected Development Indicators in Eastern Indonesia

	Ratio per capita HH Exp 1993÷87	Gr life expect-ancy at birth 1980-90	Gr infant mort-ality rate 1980-90	Gr rural M&S P&M 1987-92	Gr illiter-acy rate 1980-90	Gr HH with electri-city 1980-90	Gr depend-ency ratio 1980-90	Education: Gr >10 with 9 years BE male (%) 1980-90	Education: Gr >10 with 9 years BE female (%) 1980-90	Gr Gini Index 1990-93
West Nusa Tenggara	1.92	6.9	-23	-2.7	-14.6	33.5	-8.2	6.7	10.7	-0.0345
East Nusa Tenggara	1.78	9.9	-40	0.8	-13	10.5	-3.2	4.9	7.9	-0.059
East Timor	2.10	na	na	2.9	na	na	na	na	na	-0.0096
North Sulawesi	1.78	6.4	-32	-2.3	-4.3	33.7	-23.1	5.5	6.6	-0.0118
Central Sulawesi	1.86	7.1	-29	-9.3	-6.9	17.5	-15.5	6.2	8.9	0.0241
South Sulawesi	2.05	8.2	-37	-3.3	-15.8	26.1	-16.2	6.7	9.8	-0.0345
South East Sulawesi	2.26	7.7	-34	-2.3	-13.9	13.1	-11.2	5.9	10.9	-0.0345
Maluku	2.00	9.1	-38	-2.8	-9.6	22.3	-6.3	5.1	7.2	0.0357
Irian Jaya	2.07	5	-24	-7.6	-16.7	13.3	-0.1	7.1	10	0.0389
All Indonesia	1.96	7.6	-35	-1.1	-12.9	32.6	-11.3	6.4	8.6	0.0204

[a] GR = Growth (in indicators of Tables 5.5 and 5.6, over year shown).
[b] M&S = Moderate and Severe.
Source: Miscellaneous unpublished document.

Indonesia during 1980-90 has been faster than the national figure (Table 5.7). There are also more provinces in Eastern Indonesia experiencing improvements than those suffering from deterioration in their rural PEM, and all those improvements are occurring at a faster rate than at the national level. Only two provinces suffer from a worsening PEM , namely, East Nusa Tenggara and East Timor. There are only three provinces in Eastern Indonesia recorded as having a slower decline than the national average in illiteracy rates. Again excepting only three provinces, the trend in income distribution in Eastern Indonesia during 1990-93 has been encouraging.

On the other hand, life expectancy performance shows mixed results: only about half the eastern provinces have produced a greater number of additional years of life expectancy than the national average (Table 5.7). Also, there are only two eastern provinces registering faster increases in the number of households with electricity. Another mixed result can be detected in the trend in the labour force's educational level. For the male category, only three provinces posted higher rates of improvement during 1980-90, but for the female category, five provinces showed an improvement, the most dramatic being South East Sulawesi, which increased from a mere 5.9 per cent to 10.9 per cent.

Perhaps the most striking trend is found in the often quoted indicator of GRDP. As shown in Table 5.8, during 1988-93 the rate of growth of non-oil GRDP in Eastern Indonesia was faster than the rate in Western Indonesia, namely, 8.5 versus 7.7 per cent. When the four Kalimantan provinces are included, the better growth position of Eastern Indonesia is still pronounced. True, the fastest growth took place in the 'low-base' areas of Irian Jaya and East Timor, but even for four other Eastern Indonesia provinces the growth rate was still higher than the national average. Looking at the more recent period, 1990-93, six of the nine provinces registered faster growth rates than the national average. Basically, a similar picture can be shown for the case of total (including oil) GRDP. The agricultural and manufacturing growth rates underpinning these figures have already been presented in Table 5.3.

As noted earlier, the nine provinces in Eastern Indonesia comprised a mere 13.2 per cent of total population in 1993. It is expected that these areas will have a relatively faster population growth. During 1988-93, the population growth rate in Eastern Indonesia was registered at 2.3 per cent, higher than the rate in Western Indonesia (1.8 per cent) (Table 5.8). Yet the per-capita GRDP growth of Eastern Indonesia was, on average, still faster than the growth in Western Indonesia of 6.1 compared to 5.7 per cent.

Table 5.8: *Trends of GRDP per-capita non-oil GRDP and non-oil GRDP population in Eastern Indonesia*
(percentage annual growth)

	1988-90 GRDP/Cap	1990-93 GRDP/Cap	1988-93 GRDP/Cap	1988-90 GRDP	1990-93 GRDP	1988-93 GRDP	1988-93 Pop	1990-93 Pop	1990-93 Pop
Western Indonesia	5.78	5.60	5.67	7.96	7.38	7.61	2.06	1.69	1..84
Eastern Indonesia									
West Nusa Tenggara	6.62	5.25	5.79	8.91	7.09	7.82	2.16	1.75	1.92
East Nusa Tenggara	4.40	5.88	5.29	6.29	7.95	7.28	1.80	1.95	1.89
East Timor	4.85	6.69	6.11	9.43	9.71	9.60	4.37	2.56	3.28
North Sulawesi	6.00	7.72	7.03	7.73	9.25	8.64	1.63	1.42	1.50
Central Sulawesi	5.79	5.48	5.60	8.78	8.61	8.68	2.82	2.97	2.91
South Sulawesi	4.44	6.49	5.67	6.61	8.33	7.64	2.08	1.72	1.87
South East Sulawesi	7.77	3.76	5.35	11.77	7.43	9.14	3.71	3.53	3.60
Maluku	2.99	3.13	3.08	8.35	5.80	6.81	5.21	2.59	3.63
Irian Jaya	11.79	8.58	9.85	15.55	12.53	13.73	3.37	3.64	3.53
Total	5.83	6.20	6.05	8.52	8.49	8.51	2.55	2.16	2.31
All Indonesia	5.76	5.63	5.69	8.01	7.48	7.69	2.13	1.75	1.90

Source: Biro Pusat Statistik, 1989-94

Critics of aggregate data such as GRDP, be it per capita or total, would contend that GRDP is a production-based measure that does not necessarily correspond with the actual welfare of the local population. In other words, the above trend only indicates the changes in the relative position of 'Eastern Indonesia,' and not necessarily of Eastern Indonesians. Hence, indicators that are more related to the personal income of the local population are more important. One such indicator is the per-capita consumption expenditures of Eastern Indonesians. Unfortunately, there is no reliable relevant price index one can use to measure changes in real consumption; worse still, comparable price data for rural and urban areas do not exist. Notwithstanding these limitations, if the effect of differential price changes is omitted, during 1987-90 per-capita consumption in the rural and urban areas of Eastern Indonesia grew faster than in Western Indonesia. As reported in Table 5.4, the ratio of per-capita consumption of Eastern Indonesia and Western Indonesia increased from 87 to 91 per cent and from 84 to 87 per cent, for rural and urban areas respectively.

There was a deterioration during 1990-93, when the ratio dropped to 91 per cent for rural and 82 per cent for urban areas. Total per-capita consumption of Eastern Indonesia reached 79 per cent of that of Western Indonesia in 1993, a reduction from 83 per cent in 1990, but relatively the same as the ratio in 1987. There was, however, an improvement for rural Eastern Indonesia between 1987 and 1993. Furthermore, as shown above in Table 5.7, there was significant interregional variation; four provinces, West and East Nusa Tenggara and North and Central Sulawesi, posted a ratio between household per-capita consumption in 1993 and 1987 that was lower than the national figure, while the ratios for the five other Eastern Indonesian provinces were all greater than the national average.

In 1990-93 when Eastern Indonesia experienced high rates of growth of per-capita GRDP, its interregional disparity in this measure also improved, albeit slightly. As reported in Table 5.9, the entropy for Eastern Indonesia during this period increased from 2.1259 to 2.1270[4]. Although very small, this remains an important improvement, given the fact that during 1987-90 the disparity was still shown to be widening. Interestingly, during the same period the interregional disparity in Western Indonesia had a very similar

---

[4] Entropy, often denoted by H, is defined as: $H = \sum_i^N (p_i \ln (p_j))$; where $p_i = n_i/N$. It is a measure of dispersion of a certain activity (in this case, per-capita GRDP). Its value ranges from a minimum of 0, if $n_i/N = 1$ and $n_i/N = 0$ for all j not equal to i, to a maximum of $\ln(k)$, if $n_i = n_j$ for all i and j. The greater the value of H, the larger the dispersion of per-capita GRDP.

pattern, that is, worsening and then improving, with the following entropy: 2.7803, 2.7722 and 2.7746 in 1988, 1990 and 1993 respectively[5]. Up to this point, therefore, the dynamic trend of aggregate data as well as of per-capita household consumption has not been discouraging.

Table 5.9: *Trends of interregional and intraregional disparity based on per-capita GRDP, Indonesia 1988-93*

	1988	1990	1993
Entropy[a]:			
Total 27 regions	3.1708	3.1641	3.1651
Western	2.7803	2.7722	2.7746
Eastern	2.1536	2.1259	2.127
Ratio of entropy:			
West/East	1.291	1.304	1.3045

[a] See footnote 4 of text.
Source: Calculated from BPS's GRDP data.

The regional investment data collected by the Biro Pusat Statistik (BPS) are more or less reflected through what is known as the 'gross domestic fixed capital formation' (GDFCF)[6]. Despite the much lower share in this of Eastern Indonesia (only around 5.7 per cent in 1993), the recent growth of investment in this region has been recorded as higher than the national average, although interregional variation is also pronounced. At one extreme, Central Sulawesi posted an annual growth in 1990-93 of 23 per cent (Table 5.10), but at the other extreme investment growth in North Sulawesi and Irian Jaya was a mere 5.4 per cent. The rate for all Eastern Indonesia was 11.8 per cent, which was more than four percentage points higher than the national average. Even taking into account the 1988-90 period, during which the rate of expansion in Western Indonesia was higher than in Eastern Indonesia, the average growth for the entire period of 1988-93 in Eastern Indonesia remained faster than in Western Indonesia (Table 5.10).

---

[5] With such patterns, overall the nation's interregional disparity worsened during 1988-90, but improved from 1990 to 1993.
[6] These data unfortunately are reliable only for the total category (including oil and gas). Private investment data (PMDN and PMA) are not good sources of information for our purpose mainly because they reflect only 'approved investment'.

Table 5.10: *Annual growth of gross domestic fixed capital formation at 1983 prices, and ICOR in Eastern Indonesia, 1988-93*

	1988-1990	1990-1993	1988-1993	1988-1993
	Annual growth %	Annual growth %	Annual growth %	ICOR[a]
Western Indonesia	11.14	7.03	8.66	3.37
Eastern Indonesia				
West Nusa Tenggara	14.09	9.14	11.09	3.01
East Nusa Tenggara	15.11	10.94	12.59	2.10
East Timor	12.40	14.18	13.47	2.88
North Sulawesi	2.85	5.37	4.35	1.92
Central Sulawesi	4.83	23.03	15.40	2.20
South Sulawesi	10.01	13.55	12.12	2.09
South East Sulawesi	7.28	14.13	11.34	1.99
Maluku	15.42	9.75	11.98	2.36
Irian Jaya	6.45	5.37	5.80	0.81
Total	9.82	11.78	10.99	2.00
All Indonesia	11.07	7.28	8.78	3.25

[a] ICOR (Incremental capital-output ratio).
Source: Biro Pusat Statistik, 1988-94.

Although 1990-93 was the period of tight money policy, during which national growth slowed down, GDFCF in Eastern Indonesia accelerated. This suggests the need for caution in analysing the impact of national or macroeconomic policy on regional development and particularly on the disparity between Eastern Indonesia and Western Indonesia. Table 5.11 provides a further indication of difference. While credit expansion during that period understandably slowed down, the sharpest drop being in Java, credit growth in Eastern Indonesia accelerated from 2.2 to 3.5 per cent, although rates in Western Indonesia were still much higher than in Eastern Indonesia. Hence, there was no uniform pattern of impact between regions.

Table 5.11: *Growth rates of credits in rupiah of deposit money banks by region under the tight money policy (in percentages)*

	1990-91	1991-92
DKI Jakarta	16.4	6.2
Java	14.0	6.2
Sumatra	6.0	5.3
Java & Sumatra	12.8	6.1
Eastern Region	2.2	3.5
Indonesia	11.9	5.9

Source: Bank Indonesia, 1995.

Another example pertains to the recent drop in the growth of non-oil exports. It is now known that 1994 was among the worst years for the performance of Indonesia's non-oil exports (growing by less than 13 per cent in value). This is also apparent in the growth rate of recorded volume of exports under the 'tramps' category, in which the figure for major ports in Western Indonesia dropped, but on the contrary accelerated in Eastern Indonesia (Table 5.12). It is therefore not too surprising that Eastern Indonesia has posted a higher growth rate of GRDP, total and per capita, as well as faster growth in investment.

Table 5.12: *Volume of transported non-oil exports by type of service (annual percentage growth, 1993-94)*[a]

	Liners	Tramps	Total
Eastern Indonesia[b]	-28.80	33.70	33.44
Western Indonesia[b]	-41.96	-0.98	-10.52
Total	-34.10	28.63	28.23

[a] January-November.

[b] Relating to major export ports: Belawan and Tanjung Priok (Western Indonesia), and Surabaya and Ujung Pandang (Eastern Indonesia).

Source: Biro Pusat Statistik, 1995b.

How efficient are these investments? By adopting a proxy indicator of incremental capital-output ratio (ICOR) for the 1988-93 period, the average ICOR in Eastern Indonesia is clearly lower than the national ICOR at 2.0 versus 3.4 (Table 5.10). Whether this is due to the more capital-intensive nature of investment in Western Indonesia needs to be examined further. Nonetheless, the assertion that Eastern Indonesia's provinces are generally less efficient than those of Western Indonesia appears to be unfounded. Even when shorter time periods are used to calculate the ICOR (1988-90 and 1990-93), the picture remains the same.

Let us look at data at the sectoral level and at manufactures. The proxy indicator of value-added to output ratio (VA/O) is plagued with numerous limitations; but unless a systematic model is adopted, remains the most readily available indicator that can be used to provide rough estimates of efficiency. As shown in Table 5.13, the VA/O in Eastern Indonesia is persistently higher than the national average. Six out of nine two-digit ISIC (International Standard Industrial Classification) industries showed an increase in the ratio during 1990-92. Interestingly, the VA/O ratio of all these six industries is greater in Eastern Indonesia than in Western Indonesia. Caution should be used, however, with regard to price changes, since the lower prices of intermediate inputs in Eastern Indonesia could have easily augmented the ratio in the region. Nonetheless, the assertion that industrial efficiency in Eastern Indonesia is lower than in Western Indonesia is not supported by data on VA/O ratio.

Why do these trends seem 'inconsistent' with the widespread perception of Eastern Indonesia? The most probable explanation is that surviving industries in Eastern Indonesia, the number of which is much smaller than in Western Indonesia, are the efficient ones. The observed data quoted earlier (Tables 5.3 and 5.13) refer to these remaining industries. This does not mean that new entrants would easily reach the same level of efficiency in Eastern Indonesia. On the contrary, given the constraints of infrastructure and human resources, private investors generally have difficulty in anticipating an exemplary prospect of efficiency in Eastern Indonesia. The pull factors of Western Indonesia are still too much to reverse the current trend of investors' locational decisions.

Notwithstanding these phenomena, certain dynamic trends that are more encouraging than most people would have thought can be found in the relative position of Eastern Indonesia, particularly during recent years (1990-93). It is likely that the general perception favouring an acceleration of growth in Eastern Indonesia is based on the existing absolute position of Eastern Indonesia, which is indeed still far behind the progress occurring in

Table 5.13: *Value-added ratio in 2-digit ISIC[a] categories in Eastern Indonesia, 1990-92*
(percentages)

	ISIC 31[a]			ISIC 32[a]			ISIC 33[a]			ISIC 34[a]			ISIC 35[a]		
	1990	1991	1992	1990	1991	1992	1990	1991	1992	1990	1991	1992	1990	1991	1992
Western Indonesia	35.9	39.4	39.8	31.8	27.8	31.7	33.5	32.8	36.8	32.1	35.8	36.5	28.5	31.3	30.5
Eastern Indonesia															
West Nusa Tenggara	24.7	23.8	20.5	27.8	29.2	36.9	51.9	41.1	20.2		46.5	17.8			30.2
East Nusa Tenggara	39.7	50.2	29.4	85.4	49.5	33.1	47.0	45.7	52.0	80.4	46.5	62.1	18.2	40.1	36.9
East Timor	13.9	10.0	20.8			61.2	34.2		20.3				19.7	54.0	46.9
North Sulawesi	19.3	28.8	25.9	34.3	38.1	34.4	31.0	43.8	71.3	39.2	66.9	46.9	39.2	28.5	28.1
Central Sulawesi	18.7	8.4	7.7	89.9			33.8	34.0	39.3						
South Sulawesi	26.3	22.3	22.8	23.4	24.9	34.6	41.3	27.8	29.3	17.7	19.0	28.3	40.1	37.4	32.6
South East Sulawesi	37.8	26.3	25.0				5.15	43.0	49.0						100.0
Maluku	26.5	17.9	24.8				36.8	36.8	39.3	58.7	64.4	83.2	60.1	52.4	58.7
Irian Jaya	24.9	24.9	24.5	76.3	43.9	39.4	41.6	42.3	46.7	32.5	50.4	54.1	47.8	24.2	80.1
Total	23.8	22.1	23.7	39.8	38.7	41.2	38.4	35.7	40.3	23.3	28.6	43.8	49.3	45.4	50.2
All Indonesia	35.5	38.7	39.3	31.9	27.9	31.8	34.0	33.1	37.1	32.0	35.7	36.5	28.6	31.3	30.6

[a] ISIC 31 = Food, beverages and tobacco; ISIC 32 = Textiles, clothing and footwear; ISIC 33 = Wood products; ISIC 34 = paper products;
ISIC 35 = Chemicals.
Source: Biro Pusat Statistik, 1989-95.

Table 5.13 (continued)

	ISIC 36[b]			ISIC 37[b]			ISIC 38[b]			ISIC 39[b]			Total		
	1990	1991	1992	1990	1991	1992	1990	1991	1992	1990	1991	1992	1990	1991	1992
Western Indonesia	34.0	38.2	41.0	36.1	28.9	39.1	28.5	29.5	38.3	33.2	35.6	48.8	32.3	32.6	35.9
Eastern Indonesia															
West Nusa Tenggara	38.9	35.7	45.0				36.1	36.2	38.6				31.0	28.9	24.7
East Nusa Tenggara	42.8	37.1	37.2				40.3	41.7	36.4				40.2	40.0	37.8
East Timor	79.5	48.7	52.4				69.4	64.9	65.1				25.9	16.3	26.4
North Sulawesi	22.7	39.3	40.4	12.2	2.1	9.6	43.5	27.2	46.0				21.0	29.6	30.0
Central Sulawesi	25.2	56.0	49.3										30.8	24.4	34.4
South Sulawesi	56.7	57.6	40.4	15.5	18.9	20.3	77.5	52.9	32.0	7.3		50.5	38.0	32.1	28.7
South East Sulawesi	76.1	61.1	66.5				69.5	36.4	40.5				47.6	35.1	38.0
Maluku	50.0	42.1	42.7				40.9	43.2	69.2				38.0	37.3	39.6
Irian Jaya	39.1	40.8	40.6				67.7	50.9	59.4				33.2	28.2	39.1
Total	55.0	55.5	40.8	14.7	15.1	17.6	67.7	45.6	85.6	57.8	47.4	41.0	35.5	33.0	37.3
All Indonesia	35.3	39.0	41.0	36.0	28.8	38.9	28.6	29.6	38.6	33.5	35.8	48.7	32.4	32.6	36.0

[b] ISIC 36 = Non-metallic minerals; ISIC 37 = Base metals; ISIC 38 = Metal goods; ISIC 39 = Miscellaneous.

Table 5.14: *Regional allocation of total Inpres funds - 1984/85 - 1994/95*
(percentages)

	1984/85	1987/88	1990/91	1994/95
Western Indonesia	65.91	66.68	60.99	60.25
Eastern Indonesia (EI-Plus)				
West Nusa Tenggara	2.66	2.31	2.15	2.14
East Nusa Tenggara	3.02	2.75	3.37	3.99
East Timor	1.72	1.95	2.42	2.30
West Kalimantan	3.42	3.18	3.80	3.45
Central Kalimantan	2.23	2.17	2.81	2.87
South Kalimantan	2.89	2.77	2.85	2.73
East Kalimantan	2.36	2.34	2.98	2.75
North Sulawesi	2.15	2.29	2.59	2.52
Central Sulawesi	2.11	2.30	2.59	2.77
South Sulawesi	4.83	4.41	4.15	4.57
South-east Sulawesi	1.68	1.90	2.07	1.97
Maluku	2.12	2.37	2.53	2.77
Irian Jaya	2.89	2.58	4.70	4.93
Total	34.09	33.32	39.01	39.75
All Indonesia	100.00	100.00	100.00	100.00

Source: Ministry of Finance, (1995).

the rest of the country, rather than on its dynamic trend. This argument will suffice to answer the question 'Why Eastern Indonesia?'

In an era of increasing roles for the private economy, one opinion would propose that further acceleration of growth in Eastern Indonesia be fostered by inflows of private investment in the region. On the other hand, others will argue that, based on past experience, the lack of spill-over effects of private investment inflows on local people's welfare suggests that a major overhaul in the industrialisation strategy for Eastern Indonesia is required. Whichever view triumphs, one thing is clear: the role of government remains needed. It is probably even more needed in the epoch of liberalisation and market economy, if an improved pace of development in Eastern Indonesia is to be aimed at. One of the important roles of government, given the nature of the prevailing political system, is in financial resource allocation.

Financial transfer policy and the relative position of Eastern Indonesia

At this juncture it is important to note that the term 'Eastern Indonesia' basically carries a connotation of less developed regions, based upon which the intervention of government is strongly justified. It is in this context that the present author is inclined to include the four provinces of Kalimantan in Eastern Indonesia, in the following discussion of the government's financial transfers. For convenience, the term 'Eastern Indonesia-Plus' will be used to refer to the nine provinces of Eastern Indonesia plus the four in Kalimantan. The two major categories of central-regional transfers are *Inpres* (*Instruksi Presiden*) [Presidential Instruction for Special Grants Programs] and DIP (*Daftar Isran Proyek*) [Development Budget Allocation]. Loosely interpreted, the first is more regional-oriented, while the latter is primarily sectoral-oriented. A number of studies has linked this distinction with the issue of decentralisation and increased autonomy for the regions. As shown in Table 5.14, the proportion of total *Inpres* that goes to Eastern Indonesia-Plus is lower than that accruing to regions in Western Indonesia. It should be explaind that total *Inpres* funds are divided into 'block' and 'sectoral' proportions. But with the Eastern Indonesia-Plus share of block *Inpres* only around 30 to 33 per cent, and the region's share of sectoral *Inpres* less than half, during 1984/85-1994/95, the Eastern Indonesia-Plus share of total Inpres has been consistently below 40 per cent. Following the budget retrenchment of 1986 caused by a drop in the price of oil, total *Inpres* in

Table 5.15: *Total Inpres per capita, 1984/85 - 1994/95*
(Rp.000)

	1984/85	1987/88	1990/91	1994/95
Western Indonesia	6.55	4.39	9.14	19.6
Eastern Indonesia (EI-Plus)				
West Nusa Tenggara	11.67	6.68	14	30.1
East Nusa Tenggara	13.35	8.1	22.7	57.5
East Timor	37.1	27.1	71	141
West Kalimantan	16.14	9.72	25.8	48.9
Central Kalimantan	31.07	17.4	44.3	91.6
South Kalimantan	16.64	10.5	24.1	48.7
East Kalimantan	21.31	13	35	62.4
North Sulawesi	12.4	8.85	23	48.9
Central Sulawesi	19.01	13.4	33.5	73.5
South Sulawesi	10.01	6.13	13.1	31.1
South-east Sulawesi	20.08	14.3	33.6	64.5
Maluku	19	13.6	30	68.7
Irian Jaya	28.13	15.9	63.4	133
Total	15.97	10.2	26.4	56.6
All Indonesia	6.98	4.6	10.4	22.3

Source: Calculated from Table 5.14.

absolute terms declined, whereas DIP funds continued to increase, albeit slowly. During the same period, the Eastern Indonesia-Plus share of total *Inpres* slightly decreased to 33 per cent, then jumped to almost 40 per cent from 1990/91 until 1994/95. The effect of the 1990 presidential speech appears to have been significant.

Why are the important regional oriented funds such as *Inpres* allocated mostly to the more developed Western Indonesian regions? Many would argue that such an allocation is consistent with disparities in population size (the Eastern Indonesia-Plus population share is only 18.6 per cent of the national total). In addition, it is also consistent with regional contributions to the national product, for only 18 per cent of total GDP is produced by Eastern Indonesia-Plus. It is therefore often concluded that *Inpres* transfers have been based on a lopsided set of criteria, focusing mainly on 'requirements,' and even then the criterion used (population size) is static and narrowly defined with very little emphasis on regional 'potential.' No significant correlation can be found between per-capita GRDP and the size of transfers. The same is true of the correlation between *Inpres* transfers and some incentive criteria (for example, tax efforts and the regional prospect of commercial activities).

When population size is included, recent figures indicate that in per-capita terms *Inpres* allocated to Eastern Indonesia-Plus is about three times larger than that to Western Indonesia (Table 5.15). By 1994/95, the top four recipients of per-capita *Inpres* were all in Eastern Indonesia-Plus (East Timor, Irian Jaya, Central Kalimantan and Central Sulawesi). The figures for the first two provinces have increased most dramatically since 1984/85. It should also be noted that virtually all provinces in Eastern Indonesia-Plus receive a greater amount than the average per-capita for the whole country. But for some eastern provinces with low population densities, notably Irian Jaya, per-capita-based financial transfers do not make sense. One often quoted example in this regard is the financial transfer for road construction. With a fixed per-unit cost of construction, and given the fact that in many cases roads to be constructed in this region have to cover a very long distance, it would be unrealistic to expect such projects to be completed when the financial resource is limited because of the low population size.

DIP expenditures, which are primarily sectoral oriented, have a similar regional distribution (Table 5.16). The share going to Eastern Indonesia-Plus is even lower than in the *Inpres* case. While the portion of the DIP for Eastern Indonesia-Plus was recorded at about 20 per cent in 1984/85, the plunge of oil prices in 1986 led to a sharp decline in the Eastern Indonesia-Plus portion to around 13 per cent. This is in spite of the absolute increase in

Table 5.16: *Regional allocation of total DIP funds, 1984/85 - 1994/95*
(percentages)

	1984/85	1987/88	1990/91	1994/95
Western Indonesia	80.65	87.40	81.72	82.83
Eastern Indonesia (EI-Plus)				
West Nusa Tenggara	0.86	0.57	1.14	1.00
East Nusa Tenggara	1.21	1.20	1.29	1.20
East Timor	0.69	0.42	0.47	0.69
West Kalimantan	1.97	0.51	1.42	1.29
Central Kalimantan	1.33	0.35	0.84	1.15
South Kalimantan	1.56	1.18	1.79	1.41
East Kalimantan	1.78	0.96	1.85	1.62
North Sulawesi	1.20	1.28	1.33	1.04
Central Sulawesi	1.19	0.60	1.23	1.01
South Sulawesi	2.39	3.33	3.19	2.65
South-east Sulawesi	1.39	0.60	0.82	0.88
Maluku	1.29	0.80	1.12	1.17
Irian Jaya	2.49	0.80	1.78	2.05
Total	19.35	12.60	18.28	17.17
All Indonesia	100.00	100.00	100.00	100.00

Source: Ministry of Finance, (1995).

the DIP allocation for the whole nation in 1984/85 - 1987/88. There was in fact a 28 per cent drop in the absolute DIP funds for Eastern Indonesia-Plus. It is against such a trend that pressures to raise the Eastern Indonesia-Plus portion of both *Inpres* and DIP have escalated.

The stress on Eastern Indonesia in the 1990 presidential speech intensified such pressures and secured a response. Indeed, by 1994/95 the absolute amount of DIP allocated to Eastern Indonesia-Plus had more than tripled, giving Eastern Indonesia-Plus a more than 17 per cent share in total DIP funds. Yet this percentage figure is still lower than that in 1984/85[7].

Contrary to the case of *Inpres*, in per capita terms the DIP allocation to Eastern Indonesia-Plus in 1994/95 was lower than to Western Indonesia, that is, Rp89000 versus Rp99000, while a decade ago it was the reverse (Table 5.17). DKI Jakarta, being the capital city, absorbed the biggest per-capita funds, namely, Rp286,000 and 761,000 in 1984/85 and 1994/95 respectively. This figure is over fourteen times the per-capita DIP in West Nusa Tenggara, the lowest recipient in Eastern Indonesia-Plus and the second lowest in the whole country.

To unfold the potential resources of most regions in Eastern Indonesia-Plus would undoubtedly require greater attention, including larger funds allocations, to this region. In light of the positive role of *Inpres*, if the gap in standards of living between Eastern Indonesia-Plus and Western Indonesia is to be reduced, the portion of *Inpres*-type transfers allocated to Eastern Indonesia-Plus would have to be augmented as well. Further analysis of the impacts of Inpres and DIP allocations on interregional growth and welfare would clarify the assertion[8].

In the following analysis, the question of particular interest is: which type of transfer is more effective for the improvement of Eastern Indonesia's relative position? For this purpose, a multiplier analysis using an Interregional Social Accounting Matrix (IRSAM) accessed by Azis (1995) is conducted.

---

[7] In the case of *Inpres*, the share allocated to Eastern Indonesia in 1994/95 was approximately seven times larger than the allocation in 1987/88.

[8] There is no easy way to trace the impacts of central-regional transfers on equity. It would clearly be necessary to capture both the direct and indirect effects of the transfers on incomes and other welfare indicators. This could be done by making use of multipliers calculated from a set of data interconnecting central-local transfers and various economic sectors, factors of production, and different household institutions. Information of that sort is typically available from a 'Social Accounting Matrix' (SAM). The multiplier analysis conducted here uses an interregional SAM based on the most recent 1990 SAM.

Table 5.17: *Total DIP per capita, 1984/85 - 1994/95 (Rp'000)*

	1984/85	1987/88	1990/91	1994/95
Western Indonesia	43.1	49.2	48.9	98.5
Eastern Indonesia (EI-Plus)				
West Nusa Tenggara	20.3	13.9	29.7	51.5
East Nusa Tenggara	28.7	30	34.8	63
East Timor	80.4	49.3	55.4	155
West Kalimantan	50	13.3	38.5	66.7
Central Kalimantan	99.7	23.9	53.2	134
South Kalimantan	48.3	37.9	60.7	91.7
East Kalimantan	86.4	45.5	86.9	135
North Sulawesi	37.3	42.1	47	73.6
Central Sulawesi	57.7	29.9	63.3	97.9
South Sulawesi	26.6	39.5	40.2	65.7
South-east Sulawesi	89.5	38.7	53.6	106
Maluku	62	38.9	53.2	106
Irian Jaya	130	42.1	95.9	203
Total	48.8	32.8	49.5	89.2
All Indonesia	37.5	39.2	41.5	81.4

Source: Calculated from Table 5.16

Two counterfactual scenarios with respect to DIP and *Inpres* allocations are generated, both moving from the *baseline scenario* of Table 5.18. *Scenario 1* (Table 5.19) is to reduce some Rp1.9 trillion of DIP funds and to reallocate the funds through *Inpres* programs by placing only slightly greater emphasis on Eastern Indonesia-Plus (Rp1 trillion to Eastern Indonesia-Plus and Rp0.9 trillion to Western Indonesia). *Scenario 2* (Table 5.20) is to do the reverse, that is, to shift *Inpres* funds to DIP, again by allocating Rp1 trillion and Rp0.9 trillion to Eastern Indonesia-Plus and Western Indonesia respectively[9].

As shown in Tables 5.19 and 5.20, in terms of output generation transfers through *Inpres* are superior to those through DIP. Total GDP under Scenario 1 is larger than that under Scenario 2[10]. The Eastern Indonesia-Plus share of GDP is also higher under Scenario 1. In fact, Scenario 2 produces a worsening interregional distribution of GRDP, in particular between Western Indonesia and Eastern Indonesia-Plus, even when compared with the baseline or actual case (compare Tables 5.18 and 5.19). Interestingly enough, both scenarios produce better welfare effects (measured by household incomes in relative and absolute terms) for Eastern Indonesia-Plus as well as for the total off-Java region. In this case, however, greater effects are produced under Scenario 2. It would be interesting to find out whether a better position for Eastern Indonesia-Plus in terms of these incomes under Scenario 1 compared to Scenario 2 could have been generated by altering the hypothetical sectoral allocation of *Inpres*. At any rate, this analysis indicates that there is still room for improvement in the existing allocation. It is also important to note that although Scenario 2 gives larger Eastern Indonesia-Plus shares of household income, as well as of labour and capital incomes, in absolute terms Scenario 1 generates larger sizes for these incomes.

A similar approach could be applied, should we wish to analyse the impact of DIP and *Inpres* transfers upon relative income distribution in each region (interregional disparity). Unfortunately, to insert a list of different income groups for each region in the original SAM would involve a

---

[9] As stated elsewhere in the paper, *Inpres* allocation is more flexible in the sense that its sectoral allocation can be determined, albeit not entirely, by the provincial governments. This feature is also reflected in the exercise, notably in the hypothetical allocation of *Inpres* funds between sectors.

[10] The figures in the tables are measured in terms of ratio to the baseline (actual) scenario shown in Table 5.18. The small deviations should not hinder the essence of the analysis; they simply reflect the use of a small 'shock' (Rp1.9 trillion) in the exercise.

Table 5.18. *Baseline scenario (Rp billion)*

	Household income	Labour income	Capital income	GRDP
Java				
West	46,468.58	30,619.21	28,984.47	59,603.68
Central	22,180.33	14,295.49	10,140.67	24,436.16
East	31,805.35	17,762.34	13,337.36	31,099.70
Total	100,454.27	62,677.04	52,462.49	115,139.53
Sumatra	32,141.55	19,161.56	29,061.99	48,223.55
Western Indonesia				
Kalimantan	9,769.94	6,219.39	11,395.18	17,614.57
Sulawesi	8,780.07	4,763.01	3,561.82	8,324.83
Other areas	9,679.81	5,365.69	5,087.13	10,452.83
Total	132,595.81	81,838.60	81,524.48	163,363.08
Eastern (EI-Plus) Indonesia	28,229.81	16,348.09	20,044.13	36,392.22
All Indonesia	160,825.63	98,186.68	101,568.62	199,755.30
Shares (%):				
Java	62.46	63.83	51.65	57.64
Western Indonesia	82.45	83.35	80.27	81.78
Eastern (EI-Plus) Indonesia	17.55	16.65	19.73	18.22

Source: Recalculated from Azis (1995).

104

Table 5.19: *Counterfactual scenario (base line of Table 5.18=1): Rp1.9 trillion shifted from DIP to Inpres Rp1 trillion for off-Java and Rp0.9 trillion for Java*

	Household income	Labour income	Capital income	GRDP
Java				
West	1.0018	1.0007	0.9995	1.0001
Central	1.0023	1.0028	1.0018	1.0024
East	1.0032	1.0021	1.0016	1.0019
Total	1.0024	1.0016	1.0005	1.0011
Sumatra	1.0084	1.0131	1.0050	1.0082
Western Indonesia				
Kalimantan	1.0059	1.0105	1.0020	1.0050
Sulawesi	1.0087	1.0148	1.0110	1.0132
Other areas	1.0075	1.0141	1.0078	1.0110
Total	1.0038	1.0043	1.0021	1.0032
Eastern (EI-Plus) Indonesia	1.0073	1.0129	1.0051	1.0086
All Indonesia	1.0044	1.0057	1.0027	1.0042
Shares (%):				
Java	62.33	63.57	51.54	57.46
Western Indonesia	82.40	83.23	80.22	81.70
Eastern (EI-Plus) Indonesia	17.60	16.77	19.78	18.30

Source: Recalculated from Azis (1995).

Table 5.20: *Counterfactual scenario (base line of Table 5.18=1): Rp1.9 trillion shifted from Inpres to DIP Rp1 trillion for off-Java and Rp0.9 trillion for Java*

	Household income	Labour income	Capital income	GRDP
Java				
West	1.0029	1.0026	1.0031	1.0029
Central	1.0016	1.0013	1.0013	1.0013
East	1.0023	1.0016	1.0017	1.0016
Total	1.0024	1.002	1.0024	1.0022
Sumatra	1.0041	1.0057	1.0026	1.0039
Western Indonesia				
Kalimantan	1.0045	1.0063	1.0032	1.0043
Sulawesi	1.0048	1.0074	1.0051	1.0064
Other areas	1.0047	1.0077	1.005	1.0064
Total	1.0028	1.0029	1.0025	1.0027
Eastern (EI-Plus) Indonesia	1.0047	1.0071	1.004	1.0054
All Indonesia	1.0032	1.0036	1.0028	1.0032
Shares (%):				
Java	62	64	52	58
Western Indonesia	82	83	80	82
Eastern (EI-Plus) Indonesia	18	17	20	18

Source: Recalculated from Azis (1995).

sweeping task that is not feasible at this stage of the present writer's research. A much simpler approach is taken, however, to observe the link between transfer and interregional disparity. By assuming that the effects of central-regional transfers on the income generation of each household category will require two or three years' time lag, and by using a single indicator to reflect the status of income distribution in each region (that is, a regional Gini index, the trend in which was shown above in Table 5.7), a cross-regional correlation between changes in this indicator and the level of transfers in a particular period can be measured[11].

Figure 5.1 provides the overall picture[12]. During the early period (1984-87), there seems to be a pattern, albeit not a very strong one, in which more Eastern Indonesia-Plus provinces — denoted by bold name labels — are concentrated in the upper-left quadrant. Only four out of thirteen provinces in Eastern Indonesia-Plus are not in this quadrant. This may suggest that while all Eastern Indonesia-Plus regions had relatively high per-capita *Inpres* in 1984 — being above the average per-capita *Inpres* identified by the horizontal line — most of them experienced an improvement in their interregional income distribution[13].

But Figure 5.2 shows that in more recent years (1990-93) this pattern has weakened, with eight Eastern Indonesia-Plus provinces remaining in the upper-left quadrant. Central Sulawesi, ranked the fifth largest recipient of per capita *Inpres* (or the fourth in 1994/95), seems to have suffered from increased income disparity during recent years. Obviously, there are other and possibly more important factors affecting relative income distribution in this province. *Inpres* transfer is probably only a small contributor to this trend. The same is true for other provinces. Persistent monopoly or oligopoly practices in some sectors, and inflows of private investment with little spill-over effects on the local peoples' welfare, are two examples of factors other than central-regional transfers that may have affected the condition of interregional disparity in Eastern Indonesia-Plus.

---

[11] Lack of complete year-to-year data on the Gini index makes time series correlation impossible.

[12] In Figure 5.1, the x-axis represents the growth of the Gini index and the y-axis reflects the levels of per-capita *Inpres*. The two lines inside the box denote the average level.

[13] The zero-vertical axis, not shown in Figure 5.1, actually lies just to the right of West Nusa Tenggara, suggesting that all Eastern Indonesia provinces in the upper-left quadrant have negative growth of Gini index (improved relative income distribution).

Figure 5.1: *Per capita Inpres, 1984-85, and the trend of Gini index, 1984-87*

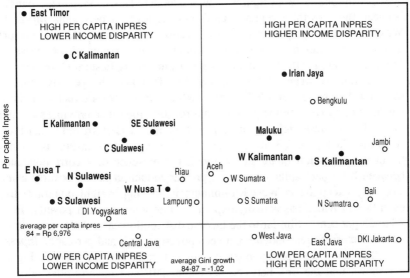

Figure 5.2: *Per capita Inpres, 1990-91, and the trend of Gini index, 1984-87*

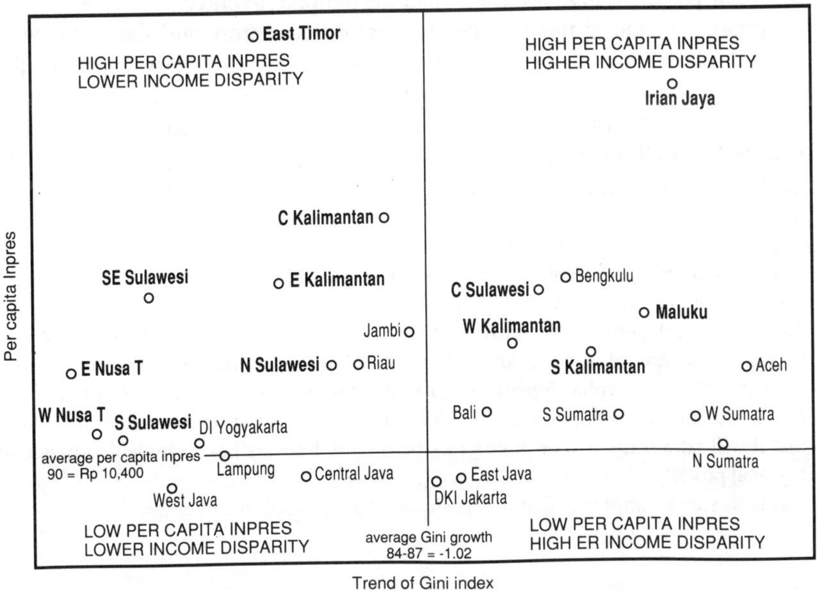

Notwithstanding these factors, Figures 5.1 and 5.2 show that the effects of *Inpres* are generally more prominent in Eastern Indonesia-Plus than in Western Indonesia. Both figures show a complete lack of systematic pattern between the growth of regional Gini and the level of per-capita *Inpres* in Western Indonesia provinces. This seems consistent with the present author's observation elsewhere pertaining to the greater effectiveness of *Inpres* transfers for the low-income regions, including Eastern Indonesia.

The link between central-regional transfers and the poverty level is shown in Figures 5.3 and 5.4[14]. Only eighteen provinces are included, since consistent and comparable poverty data for the nine other provinces are not available. Of these eighteen, nine provinces are in Eastern Indonesia-Plus. As shown in Figure 5.3, the majority of Eastern Indonesia-Plus provinces lie in the upper-left quadrant, implying the presence of a correspondence between high per-capita *Inpres* and greater reduction in the poverty level. The only exception is West Kalimantan in the upper-right quadrant. But even this province has actually experienced an alleviation in poverty, from 28 to 25 per cent[15]. Similar to the income distribution case, there seems to be a lack of close correspondence between poverty trends and per-capita *Inpres*.

What about the correspondence with DIP transfers? In general, Figure 5.4 shows that the link between per-capita DIP and poverty alleviation is much weaker than in the preceding case. Only two Eastern Indonesia-Plus provinces (North Sulawesi and South Kalimantan) are located in the upper-left quadrant. Conditions with regard to poverty in East Nusa Tenggara, South Sulawesi and West Nusa Tenggara have improved, despite the fact that their per-capita DIP is lower than the national average.

Finally, in the analysis of central-regional transfers and their link with poverty alleviation, there is perhaps nothing more contemporary than the *Inpres Desa Tertinggal* (IDT) program. The introduction of this program was stated in the President's 1994 speech, but it was actually formalised a year before by Presidential Instruction No. 5/1993. The important rationale of the program is that there were still around 25 million people living under

---

[14] The *x*-axis of these figures represents the ratio between the average poverty level — measured as the percentage of population living below the poverty line — in 1993 and 1990. Since many provinces experienced a poverty reduction during this period, most are plotted on the left-side of the inner vertical line. The *y*-axis indicates the per-capita *Inpres* in 1990/91, the national average of which was Rp10,400 (the inner horizontal line). The choice of this period is made on the basis that it will take some two or three years before the transfer has formidable impact on regional poverty.

[15] It is its rate of improvement that is slower than the national average.

Figure 5.3: *Per capita Inpres, 1990-91, and average poverty level change, 1990-93*

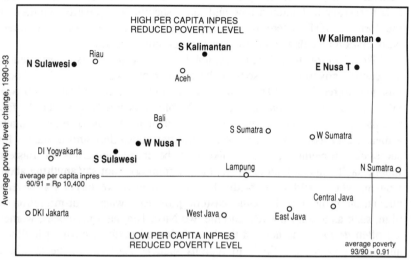

Average poverty level change, 1990-93

Figure 5.4: *Per capita DIP, 1990-91, and average poverty level change, 1990-93*

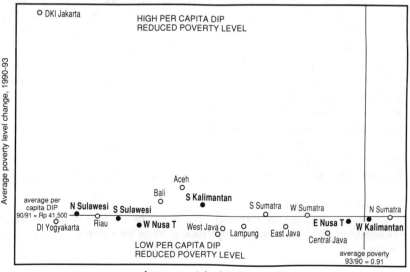

Average poverty level change, 1990-93

the poverty line in 1993, despite the continued decline in the number over the previous decade. In the context of the *Repelita* VI target of reducing the number to only 12 million by 1998/99, the government seems to believe that it is necessary to launch a new and more specific anti-poverty program in the form of IDT. There is also a strong intention to ensure the direct participation of village communities through this program.

Like all *Inpres* transfers, the regional allocation of IDT is determined by the central government based on the number of poor villages. Each poor village is to receive Rp20 million, to be paid in two stages. About 7,000 poor villages in Eastern Indonesia-Plus are eligible to receive IDT. Given the fact that the program has only recently been implemented, it is too early to make a meaningful assessment, except to note that constraints and obstacles for successful implementation are likely to be more numerous in Eastern Indonesia. To make matters worse, the program does not say anything about women, who would undoubtedly be the most effective target for poverty alleviation programs. In some eastern provinces where out-migration is high, such as South Sulawesi and the two Nusa Tenggara provinces, women are often *de facto* the head of the household and perform most agricultural and food producing tasks[16]. In regions such as Eastern Indonesia where poverty simply means food insufficiency, it would be sensible to address the needs of women in any poverty alleviation program.

Liberalisation policy: how it affects Eastern Indonesia

The stream of liberalisation and export-oriented policies has produced improvements in a number of macroeconomic variables. It is not difficult to find studies praising the achievement of the Indonesian economy during the last decade. It is less easy to scrutinise the impacts of policy reform on regional development, in particular on the development of Eastern Indonesia. In such circumstances, perceptions based on casual observations and isolated cases that may not be valid across regions often come up as an alternative. Unfortunately, no appropriate policy can be formulated if it is based only on observations of this kind.

For example, an exchange rate adjustment (that is, devaluation) is still often viewed negatively from the regional perspective. Many Eastern Indonesia provinces, according to this view, have not really benefited from

---

[16] Out-migration is due to a number of reasons, the most prominent of which (especially in Nusa Tenggara) is population pressure on cultivable land in these provinces.

increased exports. Is this really so? Or is it that for reasons other than exchange rate adjustment Eastern Indonesia's exports could not be boosted? The debated issues become even more complex when the question is raised with regard to the linkage, or lack of it, between increased exports or increased production for that matter and the income or welfare position of the local people. Obviously, there is no easy answer to these inquiries. One thing is certain, however; the indirect effects of changing macroeconomic variables on welfare indicators cannot be excluded from the analysis. Furthermore and ideally, commodity by commodity exports from Eastern Indonesia should be evaluated and linked with price changes due to exchange rate adjustment.

The popular notion that exchange rate adjustment or an export-oriented strategy will tend to worsen income distribution is probably also influenced by the findings of a number of studies in Latin American countries. There, most export commodities, including plantation products, come from relatively large estates. This may not be the case in Indonesia. As noted in Table 5.2, the contribution of smallholder tree crops in Eastern Indonesia is quite considerable (20.5 per cent of the nation's product from this subsector), given the fact that Eastern Indonesia's portions of GRDP and of the agricultural sector are only 8 and 15 per cent respectively. The largest contributors are South Sulawesi (5.6 per cent) and North Sulawesi (4.2 per cent). Looking at each province's production structure, on average the Eastern Indonesian provinces have a greater share of smallholder value-added than in Western Indonesia (Table 5.1), and more importantly the gap has tended to widen over time from 6.1 versus 2.5 per cent in 1988 to 10.6 to 2.4 per cent in 1993. Hence, the smallholder cash-crop sector is quite important for the region's economy. In fact, in 1993 the share of smallholder production in Eastern Indonesia's GRDP was higher than the share of the entire manufacturing sector.

If a considerable portion of these smallholder products are exported, one might easily predict the potential benefits that may accrue to Eastern Indonesia. Of course, a change in prices, or exchange rate adjustment, is only one determinant; there are other factors that may operate against further export growth of the region, such as inadequate infrastructure, lack of finance and limited human resources. But the assertion that exchange rate adjustment will produce detrimental effects on Eastern Indonesia is most likely unfounded although such a conclusion cannot be generalised across the region and for all cases.

Without considering the precise proportion of output that is exported, we can note that during the height of the period of export-oriented strategies, the growth of the smallholder sector in Eastern Indonesia was significantly faster than the growth of large estates, 11.7 versus 8.7 per cent annually during 1988-93 (Table 5.3). This figure would have been higher if the negative growth in East Timor had been excluded. The highest rate of increase of 25.7 per cent occurred in South East Sulawesi.

The period of robust growth in the Indonesian economy was characterised by a vibrant manufacturing sector and non-oil manufactures in particular. Various policies since the mid-1980s have been directed toward pushing this sector to expand further, especially those activities with export-oriented attributes. With regard to the performance of Eastern Indonesia in this respect, the value-added growth of non-oil manufactures during 1988-93 was faster than in Western Indonesia, 12.2 versus 10.5 per cent (Table 5.3). Even small and home industries have posted a higher rate of growth in Eastern than in Western Indonesia. Such a trend could become the basis for improved income distribution within Eastern Indonesia, as indeed has been detected by the trend in the Gini index shown in Table 5.7.

To what extent does the new policy environment affect the relative position of Eastern Indonesia's income and GRDP? Table 5.21 reports some results of simulation of increased investment and exports based on the 1990 Interregional Social Accounting Matrix. In Simulation I, attempts are made to emulate as closely as possible the actual trends in exports and private investment by location. This should reflect the trade and investment liberalisation policy of the country. Under this scenario the relative position of Eastern Indonesia has improved from 11.48 to 11.73 per cent for household income, and from 9.4 to 9.95 per cent for GRDP. This is consistent with the trend of improved GRDP distribution during 1990-93 discussed earlier.

In Simulation II, the government is assumed to raise its investment in regions outside Java, presumably in Eastern Indonesia, by allocating block funds that enable provincial governments to increase their investments in three categories: the economic, social and general sectors. Through augmented labour and capital incomes, the relative position of Eastern Indonesia in total GRDP is improved further under this scenario, and so is household income. Two interesting phenomena are learned from such an exercise. First, by comparing Simulation I and Simulation II, we can see that the magnitudes of increase in Western Indonesia remain greater than those in Eastern Indonesia, even after greater allocation of government investment is made to Eastern Indonesia[17]. This suggests something about the linkages

---

[17] In fact, for Java alone, the magnitude of increase is already greater than for the whole of Eastern Indonesia.

Table 5.21: *Simulation results of increased exports and investment mostly in outside Java*

	Baseline			
	HH income	Labour Income	Capital income	GRDP
Java	100454.3	62677.0	52462.5	115139.5
Sumatra	32141.5	19161.6	29062.0	48223.5
Kalimantan	9769.9	6219.4	11395.2	17614.6
Sulawesi	8780.1	4763.0	3561.8	8324.8
Others	9679.8	5365.7	5087.1	10452.8
Indonesia	160825.6	98186.7	101568.6	199755.3
Eastern Indonesia	18459.878	10128.7	8648.951	18777.651
EI Share	11.48%	10.32%	8.52%	9.40%

	Simulation 1: 'Actual'			
	HH income	Labour Income	Capital income	GRDP
Sumatra	35352.5	21232.2	33314.9	54547.1
Kalimantan	11036.4	7019.6	13638.3	20657.9
Sulawesi	9378.4	5213.4	4003.7	9217.0
Others	10273.5	5914.9	5756.0	11670.9
Indonesia	167502.4	101766.7	108235.2	210001.9
Eastern Indonesia	19651.90953	11128.26526	9759.677256	20887.94252
EI-Share	11.73%	10.94%	9.02%	9.95%

Table 5.21 (continued)

| | Simulation 2: 'Actual' Plus GI | | | |
	HH income	Labour Income	Capital income	GRDP
Java	102794.1	62968.2	52004.7	114972.9
Sumatra	36419.0	21947.9	34469.9	56417.8
Kalimantan	11473.1	7319.6	14299.8	21619.4
Sulawesi	9630.2	5284.4	4163.0	9457.4
Others	10542.7	6128.9	5995.6	12124.5
Indonesia	170859.1	103749.0	110933.1	214682.0
Eastern Indonesia	20172.87776	11513.33438	10158.6402	21671.974 57
EI-Share	11.81%	11.10%	9.16%	10.09%

Source: Recalculated from Azis (1995).,

between Eastern and Western Indonesia. The *interregional* multiplier (between Western Indonesia and Eastern Indonesia) seems greater than the *intraregional* multiplier within Eastern Indonesia. Nonetheless, this does not change the conclusion with regard to the improved relative position of Eastern Indonesia.

Second, even with such special government efforts to reduce the Eastern Indonesia-Western Indonesia gap, which would lead to the improved relative position of Eastern Indonesia, the share of GRDP and household income in Eastern Indonesia remains small (barely two-digit). Measured in per-capita terms and assuming no change in population size, the per-capita GRDP gap between Western Indonesia and Eastern Indonesia remains large (Eastern Indonesia's share is roughly 76 per cent of Western Indonesia's total). Hence it must be realised that the gap between Western Indonesia and Eastern Indonesia will not disappear within the foreseeable future, even if a massive government investment is allocated to this region. Does this suggest that the private sector should play an increasing role and if so what kind of role? In what types of activities would private involvement really provide greater net benefits to local people in Eastern Indonesia?

While the above exercise sheds some light on the repercussions of investment and trade liberalisation policies on the trend in the Western-Eastern Indonesia gap, not all deregulation policies will guarantee an improvement in Eastern Indonesia's relative position. A notable example is the 1988 shipping deregulation. It is believed that during the few years following the announcement of the package, many provinces in Eastern Indonesia lost ground to Western Indonesia in terms of the total share of fisheries exports. There is, however, an interregional variation of the effects. For places farthest away from Western Indonesia port centres, such as Biak and Sorong in Irian Jaya and Ambon in Maluku, the absence of direct competition with Western Indonesia enabled them to prevent their exports from declining. On the other hand, for places like Ujung Pandang proximity to Western Indonesia caused the detrimental effect on fisheries exports to be quite considerable. Largely because of this phenomenon, during 1988-93 the value-added of the fisheries sector in South Sulawesi recorded the lowest growth rate (a mere 5 per cent) among the eastern provinces (Table 5.3).

However, just because there is a widespread belief that fishermen are generally among the poor, such a trend does not automatically worsen their situation with regard to poverty in Eastern Indonesia and certainly not across all provinces in the region. Many fishing activities in Eastern Indonesia are only part-time jobs for the local population. Furthermore, several studies have shown that fishermen in Eastern Indonesia, particularly in the Makassar Straits, tend to have higher incomes than full-time operators. This does not mean that efforts to improve the welfare of full-time fishermen in Eastern Indonesia, such as the Buginese and the Bajao, are unimportant. But in terms of priority, attention ought to be given to activities from which the main source of income of most fishermen in Eastern Indonesia comes.

A somewhat opposing example is found in the area of trade in livestock, which is another important source of the economy of some Eastern Indonesian provinces (in West Nusa Tenggara, for example, more than 20 per cent of GDP originated in this subsector). The current policy of a maximum quota for inter-island exports and hence a non-liberalisation policy is weakly justified by the argument that it is necessary to maintain a stable population in the respective provinces. This restriction policy has prevented increased production of live animals in Eastern Indonesia. The most affected producers are the smallholders, since export permits are usually granted to the larger traders. Their relative position is made even worse by the fact that there is a considerable price differential between export and local prices (up to 30 per cent). A critical assessment of this restriction is therefore necessary.

Similar restrictions that need to be reviewed seriously concern the import ban on dairy breeds and the export ban on live cattle for slaughter. Furthermore, there are reports indicating that the prohibition on crossbreeding has considerably limited the options for cattle farmers and prevented them from having the possibility of earning higher income. While livestock play an important role in Eastern Indonesia's economy, there is reason for concern that the gap in growth rate has reversed from faster to slower than Western Indonesia's growth during 1988-90 to 1990-93.

Despite the fact that the national policy of trade reform through the removal of tariff barriers is applied across regions, and that the nature and size of its effects on Eastern Indonesia therefore depend very much on the region's export structure, there is still a considerable number of non-tariff barriers in Eastern Indonesia hindering increased production and interregional (domestic) trade expansion. It is in this area that the liberalisation policy can have favourable impacts on Eastern Indonesia's economy. On the investment deregulation front, it has often been found that nationally imposed liberalisation policies, such as removing activities from the negative list, did not help Eastern Indonesia's relative position very much, even if the region had potential in such activities. Numerous reports indicate that the unfavourable attitudes of certain local officials exacerbate the problem further. The term 'deregulation in talk, regulation in action' is not infrequently found in reality. Yet, as verified by the earlier simulation exercises, there is a strong likelihood that if actual exports and investment expanded Eastern Indonesia's relative position in terms of GRDP as well as household income could be enhanced.

The meaning of industrialisation and decentralisation policies for Eastern Indonesia

Given the distinct physical, economic and social settings of Eastern Indonesia, any appropriate development and industrialisation strategy for the region must be region specific. Various studies have already pointed out that a number of large industries in Eastern Indonesia, mostly resource based, both privately and publicly owned, have failed to generate meaningful spill-over effects for the local population, even if their presence inflates the region's aggregate investment and production levels. The present author has written a number of research reports, papers and articles over the past decade, cautioning against the use of aggregate data to indicate the actual welfare of local population, and stressing the danger of relying too heavily upon these aggregate data in evaluating regional development performance.

The industrialisation process that prevails in Western Indonesia is not suitable for Eastern Indonesia. Still worse, it may even be detrimental to the vast natural resources of the region. Alternatively, activities by private indigenous investors should be promoted, even if they are small- or medium-scale industries. In this respect, numerous reports point to the lack of access to financial resources as one of the major obstacles, despite the growing number of commercial banks in many provinces outside Java, albeit mostly in Western Indonesia, and the spread of *Bank Perkreditan Rakyat* (BPR, [People's Credit Bank]) during the last couple of years.

Many suggest that agriculture-related activities, including agribusiness, offer potential for further regional growth. But in this sector, too, Western Indonesia has managed to attract more investors. Furthermore, this sector is accessible only to those with access to relatively large capital, which is another factor constraining a speedy growth of investment in Eastern Indonesia. For example, the nation's potential and fast-growing crude palm oil (CPO) industries, whose role in non-oil exports is predicted to replace those of textile and wood products (whose production is often clouded by issues of human rights and sustainable forest management), are traditionally the 'domain' of Sumatra and Kalimantan, not Eastern Indonesia.

Eastern Indonesia and more specifically North Sulawesi may be attractive for crude coconut oil (CCO) industries. Unfortunately, investors' interest in CCO has, so far, been minimal. The May 1995 deregulation package, in which a number of industries, including those producing CPO, were removed from the negative investment list, will probably boost the development of new CPO and CCO industries. But it is highly unlikely that Eastern Indonesia will be the preferred destination for such industries.

In the past, small-scale activities in Eastern Indonesia have proven capable of growing at a faster rate than large ones, as demonstrated earlier through the case of smallholder production (Table 5.3). If the trend is to be continued, however, a specific set of policies that will enable the physical infrastructures and human resource conditions of the region to improve is needed. These policies should be designed in such a way that private participation can be encouraged. Although it may sound like a cliché, there seems to be no approach other than joint public-private operations that can be expected to improve the physical and social infrastructures of many parts of Eastern Indonesia.

Within the agricultural sector, fisheries is the next most important after the smallholder cash-crops subsector in the Eastern Indonesia provinces. Its average share in Eastern Indonesia's GRDP is recorded at close to 6 per cent, compared to only 1.4 per cent in Western Indonesia (Table 5.1). The region's contribution to the national fisheries sector is more than 26 per cent (Table 5.2). The trend of this sector in Eastern Indonesia also shows a stable growth rate at almost 9 per cent per annum during 1988-93. Such a trend is important, since national average growth has slowed to just over 7 per cent.

The demand prospects of this sector are bright. Local consumption in Eastern Indonesia itself is considerably higher than in Western Indonesia, and the income elasticity of fish demand remains greater than unity. In terms of export volume, Eastern Indonesia contributes slightly more than 30 per cent of the nation's fisheries exports. Shrimps and frozen tuna are among the top fishery products exported from Eastern Indonesia ports; the first is dominant in Maluku and South Sulawesi, while the latter is largely exported from South East Sulawesi, North Sulawesi and East Nusa Tenggara. Since fishing in Eastern Indonesia is predominantly carried out without boats and is small-scale in nature, there is a tendency for public-supported programs to be directed towards improving fishing technology. However, as noted earlier, most fishermen in Eastern Indonesia are part-time operators; only small proportions of fishing activities are operated by permanent fishermen. Yet the latter generally have lower household incomes than the former. Therefore, the policy to improve fishing technology must be carefully designed so that part-time fishermen will not lose the opportunity to earn higher and more secure income from other activities[18]. In other words, concerted policies with other agencies must be in place. Unfortunately, whenever inter-agency coordination is required it is often found that the difficulties in Eastern Indonesia are greater than in Western Indonesia. This is another example showing what the term 'industrialisation' (in this case, modernisation of fishing technology) means to Eastern Indonesia.

Another agricultural subsector that is very important in Eastern Indonesia is livestock. Although Eastern Indonesia's contribution to total national livestock (roughly 16 per cent) is less than in the fisheries case, in some provinces the share of this subsector in total GRDP can be as high as 11 per cent, as is the case in East Nusa Tenggara (Table 5.1). A high and accelerating annual growth rate for this subsector is found in Central Sulawesi, where it rose from 12 per cent during 1988-90 to 25 per cent in 1990-93.

The 'industrialisation' of this sector is often interpreted as moving to the upper ladder by producing and exporting meat rather than live animals. But here too we should again be cautious about whether such a goal is truly realistic for Eastern Indonesia. Reports indicate, for example, that there are only two class B slaughterhouses in Eastern Indonesia. Furthermore, even if the number of slaughterhouses was increased, exporting meat to other regions like Java would involve high transport costs. The estimated cost of transporting frozen meat from Lombok is estimated at US$0.20 per kg, compared to between US$0.10 and US$0.15 per kg live weight. Exports to foreign countries are even less likely. In this context, other policies capable of sustaining increased productivity and higher income from traditional farms, which produce the greater part of the region's output, are more urgently needed.

Among the important policies in this category are the provision of critical inputs such as mineral supplements, technical supports for improved breeding systems, and methods to deal with livestock diseases and intensive fattening. The involvement of the private sector in this area is increasingly needed. Thus, 'industrialisation' for the livestock subsector in Eastern Indonesia should be aimed at increasing the welfare of smallholders and small farmers.

---

[18] Another important policy has to deal with the risk of overexploitation, particularly due to frequent violations of territorial waters in Eastern Indonesia by foreign vessels. Monitoring of activities by foreign vessels is far more of a problem in Eastern than in Western Indonesia's waters. More detail is given by James Fox in Chapter 8.

Last but certainly not least is the trade sector. In discussions of this sector in Eastern Indonesia, 'industrialisation' should not be associated with increased modern trading activities, because the activities covered within the trade sector itself may be different. It is not unusual for women to be more involved in small trading activities than men. Their trading activities may already contribute significantly to the marketing system for a number of locally produced goods. Hence they provide one of the most important services for the production sector in Eastern Indonesia. Unfortunately, the funding needed to enhance their activities is often difficult to obtain, since financial lending practices are usually less favourable in that they furnish smaller access to women than to ,men. Formulating a special policy to counter such a trend is therefore necessary.

With respect to the human factor, there are numerous reports indicating that a number of development programs, even those designed with a bottom-up framework, have not succeeded in many Eastern Indonesia provinces. The primary culprit appears to be the mental attitudes rather than the educational level *per se* of certain local government officials. The more such stories occur, the less effective is the decentralisation process likely to be. This is not a problem that can be solved in the short term, but efforts at least to ameliorate the situation must be put in place soon. The timing could not be more appropriate than now, since in this current year through government regulation PP No 8/1995, a new policy of decentralisation using *daerah percontohan* with 26 district areas is being implemented. The objectives of the policy are to increase autonomy or decentralisation, and to promote a more rational, lean and responsive administration. The whole idea was prompted by one major goal, namely, to improve service to the public and to promote regional development.

According to the annex to PP No 8/1995, nineteen activities are to be transferred[19]. Basically, the transfer of responsibility has to be followed by transfers of funding, staff and assets. After two years these nineteen activities will be extended to all second-tier authorities. Inside sources confirm that innovations in these *kabupaten percontohan* are viewed as the pattern to be adopted in all districts, rather than as pilot studies that may be

---

[19] Activities include agriculture, animal husbandry, fishery, sea-water fishery and forestry (including small-scale rubber estates), plantations, transmigration, general government (mostly administrative matters), social affairs, cooperatives and supervision of small-scale entrepreneurs, forestry, tourism, public works, land transportation, mining, trade, health, labour matters, industry, and education and culture,

abandoned if found ineffective. Hence, it is a 'point of no return' type of policy.

Since one *kabupaten* is selected in each province except DKI Jakarta, nine *kabupaten* in Eastern Indonesia have been designated as trial areas[20]. As expected, implementation of the program has not been smooth. After the first year, even more problems are expected to appear. For example, there are reports indicating that some transferred assets are not only unusable but even add financial burdens for services and maintenance to local governments. Given the level of development and the relative position of human resources, the problems found in Eastern Indonesia are more numerous than those in Western Indonesia. Furthermore, within each sector there is no clarity in terms of precisely what activities are to be transferred and who is really transferring them, despite the stated activities listed in the annex of the PP. Since the ultimate targets are the districts, there are issues that need to be clarified by local regulations (*Perda*) in addition to the PP. Again, in this area too it can be expected that implementation in Eastern Indonesia will be far more difficult than in Western Indonesian districts.

There is a general feeling that the whole program has not really been planned carefully. This adds to the already difficult task of changing the attitudes of officials on both the giving end (central and provincial) and receiving end (*kabupaten*). The risk is also high, especially in Eastern Indonesia, that if for some sectoral activities things do not work as expected, certain functions will tend to be retained by either sectoral ministries through *Kanwil* or provincial governments through *Dinas Tk 1*. In other words, there will very likely be pressures to re-establish central or provincial offices in the *kabupatens*. This is precisely what the new policy is endeavouring to dismantle, since such a situation will not promote decentralisation.

Given the 'point of no return' nature of the program and the need for greater regional autonomy, a series of improvements has to be made as soon as possible. Funds need to be switched from DIP to *Inpres* or block grant styles of transfer. As demonstrated by simulation exercises earlier, this would be particularly beneficial to Eastern Indonesia's provinces. Clarification also needs to be made with respect to budget splitting, the transfer of staff and rules on transfers of assets. Given the initial relative position of provinces in Eastern Indonesia, considerable support, including a longer period allowed in order to reach a certain 'target,' has to be given to these regions.

---

[20] The Districts of Minahasa, Donggala, Gowa, Kendari, Badung, Central Lombok, South Central Timor, Aileu, Central Maluku and Sorong.

A rejoinder: yes, no, no, yes

This chapter is intended to provide only a general overview of regional development, with particular emphasis on Eastern Indonesia. More specific issues and sectors are discussed in greater detail elsewhere in the book.

A set of economic and social indicators elaborated in this chapter suggests that there is a rationale for looking at Eastern Indonesia, as distinct from, and generally less developed than, Western Indonesia. Interregional variation cannot be ignored, however. The relative position of North Sulawesi, for example, is not only better than the rest of the Eastern Indonesian provinces, even better than some western provinces. On the other hand, a look at the average welfare and poverty of the local population instead of the aggregate output of the region reveals that the two Nusa Tenggara provinces and Irian Jaya are the least developed and the poorest in Eastern Indonesia, if not in the whole nation. Hence the diversity within Eastern Indonesia has to be fully recognised. It is in this respect that the development strategy adopted for Eastern Indonesia ought to be region-specific. In many cases, the strategy applied in the more developed western provinces should not be emulated.

It would perhaps be appropriate to summarise the discussion by posing the following four questions. Has Eastern Indonesia's development been lagging behind Western Indonesia's? Is the trend in the Eastern Indonesia-Western Indonesia gap showing a divergent path? Is the current national policy of liberalisation in trade and investment detrimental to Eastern Indonesia's relative position? Should broader measures of the welfare of the local population be used in addition to aggregate data such as GRDP and investment? The rejoinder: yes, no, no, and absolutely yes.

6

The Socio-economic Development of Eastern Indonesia: The Role of Government

Ben Mboi

Introduction

Entering the Second Period of Long Term Development (PJP II) from 1994-2019, the Indonesian government has embarked on at least three strategic economic policies: 'Going global, going industrial and going east'. The Asia-Pacific Economic Conference (APEC) in 1994 ended with the Bogor Declaration giving a signal: the beginning of the liberalisation of the economy in the Pacific area, a policy with serious implications in terms of government and governance.

I have been asked to talk about the role of government in the socio-economic development of Eastern Indonesia[1] but I prefer to discuss the role of local government. Why do I choose local government? Concurrent with the globalisation and industrialisation processes, there has been a strong tendency in Indonesia from 1990 on, started by none less than President Soeharto himself, to think more about local government. On 25 April 1995, he made an interesting remark about local autonomy which I think it is worthwhile quoting to provoke new thinking about autonomy and decentralisation in Indonesia. President Soeharto said:

> In the management of local autonomy, we are not aiming for uniformity. Uniformity about all affairs which are national by nature has already been taken up and is inherent in the form of the unitary state itself. In local autonomy our attention should be concentrated on the effectiveness, efficiency and harmony of governance,

---

[1] I understand that the provinces belonging to Eastern Indonesia are provinces in Kalimantan, Sulawesi and Nusa Tenggara as well as Maluku and Irian Jaya.

given the socio-economic and cultural conditions of the particular area.

This means that in implementation, opportunities will be open for variations and differences. For instance, there will be differences between districts (*kabupaten*) which are agrarian such as in Java and Sumatra and districts in maritime provinces like Maluku. That is one of the manifestation of our national motto: Diversity in Unity.

Eastern Indonesia started to be an issue of local and national discussion from the time of the 'Seminar on Indonesia Bagian Timur (Eastern Indonesia)', which took place in 1981 under the auspices of the Provincial Government of East Nusa Tenggara and the Nusa Cendana University in Kupang. Thereafter there were some pragmatic approaches by the then Minister of Defence, General M. Jusuf, who invited big conglomerates to the eastern provinces. President Soeharto revived the issue again around 1990/1991.

The issue of Eastern Indonesia seems to have been forced upon us for several reasons. First is the fact that there are still poor people and poor areas, despite the five development plans (*Repelita*) which we have implemented. Socio-economic development in Eastern Indonesia then is a war on two fronts: improving the difficult and inconvenient life of the people on one side, growth and change on the other side. Those in charge of development in the region have to be aware of this fact and keep it in mind with every step they take. Secondly, there is increasing awareness and political pressure to abolish or at least to mitigate the welfare discrepancy between Western and Eastern Indonesia. Thirdly, with Indonesia going global and industrial, it would be ironic if one large part of the country was still backward, an issue that would touch the dignity and the integrity of the nation. Because of this the issue of Eastern Indonesia has become a nation-building issue, and thus a political issue.

The spirit, enthusiasm and the political will to go east have been aroused, but it is still not very clear whether the development approach should be 'sectoral' or 'territorial/decentralised' or 'what'. All options have their strengths and weaknesses.

Up until now, decentralisation laws have treated local societies only as political, legal and administrative communities[2]. But societal changes following 25 years of economic development demand that the local societies

---

[2]*Daerah* means 'a legal' juridical community within a circumscribed physical boundary, which has the right to take care of its own household' (Decentralisation Law No. 6/1974).

be looked upon also as economic and cultural communities. This needs harmonious administration. The purpose of using an economic entry point *vis-à-vis* the role of government is to explore the possible new role of local government (provincial and district) in the future, taking into consideration the sociological changes that Indonesia is facing and particularly economic, political and cultural realities.

Concurrent with the new politics of globalisation, industrialisation and going east, the Indonesian government (national, provincial, and district) is embarking on another task, namely, decentralisation, with the centre of gravity of autonomy located at the district level. I would like to explore possible paradigms, which are useful for local governments in the eastern region. These governments are faced with the task 'of catching and keeping up' with other areas of the country, challenged by international and global pressure on the one side, and the pressure of poverty alleviation plus the government's own weaknesses on the other side.

In my opinion there are two different ways of viewing 'going global and industrial', and 'going east'. Going east in terms of economic development — from the point of view of the people — is going back to the basic classical definition of development: change and growth, structural and cultural changes and institution-building, which make sustainable development possible. It is my view that going east is based first of all on a sense of justice, while going global is based on a sense of business and competition. To go east we look first to the people. To go global, we look to our national economy and our competitors and partners. From these facts we can conclude that the question of approach to the economic development of Eastern Indonesia — whether sectoral or decentralised — is clear. It should be predominantly decentralised.

Those who have been participating in the development process in the area will certainly acknowledge that development in Eastern Indonesia is not simply a concern of the economy or the people's welfare, a fact we perceive and experience every day.

On the other hand, it is also our experience that local autonomy as defined by Law No 5/1974 handicaps the government in intervening in other fields of life for lack of political authority. A new paradigm of local government is needed in facing current sociological realities, whether they are political, economic, cultural or social.

Because the present paper is exploratory in nature, my opinion could conflict with common perceptions at the moment, when everybody is thinking in terms of globalisation, privatisation, deregulation and debureaucratisation, and everything else is taken for granted. I would not be astonished if there were still people thinking centralistically. However, please keep in mind the fact that the thinking of this paper is 'bottom-up', a micro approach to development problems in the eastern region.

During the last two decades, one of the obvious societal phenomena has been the great inter- or intra-provincial/district migration of population, both planned and spontaneous. This phenomenon has had positive and negative consequences, but thus far there has been little conscious awareness and perhaps no studies of the impact of the in-migrants on the local economy. Nor is there any indication of awareness of the development impact of this process, despite the fact that conflicts have occurred. These have not infrequently been ethnic conflicts based on the economic discrepancies between the local residents and the migrants.

Socio-economic features

The profile of government management and the role which it is going to play in Eastern Indonesia depend on the nature of problems in the region. These will be determined by population pressure, the structure of the economy and concern for the material welfare of the people. An illustration of the demographic and economic dynamics of the region is worthwhile, just to give a glimpse of the social and economic trends and changes in Eastern Indonesia.

Demographic and socio-geographic changes[3]

After 25 years of development, now and in the future societal dynamics will turn around the quantity, quality, and mobility of the population. In some areas the main phenomenon will be population pressure, particularly in towns and urban areas, while in other areas problems will arise because of a shortage of manpower, with all its positive and negative consequences. In a given situation, observations and planning, policy analysis and programs, should be directed to and influenced by population factors, besides being influenced by factors involving the environment and technology.

The growth rate of the population varies from province to province because of interprovincial migration, causing growth rates ranging from 1.42 per cent in South Sulawesi to 4.42 per cent in East Kalimantan (see also Table 1.6). Because of longer life expectancy, the age composition is also changing. There

---

[3] Sources for this paper are taken from three documents: (a) *Repelita VI*, Book VI; (b) *Statistik Indonesia* 1994, and (c) *Statistik Keuangan Daerah Tingkat Satu* 1988-90 [The Financial Statistics of the Provinces 1988-90].

are provinces with high in-migration,[4] as a result of official transmigration programs as well as spontaneous migration. The provinces in Kalimantan and Sulawesi as well as Irian Jaya are particularly attractive for planned migration, while other provinces are also destinations for spontaneous migrants, particularly people feeling the economic pressure in Java and Bali. Along with these are the adventurous-spirited Buginese and Makassarese, who like people from Padang have migrated over most of the Indonesian archipelago (see Figure 1.1).

Urbanisation is taking place very rapidly and has already caused social dislocation, including problems of housing and slums as well as problems of drinking water and a healthy environment. Health, education, and culture likewise face problems of many kinds, while the lack of work opportunities and unemployment of people from all levels of education in rural as well as urban situations add further dimensions. In all provinces we see new towns growing at a rate of 10 per cent per year because of young people seeking education and work. They do not always succeed in their new surroundings and ultimately give rise to social problems. There are also problems of transportation and communication, not to mention the discrepancy between agriculture and industry and between agriculture and the availability of arable land.

The high spatial mobility within and among provinces as a result of economic progress has exerted pressure for improvement in the land, sea and air transportation system since the early 1980s, combined with the opening and improvement of roads. Interprovincial and interdistrict mobility has reduced ethnic isolation. Towns are flooded with job-seekers with high school and college diplomas. On the other hand villages have become empty in part because there are no work opportunities and tragically, in part, because many young people do not want to work as farmers any more.

This mingling of people has caused a mingling of ethnic groups and of people from different religious backgrounds and socio-economic status, all with their own abstract and real interests. Encounters therefore tend to collide and be highly conflict-loaded. The pressure on the government to take a fair and correct attitude is intense. If the government posture is not right, the feeling of harmony and the sense of belonging and of being part of a community is disturbed. The physical and psychological density of population now causes so many problems that the government cannot gain a clear view of the situation, which can no longer be managed in a traditional way.

---

[4] The term 'in-migrants' is used to designate people moving into a district or province from outside the area.

It cannot be denied that the presence of the in-migrants has had positive effects for local economic development. The migrants play the role of intermediate traders between big merchants and local people. They themselves are often big traders and employers. In many areas they live separate from the local people, which often causes social jealousy and results in inter-ethnic conflicts. If we see how conflicts are solved, and how little is done to reconcile and integrate the economy of the local people and that of the in-migrants, it is clear that the developmental role of the latter is neither well appreciated nor understood. We can include, for instance, the Chinese among the in-migrants.

Because of the spread of formal education, there is considerable vertical mobility of the population, the educated forming an elite stratum in the regions. In many areas graduates are reluctant to migrate. They stay in their home town unemployed for a long time, or they go back to their village but refuse to become farmers, no matter how limited other employment may be.

Conventional social problems remain and perhaps are increasing in quality and quantity (for example, drugs, prostitution, theft, burglary etc). But the main pattern of social conflict is dominated by issues rooted in economics and relevant to marginalised groups. Thus, socio-economic discrepancies will continue to colour future social conflicts. In my opinion, conflicts based on primordial sentiments will still continue to exist but to a lesser degree. Indeed it is true that the situation will be more dangerous if primordial elements are superimposed on socio-economic conflicts, or if conflicts are portrayed as having primordial roots.

At the village level change is reflected in social disintegration from the old structure when the population was homogeneous, to a new one where it has become heterogeneous. This phenomenon can be clearly observed at the level of local leaders. In former days a leader was automatically concerned with the fate of his people, as he was part of the 'big family'. Now he has to be educated to be so. The old traditional community was secure and prosperous, because of its communality. The new plural village community experiences disintegration, and the most crucial level is that of the leadership stratum. The lower we go, the more we feel that leadership will influence the administrative capacity of the region.

Economic changes

Twenty-five years of development work has proven that economic progress depends on the availability of natural resources, on human resources including leadership at all levels, on local culture and technology, on local economic institutions like financial institutions, banks, traders and cooperatives and on such things as markets, infrastructures, roads, harbours, transportation, a supportive bureaucracy and a facilitative administration. At the same time policies and strategies devised and programs implemented by the government, supported by an appropriate administrative systems, play an important role. So if there are differences in economic progress among the provinces or between Eastern and Western Indonesia, then these factors are responsible. Changes of an economic nature, including the structure of income, are the result of interactions among these same factors.

There is no denying that past development efforts have recorded many successes in Eastern Indonesia, but the following facts must be noted in all the provinces. The economic structure is still basically agricultural, consisting of food and cash crops, wet and dry land agriculture. The efficiency of agriculture is still low, due to the lack of better technology, poor soil quality, backward cultures, remote markets, trade mechanisms that do not support farmers, ineffective cooperatives, transportation problems that caused delays and damage, unreliable cargo transportation, uncontrolled trade systems and the like. While the contribution of agriculture to the gross regional domestic product (GRDP) is shrinking, the absorption of the labour force in this sector remains above 50 per cent (Table 1.3). In East Nusa Tenggara the figure is above 70 per cent. In some provinces there is overlap between modern industries and modern agriculture on the one hand, and traditional agriculture on the other, which creates social discontinuity. Except in East Kalimantan and Irian Jaya, the role of industry and mining is still small. Looking closely, we see that the main economic activity of the local people is still agriculture. Mining and industry are in the hands of big companies.

It cannot be denied that, as in former times, the ultimate market for Eastern Indonesia is still Java, but products from Eastern Indonesia cannot compete successfully against similar commodities from Java or nearby areas, a condition which is not favourable for the income of Eastern Indonesian farmers. To modernise agriculture or to introduce industry in Eastern Indonesia is difficult, because of shortages of adequately qualified manpower. Home industry cannot be expected to be a leading subsector in the region as such activity is undertaken only part time. We can conclude that agriculture is still the main source of income, but its efficiency is too low to allow it to become an instrument to improve the welfare of the people of Eastern Indonesia. Efforts to boost efficiency should be made, simultaneously with efforts to broaden the economic base of the region.

In spite of all these difficulties there are no special facilities to encourage investors to go east or for local entrepreneurs who want to develop. There are no policies or concrete efforts at the moment to integrate high-tech, capital-intensive industries with local, slow-moving economies, or to involve the local people in the broader economy. No wonder the modern and traditional economies exist side by side, and friction occurs.

The role of government in socio-economic development

All the demographic, socio-geographic and economic changes that have occurred have implications for political life, particularly for the government and governance. At the same time, political life has a tremendous impact on socio-economic development. The traditional 'government culture' in which a government is conceived of as an organ of power to maintain rule and order, to levy taxes and to provide enough services so that there are no outbreaks of disease or hunger has not changed very much since the departure of the Dutch.

Economic development is part of a very recent government culture that includes its administrative and bureaucratic consequences. Although by definition development is a long term-process, in practice the government apparatus is still thinking and working on a 'one-year base'. Except for internationally financed programs, quite often there is no relationship between the projects of one year and those of the next. The deciding factor is finance. The way of thinking is still day-to-day, not developmental. Not infrequently routine matters are also administered as development projects, as routine funds are sometimes not available.

At the beginning of the paper it was stated that the issue of Eastern Indonesia has been raised, among other reasons, because of awareness among the political elite of the discrepancy in material welfare between Western and Eastern Indonesia. So in this paper we raise the question of the government's role in economic development. Instead of focusing on the role of the Indonesian government, I prefer to explore the role of the provincial and district governments *vis-à-vis* socio-economic development, and the constraints that accompany that role.

There are several reasons for my argument. First of all, there has been a shift from a very strong to a weaker government role in terms of financing socio-economic development, from the 1970s into the 1980s and the 1990s, as the deregulation tendencies demonstrate. Secondly, there has been an intense awareness, debate and discussion of decentralisation since the early 1990s, but it seems we have not yet reached any kind of a workable consensus about the appropriate format. Thirdly, my experience shows that there are two interesting aspects of the 'government — development relationship' in the so-called 'poor provinces'. The first is that the government influences development, and the second is the way in which socio-economic development influences the performance of the government, a fact we quite often ignore. The fourth reason is the fact that President Soeharto's speech, which I quoted in the introduction to this paper, shows a new trend towards liberalisation of the definition of decentralisation, going beyond the politico-legal and administrative dimensions of decentralisation. This fact alone will open new horizons of discussion regarding the format of local autonomy and decentralisation.

Misperceptions exist, if I may say so, on the part of many established countries about the role of the government *vis-à-vis* economic development, as if the role is unilateral only. In fact, if we talk about 'poor people and poor areas', we cannot avoid talking about 'poor local government'. The influence thus is mutually interactive.

What is the role of the government in development?

Firstly, we can consider the government as leadership. We can conclude that development in Eastern Indonesia really is an intricate social process. Eastern Indonesia is economically poor, but from the point of view of natural resources, very rich and unexploited. Sociologically it is very heterogeneous, culturally plural and in some ways backward; socio-politically it is volatile. It is an area difficult to govern, to administer and to develop economically.

Professor Jan Tinbergen, the famous Dutch economist, suggests that, all other objective economic factors being equal, there are seven preconditions for an economically backward society to improve its material welfare: (a) the people must be willing to have a better quality of life; (b) they must be willing to look far ahead; (c) they must be willing and ready to take risks; (d) they must be ready to accept new technologies; (e) they must be willing and ready to cooperate or work in collaboration with other people; (f) they must persevere, and finally (g) they must be willing to follow the rules of the game.

I agree entirely with what Professor Tinbergen has said, but having been involved for more than twenty years as a medical officer and as governor in the development of backward areas, I should add at least one other requirement for a society to progress economically: it should have good leadership.

Leadership is a quality and an activity which in a backward or underdeveloped region is an indispensable institution or factor, if there is to be progress. From what we have seen, development cannot be stimulated just by regulations, laws and instructions. Leadership is a necessary part of the system, which creates and recreates conditions for development.

It cannot be denied that the discrepancy between Eastern and Western Indonesia is accounted for, at least in part, by the difference in the quality of leadership. Java and Sumatra have a longer history of modern government. The provinces and regencies in Java date back to 1925 or even earlier as administration units, Sumatra as early as the proclamation in 1945 and Bali and South Sulawesi to 1950. I believe that makes a lot of difference. The culture is there. The intellectual capacity and experience are there. The stamina and entrepreneurial spirit of leaders and organisations are there. In the end it is the fertility of resources and imaginative enterprise that lie at the root of the material progress. The supply of entrepreneurs and of people who carry out new combinations of the means of production determines if and how quickly the people will achieve material welfare.

Was it not leadership in Germany, Japan and Russia that started modernisation? In Eastern Indonesia we need a small group of creative people, with a vision of social, economic, cultural and political changes, an elite able to look for new combinations of efforts to 'catch and keep up' with other provinces, taking into account local, regional, national and international constraints and opportunities.

To bring the people through the transition period — who knows how long it will be — and given the trends mentioned above, we need three kinds of leadership in the region: agrarian, industrial, and agro-industrial leadership. We need leaders who can communicate with and motivate the people about the possibilities, opportunities, problems and dangers of today and tomorrow, whether they be agrarian or industrial. Another responsibility of leadership is to overcome the opposition and resistance of the traditional groups on the one hand and the stubborn, conservative, power-oriented administrators and bureaucrats on the other hand.

Secondly, we can view the government as goal-setter, policy-maker, regulator and planner. These are the basic roles of the government, although it has to be acknowledged that the planning function is a very recent role with a very young planning board. In the provinces and districts no wonder these institutions are staffed with brand new personnel from the university, without any previous field experience or even a minimal knowledge of the area.

The 1993 Broad Outline of State Policy (GBHN) explicitly stipulates the political qualitative goal of the Second Long-Term Plan, which is an amelioration of material welfare through sustainable development based on self-reliance, self-confidence and the nation's own capacity. Economic welfare is a part of the nation's ideological, social, political, cultural and economic resilience.

   The qualitative aspects of development politics in the next five years are
determined every five years by the People's Consultative Assembly (MPR),
which produces the GBHN. The GBHN contains the main tasks of the
national, provincial and district governments for the next five years.
Simultaneously the provincial and the district levels promulgate their own
guidelines, taking into consideration local conditions.

   The quantitative aspects of government policies are formulated through a
presidential decree in the form of the *Rencana Pembangunan Lima Tahun
Nasional (Repelita)* or the National Five-Year Development Plan. At the
provincial and district levels they are presented through decrees of the
governors and district heads *(bupati)*.

   The quality of the plans is improving with the years as the personnel gain
experience and expertise, although a certain degree of uncertainty always
exists as the planning agencies in the provinces and districts do not have real
authority over financial aspects of the planning period. Plans are more or less
shopping lists to be sent to the central government, in this case the National
Planning Bureau which provides the finance.

   In the future there should be changes in the local planning mechanism, but
this will only be possible if there are changes in the central-provincial, and
central-district, and provincial-district political and economic/financial
relationships. For Eastern Indonesia, as a consequence of the sociological and
economic changes described above, good management of government clearly
depends on the following factors: the fact that the trend of problems in Eastern
Indonesia is determined by population pressure and the desire for better
welfare of the people living there; the socio-economic trend of the
region/provinces; the trend in technological progress and the shift from
agriculture to industrialisation, not only as a structure of the economy but also
as a structure of source of income; the trend of dynamism and the *élan* of the
local government, bearing in mind that the region is the catchment area of
changing social problems; and the willingness of the central government to
share its power and authority with local autonomous authorities and
institutions, and to push the solution of problems as near as possible to their
source, which implies decentralisation. To these factors we can add the
tendency of the government to involve non-governmental organisations in
socio-economic development through deregulation, debureaucratisation and
privatisation, which shows that it is not only the government that is able to
solve the problems of society, but that there are problems beyond the capacity
of the government, including speed and accuracy in taking action in a
democratic way. Fortunately, that is what we have already witnessed during
the 1970s, 1980s and the 1990s. On the other hand, although the central

government reacted very quickly to deregulate, privatise and debureaucratise, it did not go so far as to decentralise its power to the provincial and district governments. In my opinion, economic deregulation should be followed by political decentralisation.

As part of its Development Plan and to encourage balanced private sector investment, every five years the government produces a 'Profile of Investment' for the whole country, with specifications for each province. However, 'selling' of the profile depends on the Provincial Investment Office and the activities of private enterprises themselves. That is why we do not see a common goal among the provinces of Eastern Indonesia, to be used as *leit-motif* for economic cooperation in the region. In many instances we see interprovincial competition, without good coordination.

Speaking from personal experience, I see the following key questions as important in looking for and setting up economic development policies in Eastern Indonesia:

- How can we improve the efficiency of agriculture?
- How can we accelerate growth by expanding the economic base?
- How can we integrate the new high technology and capital-intensive economy with the slow-moving, indigenous, people's economy?
- How can we integrate the economy of in-migrants with the autochthonous people's economy, so as to create harmonious social conditions. In other words, how can we foster nation-building, and prevent social disintegration through economic efforts?

There is, however, another important question: How should we allocate or reallocate authority from the central government to the local government in order to take problem-solving as close as possible to the source of the problems?

But let me add a warning at this point. Planning is not always easy, not because of deficiencies in planning requirements but very often because the economic conditions of the area (particularly at district level) are so difficult that the local government has problems allocating its resources and tends to live day by day. Development in those areas means fighting on two fronts: fighting against poverty and at the same time trying to grow and change. Here development becomes a moral problem.

Thirdly, we can see the government as the producer of services. From the beginning, it was realised that it would be impossible to invite investors to the eastern part of Indonesia, if the only thing we have to offer is natural resources. Because of this, programs and projects during the First, Second and

Third *Repelita* consisted of infrastructure, building or repairing of harbours, roads, bridges, air-strips/ports and fuel depots, and the modernisation and expansion of telephone and telegraphic facilities and of electricity capacities.

Road improvement programs are nationwide for state, provincial, and district roads. Even village roads are being extended to stimulate the local economy. Economic institutions like banks have been introduced to the regions to help investors in financing their enterprises. Hospitals, health centres and polyclinics have been rehabilitated or built to guarantee a certain degree of health care. In many cases only very modest technology is available, but some hospitals are already able to provide specialistic services for urgent cases.

Administrative assistance for investment purposes is still very weak in the provinces and districts, and depends very much on how much Jakarta is willing to share its power with the local regional office or with the governor or district head. In my view, the service that is very much expected from the local government is creation of a social, economic and political atmosphere conducive to local investments by foreigners and non-autochthonous people. Here we see the role of the government as investment facilitator. Consultation agencies can be very useful as participatory mechanisms in laying down policies and plans.

Fourthly, we can regard the government as a fiscal agent and financier of development. The socio-economic development role of the local government cannot be effective without an adequate administrative capacity. From our experience there are at least five factors which determine the effectiveness of the government role in administering its area. The first is the size of the territory: many provinces and districts are too large for the local organisation to cover them effectively, yet on the other hand splitting into smaller areas would fragment the demographic capacity. The second is the nature of the population, that is, the quantity and quality of human resources. The third is the personnel and personnel policies of the government, both qualitative and quantitative where the policy of placement makes districts nothing more than elementary schools for government employees. The fourth is the financial capacity of the province and districts, which is very much dependent on the state subsidies from the national level through the *Inpres* programs.[5]

---

[5] *Inpres (Instruksi Presiden)* programs are intended to assure some measure of equity in allocation of national resources and the process of development. *Inpres* programs like school building and health clinics are carried out according to common guidelines throughout the country. The programs are basically 'co-administration programs', in which the purpose is already determined by the central government. These programs are also discussed by Iwan Azis in Chapter 5.

The latter do not leave latitude for local governments to talk about their own problems and their own solutions. Indeed, the main source of income of the Eastern Indonesian provinces are state subsidies and contributions. The income from their own sources is still very limited, due to the narrow base of taxation and retribution capacity. Political autonomy in the future should be understood as the broader right, capacity and responsibility of the provincial and district governments to make their own political, economic and cultural decisions. In the case of Eastern Indonesia the governor and the provincial DPRD and the *bupati* and district DPRD should be able to make those decisions. Political decision-making should not depend on the source of income, whether it comes from their own or the central government's subsidy or from elsewhere.

The last factor determining the effectiveness of government administration is the capacity of provincial and district institutions. The provincial and district organisation is still relatively young in government culture by comparison with autonomous areas in Java and Sumatra, and the organisations receive personnel from many disciplines. Creating mental cohesiveness is thus difficult.

The new paradigm of autonomy

After reading the above, one is apt to ask: what then should be the role of the local government in relation to autonomy and decentralisation politics in Indonesia? In discussing autonomy and decentralisation, I am consciously avoiding reference to decentralisation and the people's sovereignty, which usually appears in discourses about decentralisation. I take it as given.

I suggest that the principle of autonomy and decentralisation should be seen in relation to economic development and be based more on efficiency and effectiveness towards economic development. This is determined by: (a) patterns of national problems in a complex economic, social, cultural and political environment; (b) the complexity of economic problems in Eastern Indonesia, with the interweaving of social, technological and cultural aspects; (c) the risks and consequences of the processes of regionalisation and globalisation, as can be seen, for example, in the Trade Triangles; and (d) awareness of and demand for just, appropriate and speedy solutions, which means solutions as near as possible to the source of the problem.

My conclusion is that, having understood the trends and nature of changes, we need a restructuring of central-local relationships for better governance, but we must always take into consideration the administrative capacity of the local government and local community. The classic paradigm of deconcentration, devolution and co-administration should be placed in a more dynamic relationship, and the following dimensions or variables should be considered as we working out the dynamics of transfer: the types of activities to be transferred, the type of power or authority to be transferred, the levels of administration to which the power or activities are to be transferred, the organisations to which power is also transferred, and the political and/or legal mechanism needed to carry out the transfer and function thereafter.

Policies for decentralisation should not be 'flat-rate' decisions that are the same for all parts of the nation. Local conditions are determining factors, as was stated in the President's speech on 25 April 1995, when he inaugurated the Autonomy Pilot Project for 26 districts in 26 provinces. There will be differences among provinces and among districts. One other consequence is that the household of the province or districts shall be either a 'household based on material principle' and/or a 'household based on the formal or residual principle'. We have had this last mentioned principle in the Decentralisation Laws No.1/1945 and No.1/1957.

More autonomy will be difficult but not impossible. The only question is one worthy of consideration on the 50th anniversary of the Republic. Do we have the will and the courage?

The influence of socio-economic development on government in a poor province: a personal experience

Talking about government in a developing society is like talking about a hunter in the midst of a moving herd. At one time the herd is his target, at another time he is the herd's object; at all times they are each other's object.

That is the position of the government in a province like East Nusa Tenggara, a situation which many industrialised and advanced countries do not fully comprehend and appreciate. East Nusa Tenggara has been well known as a 'minus province', which is a diplomatic term for a 'poor province', meaning a province deficient in practically everything. Development that is understood by everybody on the street — perhaps also by many intellectuals — is a process to ameliorate the hardships of the people, to change the economic structure, to raise income, to provide employment, to industrialise, to build institutions for sustainable development and to create economic resilience among the people.

All this should be done by the government; all the burden is on the government's shoulders. The whole process is planned and implemented by the government. Is the government capable of doing all this work and how is it going to do the job? Does anyone really care?

It is assumed that the government is politically and intellectually capable and financially able. Where the support is to come from, is not discussed. Given that all the requirements for good development are there, donors and Western countries often misunderstand and assume that everything is fine with the local government *vis-à-vis* its development role.

I had a different perspective on government-development relationships, particularly in 'poor areas', where development is a very recent social process. My first point is the attitudinal aspect of the government: The process of development demands a positive attitude and awareness towards poverty, towards backwardness, towards planned thinking and action, and towards participatory process, as well as an awareness of the limitations on one's capacity. If Jan Tinbergen was talking of the requirements for a society to progress, those same requisites will apply for the government as guidelines.

Second is the fact that the government is traditionally conceived of as an organ of power, which makes policies and decisions, sets goals, and also punishes. Development demands a change from a power-oriented organ to a development-oriented one that receives other institutions as partners in development. But the change of attitude and development of institutional capacity have already taken 25 years and we are still discontented with what has been achieved so far. But please be aware, if you talk about 'development in terms of projects', then it could be a different story.

My third point is that the socio-economic development of Eastern Indonesia has forced the government to think in spatial dimensions, a natural way of thinking for public administrators and also in terms of inter-spatial discrepancies, which is not always easy. But the idea of Eastern Indonesia forces or teaches the government to accustom itself to thinking about discrepancies, whether interprovincial, interdistrict, intersubdistrict, and intervillage. It even forces us to think about marginalised people in the villages. It is easy to think of poor people if you have been poor yourself, but if not, you have to be taught to be conscious of poverty.

Finally, the political impact of economic development on the government and management of government can be briefly illustrated as follows. The higher the income of the people, the better the economy of the local government. The better its economy and the greater the government's income, the more leeway it has for local political, autonomous decision-making. The lower its income, the more it is financially dependent on the central government, the smaller its own leeway for decision-making, the lower the degree of autonomy and the lower the degree of local democracy. The lower its own income, the more it is dependent on sectoral and *Inpres* programs for its development plans, and the less it knows what to do. In terms of goals, local governments then are more uncertain of themselves. Consequently, a governor who is enthusiastic about developing his province should also spend a lot of time bargaining for more funds and projects and other facilities from the central government. The other side of the coin is that he will lose much of his countervailing power, a capacity very much needed in a country as plural as Indonesia. Local government is a product of its own environment. On the other hand, a good local government is a function of the size of its territory, the nature of its population, the nature of its personnel, its financial capacity and its administrative organisation. Does this imply that in poor provinces development of the 'poor people' has an influence on the development of the local government too: a chicken and egg relationship? No! No matter what, it is still the government that is responsible for the economic development of its people. But indeed, a government in a 'poor area' needs understanding.

Conclusion

The economy of Eastern Indonesia is still agriculturally based. If there is a discrepancy between the welfare of the eastern and western parts of the country, I believe from my own experience that it is due to the efficiency of agriculture. For various reasons other branches of the economy which could broaden the economic base of the region have not yet developed. The presence of big industries and mining in some provinces (East Kalimantan and Irian Jaya) can give us a false impression of the people's economy, in terms of their contribution to the Gross Domestic Regional Product. Putting those industries aside, we will have a similar picture of the people's economy in all Eastern Indonesian provinces.

In the last twenty years we have witnessed very strong interprovincial mobility. This has had positive and negative consequences for the social, economic and political dimensions of life. Despite some negative aspects, the development role of these 'in-migrants' should be appreciated and better integrated with the local economy of the people.

In the message of the GBHN, development is not only economic; it also implies political, social and cultural aspects of life, which are the constituent elements of national resilience. The role of the government is still critical in that it is leader, goal-setter, planner, policy-maker, producer of services and financier of development. But the place and role of the local government are still being questioned for their effectiveness and efficiency.

Indonesia is very serious about embarking on a new discourse on local autonomy and decentralisation. This should be welcomed, appreciated and utilised, not only as a classic power debate but also as a means to explore sincerely new paradigms of central and local government relationships, while understanding societal dynamics and constraints. The President has given the green light for such a course of action. At least the efforts of the national government to start with a Pilot Project on Local Autonomy with the centre of gravity in the districts should be appreciated.

It has been our experience that the local government-socio-economic development relationship is bilateral. The government influences economic development, and vice-versa, socio-economic development influences the performance of government. Very frequently this relationship is not well comprehended or appreciated.

7

Agricultural Development in Eastern Indonesia: Performance, Issues and Policy Options

Lucky Sondakh

Introduction: economic miracle and regional disparity

Indonesia has achieved remarkable economic success in the past two and a half decades (World Bank 1993). It has done well in sustaining rapid economic growth and reducing inequality and poverty. Over the last two decades Indonesia has been transformed from low to middle rank among less developed countries. Annual growth rates of GDP over this period have generally exceeded 5 per cent. It has managed to reduce income inequality from a Gini measure of 0.35 in 1970 to 0.32 in 1990 and in many provinces the income inequality coefficients are below 0.30 (Table 5.5). It has also been successful in reducing poverty from about 40 per cent in the 1970s to 15 per cent in 1990. The stability of the country during the period, despite some minor problems, has allowed business activity to take place.

The success, however, is not without criticism. Criticism has been launched at the way the government intervenes or regulates the market. A number of regulations in trade, marketing and prices are considered to have benefited the elites more than the society as a whole; to be responsible for the on-going high-cost economy and for a decline in the nation's economic competitiveness on the world market; to have shown little respect for the rights of (some) individuals and society; and to have widened income and regional disparity (Nasution and James 1995; Sondakh 1995; Rachbini, 1995b). Other criticisms have been focused on the way democracy has been implemented, for today the position of the state seems far stronger than that of the society. The prevalence of these shortcomings will in the long run dampen not only economic growth but also stability.[1]

The above criticism, however, seems to have been overshadowed by the numerous government achievements, for success more effectively touches the feelings of the people. Indonesia has been praised as a developing Asian country which in the last decade has experienced a miracle in its economy and deserves to have been regarded as one of the *Six Asian Tigers* (World Bank 1993). More recently, any criticisms have been strongly overshadowed by Indonesia's success in producing aeroplanes and ships, and by President Soeharto's role as the Head of the Non-Aligned Nations and his unpredicted but safe visit to Sarajevo.

This paper argues that inequality in general and regional disparity in particular remain important development issues. It is true that Indonesia has done remarkably well during the past two and a half decades. But the success has not been fairly distributed throughout the country. Some regions, mostly Java and the western islands (referred to here as Western Indonesia), have gained more from the fruits of development than have the islands of Eastern Indonesia.

The relative per-capita gross regional domestic product (GRDP) of most eastern provinces, especially East Nusa Tenggara and West Nusa Tenggara, is far lower than the national average and is just a little more than one-third of the average Indonesian per-capita gross domestic product (GDP) (Table 1.1). Take the case of North Sulawesi. According to Sondakh (1993), the per-capita GRDP of North Sulawesi was 24 per cent above the national average in 1971, but then declined to 22 per cent below the national average in 1992. In contrast, West Java, whose per-capita GRP was 25 per cent lower than the national average in 1970, increased to 14 per cent lower than the national average in 1992.

During the period from 1970 to 1990, the economy of Eastern Indonesia, which is rich in natural and agricultural resources, experienced economic growth in absolute but not in relative terms. In relative terms, the rate of growth tended to decline over time, which explains why there are more poor people in this region than in Java.[2]

---

[1] The World Bank (1995) recently released a report mentioning cartel practices in cement, plywood, paper and fertiliser, price controls in cement, sugar and rice, entry and exit controls in plywood and retail trade, exclusive licensing in clove and citrus marketing, exclusive licensing in wheat flour milling and import of soya beans and public sector dominance in steel, fertiliser and refined oil products.

[2] But see also the discussion of Iwan Azis in Chapter 5.

Table 5.5 indicates that there are relatively more people living at and below the poverty line in Eastern Indonesia (Sulawesi, Maluku, Nusa Tenggara, Irian Jaya and Kalimantan). In Sumatra and Java, the percentages of people living below the line are smaller than their corresponding shares of population. This comparison highlights some of the government's numerous shortcomings in implementing the stated objective of attaching higher priority to the development of Eastern Indonesia, even though the 1993 Broad Outline of State Policy (GBHN) seven times mentions the need to give more priority to development of the eastern islands.

One good meausre of regional inequality, the Williamson Index of Inequality, does not indicate that inequality has declined. Overall, it seems to have remained constant, if not worsened. In the mid-1970s, the coefficients varied between 0.434 - 0.463. During the period of 1983-90 the coefficients increased to more than 0.50, varying from 0.541 to 0.566. This evidence does not support the phenomenon of declining income inequality indicated by the World Bank 1993. That inequality remains a problem in Indonesia can also be seen from the fact that about 91 per cent of the population earned income less than the national average of Rp75,520 per capita per month (Biro Pusat Statistik, 1993b).

Irian Jaya had the highest per-capita GRDP of the Eastern Indonesian region in 1986, namely Rp801,306. However, most of the income did not belong or accrue to the rural Irianese community. About 82 per cent of the people of Irian Jaya live from subsistence farming; their per-capita income in 1986 was Rp200,000 or one-fourth of the province's GRDP/capita. The average per capita income of the other 18 per cent, who were mostly employed in the mining and manufacturing sectors, was Rp2 million per annum, a very wide income disparity indeed. The majority of the 18 per cent are not Irianese but 'outsiders'.

Distribution of income in the rural areas of Eastern Indonesia indicates that inequality remains a serious problem. Gini coefficients calculated for North Sulawesi are higher than the national averages of about 0.32. They vary from 0.26 to 0.60 for income, 0.18 to 0.50 for expenditure and 0.33 to 0.62 for landownership, with averages of 0.38, 0.38 and 0.47 respectively.

A more direct indication that regional inequality was getting worse up to 1989 can be seen by comparing GRDP/capita of the provinces to GDP/capita for the whole country. However, the process of deterioration seems to have halted at a stationary level. To some extent, signs of improvement are beginning to appear. During the past five years the relative income per capita of people in Eastern Indonesia has remained constant. However, it must be borne in mind that the per-capita income of the majority of people in this region is far below the national average. Even that of Irian Jaya, with the highest per-capita income, is in reality not high at all.

The President, in his speech on 4 January 1990, saw the relatively declining economic growth of Eastern Indonesia as an important development issue. He immediately instructed his government, especially the National Development Planning Body (Bappenas) and the Minister of Research and Technology, Professor Habibie, to tackle and overcome the problem. So far, however, five years after the speech of the President, neither Bappenas nor Professor Habibie and the various departments (including the Department of Agriculture) has produced well formulated or readily implementable regional development programs for Eastern Indonesia.

The main features of Eastern Indonesia

Most land in Eastern Indonesia is classed as conditionally suitable for agriculture. The extensive lowlands of South and to some extent Central Sulawesi and the volcanic soils of North Sulawesi are among the most fertile areas. The soils of East and West Nusa Tenggara and Maluku, however, are on the whole very shallow and therefore less suitable for intensive food cropping. Irian Jaya consists mainly of alluvial and marshy plains which are difficult to improve for agricultural usage. However, there are indications that several places in Membrano and Nabire have potentials for the cultivation of food and crops.

From an economic stand point, Indonesia can be divided into three sections: (a) provinces which have a predominantly mining (oil and gas) oriented economy; (b) provinces which are predominantly manufacturing oriented; and (c) provinces which are predominantly agricultural in their economy. The provinces of Aceh, Riau and East Kalimantan are predominantly oil- and gas-oriented, while East Java, West Java and Jakarta are predominantly manufacturing-oriented. The main features of the structure of Indonesia's economy excluding mining are depicted in Table 7.1 below.

Table 7.1: *Percentages of main economic sectors in GRDP (range for constituent provinces), 1993 (1983 constant prices)*

Sector		Eastern Indonesia	Western Indonesia[b]	Java
Primary[a]	(A)	16.0 - 45.0	26.0 - 48.0	1.3 - 31.0
Secondary[a]	(M)	2.0-17.0	8.6 - 24.4	16.0 - 36.0
Tertiary[a]	(S)	41.0 - 47.0	45.7 - 62.0	46.8 - 62.0

Note: [a]A = agriculture, M = manufacturing, S = services.   [b]Excluding Java
Source: Biro Pusat Statistik, 1989-94.

Table 7.1 shows very big differences in economic structure between regions. Java already has an industrially oriented economy; Eastern Indonesia is still an agriculturally oriented economy and most parts of Western Indonesia are already entering a manufacturing oriented economy.

The employment distribution of Eastern Indonesia (Table 7.2) is typical of an economy at the earlier stages of development. Between 60 and 80 per cent of the labour force are work in agriculture and only 3.2 to 9.2 per cent are employed in manufacturing. In Java, the role of agriculture has declined but that of manufacturing has increased. The amount of labour employed in agriculture is around 50 per cent and that in manufacturing is already around 20 per cent. In Eastern Indonesia the role of agriculture has been very slowly declining and, with almost no growth in manufacturing, a static expansion characterises the economy.

Table 7.2: *Distribution of employment by economic sector in Eastern Indonesia, 1990*

Province	Total ('000)	Percentages in Economic Sectors				
		(1)	(2)	(3)	(4)	(5)
West Nusa Tenggara	1,475	58.6	9.2	14.6	13.4	4.2
East Nusa Tenggara	1,589	81.3	6.8	2.9	7.7	1.3
East Timor	337	81.1	3.2	3.6	9.5	2.6
North Sumatra	1,016	65.2	5.7	10.8	15.5	2.8
Central Sulawesi	643	67.8	5.1	9.5	15.0	2.6
South Sulawesi	2,513	66.8	5.0	10.0	16.0	2.2
South-East Sulawesi	570	75.8	3.8	7.4	11.2	1.8
Maluku	650	68.5	5.6	7.9	15.2	2.8
Irian Jaya	719	69.2	2.1	6.2	19.5	3.0
All Indonesia	76,423	53.9	10.4	15.0	16.4	4.3

Note: (1) Agriculture; (2) Manufacturing; (3) Trade; (4) Services (transport, financial intermediaries, real estate, business services, public services); (5) Others (mining/quarrying; electricity, gas and water, construction and others).
Source: Biro Pusat Statistik, 1995c.

It is interesting to ask why a region with good agricultural and resource endowments has not experienced the sustained economic transformation that most developed countries have. To gain some insights into this issue it is necessary to examine two things: agricultural development in Eastern

Indonesia, and the impact of development policies on agriculture and on the economy of Eastern Indonesia.

Agriculture of Eastern Indonesia

The role of the agricultural sector

The greater part of the land in the eastern islands belongs to the 'conditionally suitable' category. Due to innovations and technological improvements in farming practices, however, the so-called 'conditionally suitable' land may be suitable for tree crops although not for the intensive cultivation of rice and other food crops. In fact Eastern Indonesia has long been the main tree-crop region. Furthermore, Maluku and later Minahasa in North Sulawesi have long been recognised as the world's main 'spice islands'. The tree crops commonly cultivated are coconuts, cloves, nutmegs, coffee, cocoa and vanilla.

A survey carried out by the Directorate General of Smallholder Agriculture (Biro Pusat Statistik 1992b) reported that 27 per cent, 21 per cent, 26 per cent and 90 per cent respectively of the country's total number of coconut, coffee, cloves and cocoa farmers are in Eastern Indonesia, which implies that the majority of farm families in Eastern Indonesia depend on tree crops (see also Table 1.4). Within the national economy, some of the crops may not be important. However, in the economy of the region and especially the economy of the people, the role of agriculture is crucially important. The majority of rural people depend very largely on agriculture for their livelihood and future. Unlike Java and the rest of Western Indonesia, where farmers can seek employment outside agriculture, the main employment source in Eastern Indonesia is farming.

It is evident that nearly half of GRDP comes from agriculture. This is far higher than the role of agriculture in the national economy, which dropped from 45 per cent in 1970 to 21 per cent in 1990. Tree-crop commodities are the main exports of Eastern Indonesia. In North Sulawesi, for example, about 86 per cent to 99 per cent of exports come from the agricultural and agroindustrial subsector. During the past ten years, exports have increased from US$35,415,887 to about US$97,729,790.

Eastern Indonesia, whose population is 15 per cent of the nation's total and whose land is about 40 per cent of the total land area of Indonesia, has 20 per cent of the country's rice fields, 26 per cent of dryland farming, 24 per cent of smallholder agriculture, 68 per cent of pasture and 36 per cent of shrimp ponds. These figures explain the importance of agriculture to the economy of not only Eastern Indonesia but also Indonesia as a whole.

Traditionally, Indonesia relies mostly on Java for its rice, sugar and corn. However, the role of Java as a food-producing island has been rapidly declining. More and more fertile land is being used for housing, infrastructure and industry. One report says that in 1994, agricultural land had declined by about 180,000 ha.[3] The shortage of land in Java for agriculture means that the 'outer islands' will have to play a more significant role in producing food to feed the nation[4]. For these islands to be able to produce food, the present unutilised and conditionally suitable land must be turned into agricultural land. Construction of irrigation networks and other infrastructure is therefore necessary. However, since population density in these islands is relatively low, extensification has been carried out, largely as a part of the transmigration program. The program has been quite successful in increasing food crops. For example, in North Sulawesi the rapid increase in output of rice and soya beans can be largely attributed to the program since 1970s. In fact, most of the fertile arable land in the outer islands has been allocated primarily to transmigrants.

Farming systems and productivity

As shown by Hardjono (1994), the land in Eastern Indonesia is vulnerable to ecological degradation. Shifting cultivation was adopted at the time where the land-man ratio favoured this form of land use. Nowadays, due to population pressure, the practice of shifting cultivation is gradually disappearing. Tree crops are suitable for the topography and soils of the eastern islands not only because they are economically profitable but also because this form of land use is environmentally sound. They can be grown in hilly areas with a slope of up to 30 per cent.

Therefore, the farming systems most commonly practised in the region involve tree crops, especially coconuts, coffee, cocoa, cloves and nutmegs. This does not mean that farmers do not grow food crops. Nearly all cultivate food crops, at least as subsistence crops to meet their own requirements. Cash is earned through tree crops. The penetration of a market or monetised

---

[3] The shortage of agricultural land in Java has forced the government to begin shifting sugar plantations to the other islands. For example, since 1987 North Sulawesi has been asked to allocate 20,000 ha of land for sugar plantations. Sugar production began recently.

[4] There is an emerging view that since the opportunity cost of land in Java has increased, the land is now considered 'unprofitable' for agriculture. Professor Sayogyo (23 August 1995, personal interview) mentioned one finding where a farmer was considering selling a parcel of agricultural land at about Rp200,000 per sqm, a price comparable to the level in big cities.

economy in rural areas accelerated the planting of tree crops as far back as the early 1900s. However, tree-crop products are subject to a relatively high degree of uncertainty . Furthermore, the supply as well as demand elasticity is in general low, which causes farmers to be easily trapped in a poverty circle. It is the high degree of uncertainty in price which forces most farmers to diversify their farming systems by intercropping.

On the other hand, the high proportion of tree crops was seen by Geertz (1963) as an indication that farmers in the 'outer islands' are relatively more dynamic and commercially oriented than those in Java. Their choice of tree crops indicates that they are willing to take risks and risk-taking is necessary for progress. Such an attitude to risk may indicate some degree of economic dynamism, but if farmers are dynamic and commercially oriented why then is no structural transformation taking place either at farm or regional level? To obtain some light on this issue, one has to examine factors affecting farm income and surplus, namely, farm size, productivity and factor prices.

Most farmers in Indonesia, including those in the eastern region, are smallholders. About 50 per cent own less than one hectare of land. Since population density in Eastern Indonesia is lower than in Java, obviously there are more smallholders and landless farmers in Java than in Eastern Indonesia. Unavailability of data from the other provinces in the region limits the present discussion to North Sulawesi.

Table 7.3 shows that the process of land fragmentation has taken place quite rapidly. In North Sulawesi, the proportion of small farms <0.5 ha increased from 26.72 per cent in 1983 to 34.3 per cent in 1987 and 47.71 per cent in 1993. As a result, more and more farmers cannot provide their basic needs from their small pieces of land. These people are therefore forced to seek income from other sources. Some migrate to urban areas, seeking formal and informal employment in town. Others remain in rural areas and secure their needs from off-farm employment (Sondakh 1993). In both absolute and relative terms, the number of farmers controlling less than 0.1 ha increased dramatically from 1.12 per cent in 1983 to 6.06 per cent in 1993. The number controlling more than 0.5 ha has decreased, as has the average size of their holdings. On the other hand, the number of small farmers increased but their average holding also decreased in size (at a lower rate). About 50 per cent of farm families are smallholders owning less than 0.5 ha.

Table 7.3: *Percentage distribution of farmers by farm size in North Sulawesi*

Source of Data	Farm Size (ha)				
	<0.5	0.51-1.0	1.1-2.0	2.1-3.0	>3.0
Agricultural Census (1983)	26.72	23.19	27.12	11.87	11.12
Puslit Unsrat[a] (1987)	34.43	23.83	24.44	8.04	9.27
Agricultural Census, 1993 (All Indonesia)	47.71	22.21	17.35	6.79	5.93

[a]University of Sam Ratulangi research centre.
Source: Sondakh 1993b.

On the whole, food-crop productivity outside Java tends to be lower than in Java. Strachan *et al.* (1990), for example, have shown the superiority of Java in rice productivity in the following figures: Java and Bali, 4.9t/ha, Sulawesi 3.8 t/ha, Kalimantan 2.6 t/ha (see also Table 1.3). Recent evidence, however, demonstrates that, thanks to the several effective agricultural development policies, the low productivity problem in North Sulawesi has been successfully overcome. Differences in productivity between Indonesia as a whole and North Sulawesi are now very slight.

The key factor in developing agriculture is for farmers to increase productivity. This is achieved through the use of more profitable farm inputs: HYVs (high yielding varieties), selected seeds, fertilisers, pest control measures and better farm practices. While it is true that North Sulawesi has probably the most fertile volcanic soils in Eastern Indonesia, the relatively slight differences in average productivity between Java and North Sulawesi may mean that the backwardness of the economy of this province in particular and the other islands in general is related to more than low agricultural productivity.

The roots of disparity

The efficacy of agricultural development policies

The promotion of rapid growth in agricultural output and productivity has become widely recognised as an essential and effective development strategy, particularly during the early stages of economic development. Growth in agricultural output and productivity is needed to secure sufficient agricultural surplus to fund the growth of non-agricultural output. If this happens, as the economy continues to grow, the share of agriculture to gross domestic product and employment will decline.

It was under this scenario that Indonesia placed high expectations on the efficacy of various kinds of 'green revolution' programs, such as *Bimas* and *Inmas* in food crops in the early 1970 and various tree-crop programs in the late 1970s. The results have been quite encouraging. Indonesia has not only achieved self-sufficiency in rice production, but has also undergone a quite rapid structural transformation of the economy. (Table 1.2). But the increasing share of manufacturing in Indonesia as a whole did not occur in Eastern Indonesia.

There are two policy options commonly employed in developing agriculture: development policy aimed at shifting the supply curve to the right and commodity and/or price policy aimed at regulating commodity markets along a given supply curve. In Indonesia, the former has been implemented through various kinds of subsidised credit programs to enable farmers to adopt high-yielding crop varieties and modern farm inputs (fertilisers, pest control etc.). The latter has been implemented through various kinds of pricing policies and commodity market regulations.

The former approach has been quite successful, especially in rice production, but the achievements of the latter are questionable. In fact, the success of the former in increasing agricultural output has been eroded by 'government failures' in regulating several commodity markets. The price of the failures has been not only economic efficiency but also regional disparity. The cost to the economy may be indicated by the relatively high domestic resource cost (DRC) of soya beans, sugar, edible oil, etc. (Sondakh 1995). In the case of sugar, quite large areas of land considered more suitable and profitable for rice have been allocated to sugar cane.

In the tree-crop subsector, 'government failures' are revealed in both types of policy measures. The failure in development policy has been demonstrated in the Smallholders Coconut Development Programs. This was a project worth US$90 million to replace 'tall' coconut trees with a hybrid variety. A project participant received an amount of about US$1000 per hectare at an interest rate of 12 per cent. The corresponding IRR (Internal Rate of Return) was calculated at 17 per cent, which was higher than the rate of interest. However, the 17 per cent IRR could only be obtained if production per hectare was 6 tonnes per annum. It turned out that production per hectare was at most 2 tonnes. The farmers who had signed the collateral for the credit were not exempt from credit repayment. In other words, the scheme has, in fact, impoverished rather than increased the income of the already low-income farmers.

Agriculture in Eastern Indonesia has the potential to transform the economy from its present agricultural orientation to the anticipated industrial orientation. The past two decades have proven that, though the soils of Eastern Indonesia are less fertile, farmers can choose crops which are suitable for the ecosystem and therefore may still farm the land productively. All this should have resulted in better economic progress for Eastern Indonesia. However, Eastern Indonesia is still lagging behind in per-capita income. What then has gone wrong with the agricultural sector?. What has been happening with agricultural production, productivity, marketing and trade in the Eastern islands?. If production and productivity have increased, why has agriculture not yielded surpluses to promote growth in the secondary and tertiary sectors?

Sondakh (1993 and 1995) has shown that the backwardness of Eastern Indonesia is only partly traceable to agriculture as such. The major determinants of the backwardness are inequality in development budget allocations, inequality in the allocation of rural credit, market distortions in commodity as well as services markets, and last but not least, production squeezing through commodity marketing and pricing policies.

Agricultural growth with increasing regional disparity

Interregional income disparity stems from differences in labour productivity, natural resource endowments and infrastructure. However, there does not seem to be any positive correlation between abundance of natural resources and income. In fact, the majority of provinces with abundant resources (Riau, Aceh, East Kalimantan and Irian Jaya) are in fact poor. The share of oil and gas and other natural resources in the GRDP of these provinces is Riau 90.5 per cent, Aceh 86.13 per cent, East Kalimantan 83.0 per cent and Irian Jaya 82.9 per cent. So when oil-gas income is excluded, GRDP/capita declines drastically.

In Eastern Indonesia,. Irian Jaya is a major producer of copper and gold (in Timika) and of timber, Maluku of timber, fish and spices and Central Sulawesi of timber, iron, copra and spices. North Sulawesi is also a major producer of copra, spices and timber and is becoming an important gold-mining province.

According to Hecksher-Ohlin's theory of international trade, differences in resource endowments and factor intensity are the roots of differences in (revealed) comparative advantages and therefore in economic growth. Based on this theory, Eastern Indonesia is more competitive in resource endowments but less competitive in labour. Java with the highest population density, has abundant labour, which enables it to specialise in manufacturing. On the other hand, Eastern Indonesia continues to rely on relatively lower value-added activities (Sondakh 1995).

The argument that scarcity of labour has constrained economic development in Eastern Indonesia is, however, misleading for two reasons. First, Eastern Indonesia remains a labour-surplus region; otherwise, it would not have the problem of unemployment. In North Sulawesi, for example, the unemployment rate might exceed 10 per cent. This year about 70,000 people are still looking for employment, 3,000 of them claiming to be university leavers. Second, even if labour was scarce, the scarcity could be easily replaced by capital; capital in Eastern Indonesia is also abundant, provided that the capital generated in the region is reinvested there.

There also is a view that people in Eastern Indonesia attach higher significance to leisure and are less productive. This assertion could also be subjected to academic debate. Most farmers in Eastern Indonesia, like farmers everywhere, have demonstrated that they are able to work hard, provided they see a reasonable reward for working. They are efficient and responsive to market stimulus. Otherwise, one would not see the currently large area of tree crops mostly planted without government subsidies since the turn of the 18th century (Sondakh 1983a).

The farmers are poor not because they do not like working or cannot increase productivity. They are poor because they do not have fair bargaining information and therefore do not have access to capital and information, and because the marketable surplus cannot be sold at market prices since the market is heavily distorted for the benefit of traders and consumers. The surplus that they produce is quite often squeezed through various kinds of commodity marketing regulations that favour urban people rather than the rural community. As a result of this fact, most farmers in Eastern Indonesia tend to leave farming and seek employment in the non-agricultural sectors.

Thus the 'relative backwardness' of a resource-abundant region like Eastern Indonesia is not explained by the fact that the people are inefficient. They are poor simply because they do not have the same access to capital, markets and information that people in other parts of the country do.

Disparity in allocation of the development budget

The proportion of the Routine and Development Budget (APBN) allocated for the islands outside Java is relatively low. North Sulawesi, with a population of 2.4 million (1.3 per cent), received only 0.59 per cent of the total Development Budget of Indonesia. By contrast, Java with a population of 60 per cent, received 77 per cent of the Budget. In short, on a per-capita basis, the Budget for Java is higher than for the other regions. The Development Budget is aimed at infrastructure development. The relatively lower Development Budget allocated for Eastern Indonesia is therefore one explanation why, during PJP I (the first period of long-term development, 1969-94), the infrastructure of Eastern Indonesia still lagged behind that of Java.

Disparity in the spatial allocation of credit

Eastern Indonesia received only 3.5 per cent of the total (subsidised) credit available from Indonesian banks. Nearly 60 per cent of the credits were allocated in Jakarta alone, and were mostly used by companies in the secondary sector. This inequality is one among many reasons why, at the regional level, the impact of recent economic reforms (deregulation) on income, employment and growth has not been as significant as its impact at the national level. In the case of North Sulawesi, the impact of recent reforms has been to increase copra prices. However, the surplus that resulted from the increase has not transformed the economy. The money mobilised by banks in Eastern Indonesia during 1970-90 was approximately Rp10.4 trillion, but the amount of credit allocated was only Rp9.6 trillion. Eastern Indonesia with 14 per cent of population receives only 3.5 per cent of credits, and less than 8 per cent of foreign and domestic investments.

Disparity in infrastructure and access to information

Infrastructure is intended to promote production and trade. However, the centres of trade have long been concentrated in Java. The proportion of commodities exported or traded through harbours in the eastern islands has been continually declining. Seaports in Java have gained more control over domestic as well as international trade. As a result, the corresponding value added of the primary sector in the Eastern islands is enjoyed not by the eastern region but by Western Indonesia.

Distortions in project bidding

Most of the public investment projects in the region are undertaken by private contractors who win contracts in a 'distorted market'. Contractors in North Sulawesi play roles mainly as subcontractors. Most of the sectoral construction projects in North Sulawesi are won by contracting companies in Jakarta, who generally have close relations with the few economic elites in the country (the so-called conglomerates). Therefore, it is very difficult for entrepreneurs in the region to become top-level professional contractors.

Decentralisation with less autonomy

It is widely known the position of the state in Indonesia remains more powerful than that of society. To hold high-level bureaucratic-structural positions, individuals must be 'politically and bureaucratically screened' by higher ranking government officials at central government level.[5] Provincial governments also have less access to global markets, compared to the provincial governments of neighbouring countries. This reduces the competitiveness of the provinces in the global market.

Production squeeze and regional disparity

The roots of disparity described above has been intensified by government policies which let the market operate at a relatively high level of market failure, which is borne by the 'weak' unfortunate people living on the periphery of the economic stages and state. Sumodiningrat (1995) refers to this government attitude as *tidak berpihak kepada rakyat* (not taking the side of the people). It is the pricing and market policies of the government which play major role in widening disparity and perhaps increasing poverty. The backwardness of Eastern Indonesia is more to do with the relatively higher proportion of agricultural and primary-sector surplus taken away or squeezed by the central government than through either market forces or investment policies.

The efficacy of pricing policies

The general policy approach

Both development and pricing policies are supposed to serve multiple development objectives to ensure that economic transformation takes place. Agricultural prices play a key role in the efficient allocation of resources within agriculture, between domestic production and imports and between the agricultural and non-agricultural sectors. Policies are generally directed

---

[5] The screening is 'understandably' necessary to guarantee national stability and security, and to ensure that the country has a strong and clean government.

towards two aspects of agricultural prices, namely, price stabilisation and changes in their respective structure. The relative price changes include: agricultural prices relative to non-agricultural prices, food grain prices relative to non-food grain prices, product prices relative to the corresponding competing goods prices and output prices relative to input prices.

Changes in relative prices will change the production, consumption, savings and investments of different income groups between producers and consumers and will therefore change the proportion of surplus for consumers, and producers. In each change there is a group that gains and another that bears the cost. Therefore, a change in relative prices is a highly sensitive issue in a developing country. Any reform of agricultural price policies thus needs to be designed in a manner that will effectively safeguard the interests of the target groups which the government wishes to protect. In Indonesia, unfortunately, the target groups for many policy changes in agriculture are not farmers.

Agricultural pricing policies in Indonesia seem to have been traditionally formulated more for the welfare of consumers than for producers. In developed economies farmers are protected, but in developing countries such as Indonesia, farmers are taxed. This approach originated from a belief that it is the role of agriculture in the earlier stages of development to bear the cost of that development.

Before the fall in prices in the early 1980s, oil and gas were Indonesia's main exports and main sources of foreign exchange. Since then, however, the roles of oil and gas have gradually and increasingly been replaced by non-oil commodities. The replacement was carried out through by deregulation on the one hand and subsidies to manufacturing exporters on the other hand (Nasution and James 1995). The reform has resulted in a fast growth of non-oil exports, which were estimated in 1992/93 to account for about 70 per cent of total exports, compared with about 20 per cent a decade earlier. In turn, the growth in exports in 1986-92 increased Indonesia's average GDP growth rate to 6.5 per cent per annum, compared with 5.6 per cent per annum in 1978-85. The rapid growth in non-oil exports has been more than enough to offset the slower growth in the traditional, resource-based foundation of the economy.

The need to increase exports is crucial for the Indonesian government at the present time. With a total foreign debt amounting to approximately US$100,000 billion and with a debt service ratio already greater than 0.3 (Table 2.3), there is not much choice for the government but to increase exports, including non-oil commodities. On the other hand, however, shortages of supply on the domestic market may encourage the government to impose export taxes or ceiling prices on the corresponding commodities. The choice depends on the value judgement of the government: is the government on the producers' or the consumers' side? Possibily it is on the side of the 'elites'. Let us see which value judgement has been adopted or exercised by the government.

Due to a regulatory policy up to 1990, copra has been obliged to fulfil domestic demand at enforced lower prices than the corresponding international terms of trade. The case of North Sulawesi shows that the majority if not all of inter-island exports consist of agricultural commodities. North Sulawesi, for example, in 1990 exported about $US100 million, a figure more or less similar to its development budget at that time. The case is similar in all provinces in the eastern islands. One of the most popular examples that show how the government has squeezed the surplus in Eastern Indonesia is that of clove marketing.

The case of clove marketing clearly illustrates how cooperatives (KUD), which are supposed to 'fight' for the interests of farmers, have turned out to be the instruments of the state in squeezing the surplus from agriculture and moving it to non-agriculture, from the periphery to the centre.

According to Hill (1989), throughout the first stage of Indonesia's long-term development strategy, the industrial sector enjoyed most favoured status, while agriculture suffered from pricing policies. In contrast with the protectionist attitude to industry, agriculture has been subject to an 'anti-protection policy'. As shown by Glassburner (1985), Eastern Indonesia in particular has been subject to 'anti-protection policies'. The degree of protection as indicated by the ERP (effective rate of protection) of certain commodities is described in Table 7.4.

The ERPs indicate that some commodities enjoy protection but others suffer from 'anti- protection'. The commodities mostly produced outside Java, such as palm and coconut oil, spices, vanilla, nutmegs and coffee, have been subject to anti-protection policies. In the 1970s, the government imposed regulations prohibiting the export of copra, despite the fact that at that time copra was fetching reasonably high prices. Exports were prohibited because copra had to be sent to Java to revive the island's inefficient coconut oil industry, at the cost of lower prices in the coconut-producing provinces. Even now, the government continues to impose ceiling prices on palm oil (Sondakh 1995).[6]

---

[6]In 1991, the government relaxed the restriction by issuing a deregulation policy known as *Pakjun* 1991, under which import of copra and coconut oil was permitted. Sondakh (1993) shows that the policy greatly increased copra exports and farmgate copra prices but resulted in a shortage of copra for coconut oil producers and

Table 7.4: *Effective rates of protection of selected industries, 1987 and 1994 (percentages)*

Industrial Sector	1987	1994
Food crops	18	15
Estate cops	14	5
Livestock	33	16
Forestry	-20	-39
Fisheries	15	32
Oil and LNG	-1	1
Mining and quarrying (exc. oil)	0	5
Food, beverages, tobacco	122	27
Textiles, clothes, footwear	102	11
Wood products	25	-5
Paper products	31	26
Chemicals	14	0
Oil refining	-1	3
Non-metal products	57	31
Basic metals	13	7
Engineering	152	100
Other manufacturing	124	22
Agriculture	16	8
Mining/quarrying (inc. oil)	-1	1
Manufacturing (inc. oil ref.)	39	18
All trade goods	16	10
Import-competing	39	22
Exports-competing	-2	-6
Manufacturing (exc. oil ref)	68	22

Source: Fane and Condon (1995).

World Bank (1993:99) shows that in contrast to the easing of import restrictions over the past nine years, Indonesian exports have recently been subject to increasing regulation and control. Export restrictions, especially before the very recent deregulation package of 23 May 1995, covered half of

refineries. To overcome this problem, export restrictions on edible oils were reimposed very recently.

the total non-oil exports.[7] Most of these restrictions are directed towards agricultural products; the proportions are shown below in percentages:

Total non-oil exports	50.9
Agriculture	62.1
Wood products	84.5
Textiles	75.1
Manufacturing	10.2

The World Bank (1993) has estimated that about US$4.1 billion worth of agricultural products, including the large cash crops rubber, palm oil, coffee and copra, are subject to some form of export restriction. Exports of many cash crops, including some of the largest export earners (crude palm oil, crude coconut oil, cottonseed oil and copra) are regulated to ensure adequate supply, that is, to provide protection for the domestic processing industry. The protectionist attitude of the government towards industry is also demonstrated by the fact that the edible oil industry also benefits from a 30 per cent nominal protection. The wholesale price of cooking oil exceeded world market prices by over 20 per cent at the end of 1992.

Not only have marketing and trade policies worked to the disadvantage of cash-crops farmers in Eastern Indonesia; the implementation of various rural credit programs has not put farmers at an advantage. There are at least two cases apart from the coconut example quoted above of farmers being impoverished by programs aimed at increasing production of export commodities. In the early 1990s hundreds of farmers in Minahasa, North Sulawesi, were granted loans to cultivate garlic and root crops. The farmers signed loan agreements under which their agricultural produce was pledged as collateral for the bank. The exporters concerned, however, failed to keep their promise to purchase the products at a price which would guarantee profits for the farmers. The results were insufficient profits for loan recipients and their subsequent inability to repay the loans, which plunged them further into poverty and widened the social gap.

A second example of policies which have accelerated regional disparity by the squeezing of a surplus through marketing regulation is discussed in detail below.

---

[7] The export restrictions took four forms: export bans (72 products), regulated exports (which can only be exported by exporters approved by the Ministry of Trade (1827 products), supervised exports (which require approval by the Ministry of Trade (105 products) and export taxes (80) products (World Bank 1993).

The special case of clove marketing

Since the early 1970s when import restrictions imposed on this commodity boosted prices considerably, clove marketing has been subject to quite intensive regulation. High prices encouraged expansion in clove-growing areas until supply exceeded domestic demand in the late 1980s. The importance of the clove trade as a source of taxes and other cash revenues has encouraged the government to tighten its control of the industry. In 1980 Presidential Decision No. 8/1980 granted a bigger role to KUDs in clove collection and distribution from farmers to *kretek* factories via inter-island traders. But because the practice of *ijon* was evident and clove traders were said to be exploiting clove producers, the government initiated a new clove marketing system in 1990, based on Ministry of Trade Decisions No. 306 and 307. Under this new system, the role of the inter-island traders was taken over by BPPC (*Badan Penyanggah dan Pemasaran Cengkeh* or the Cloves Marketing Board).

Prior to 1990, clove farmers were required to sell their output through KUDs to inter-island traders at or above the floor price of Rp 6,500 per kg. In reality, the proportion of cloves sold by farmers through KUDs was only about 6 per cent in Maluku (Godoy and Bennett 1990) and about one-third in North Sulawesi. Prices were frequently below farmgate prices, and the KUD and domestic agents did not have the financial resources to support the floor price. Although in principal these bodies were granted a domestic monopoly, effective control resided with licensed importers of cloves, who were linked to Java's *kretek* cigarette industry.

The inability of these domestic agents to secure the floor price encouraged the government to reregulate the marketing system, allowing the role of inter-island traders to be taken over by BPPC. While the marketing regulations grant an important role to KUDs in clove marketing, the KUDs seem to have changed from 'agents of rural development' to 'agents of surplus appropriation', as they are today. BPPC has been in operation since 1992. Supported by subsidised soft loans of nearly US$350 million in 1992, BPPC has been carrying out its operations with profit margins between Rp1,000 and Rp4,000 per kg. Before the regulation, this amount would have been enjoyed by clove farmers and inter-island traders.

The present marketing system seems to demonstrate rent-seeking activities within the framework of a production squeeze in economic development. Consumer and producer surpluses have been transferred from the clove producers and *kretek* factories to the main marketing agents imposed by the state: BPPC, KUDs, PUSKUD, INKUD, SUCOFINDO (see Glossary) and the government, in the last case in the form of the SRC (*Sumbangan Rehabilitasi Cengkeh* or Clove Rehabilitation Fund). It is generally known that the SRC funds are rarely used to rehabilitate the deteriorating clove industry.

These marketing agents have depressed farmgate prices and reduced factory profits. Although they argue that they have been quite helpful in stabilising clove prices, in reality clove prices at farmgate level were far below the 'floor prices' of Rp7,900 in 1992 and Rp4,000 per kg in 1994. Furthermore, major portions of the money paid to KUDs and INKUDs have not been returned to clove farmers.

The present regulation sets a 'farmgate price' of Rp4,000 per kg, including Rp1,900 as SWKP (*Sumbangan Wajib Khusus Petani* or Farmers' Obligatory Contribution) and Rp2,000 as the participation fee for the KUD. The KUDs then forward the cloves through PUSKUD to BPPC, which has the 'monopolistic privilege' of distributing cloves to *kretek* factories at prices, depending on moisture and impurities, between Rp10,000 to Rp14,000 (Table 7.5). It is not the financial institutions and KUDs that provide credits or loans to farmers to harvest their cloves. It is the farmers who provide credits for the institutions, which pay the farmers only after the *kretek* factories pay for the cloves delivered to them by BPPC.

The policy changes in the clove marketing system have caused further deterioration in the farmers' position and reduced overall economic efficiency. The former regulation enabled farmers to earn nearly 70 per cent of the cigarette manufacturers' price. Under the new regulation they obtain only a little above one-third of the price. Deregulation of the system would transfer the surplus from the agents to the producers. Long-run farmgate prices would probably be in the vicinity of Rp8,000 per kg, that is, a price differential of Rp4,000 to Rp5,000. This difference would mean a lot for the province. With production of about 30,000 tonnes in 1994/95, the difference would be around Rp150 billion (US$75 million), an amount sufficient to finance the needs of almost one year's APBN budget. However, it must be remembered that at present the market is under the influence of excess supply caused by the high clove prices of the 1970s. This implies that the current likely equilibrium price under deregulation would be far lower than Rp8,000 per kg.

The above discussion shows that the clove industry is in disarray, as a result of government regulations implemented without detailed analysis of the likely impacts on the economy as a whole. The careless formulation of policies has created a serious market distortion and considerable uncertainty in the industry. Nowadays, farmers in North Sulawesi are abandoning cloves production, since the benefits go mostly to marketing agents and certain bureaucrats. In short, agricultural policies on cloves tend to favour the state (that is, the marketing agents) at the expense of producers and cigarette factories alike.

Table 7.5. *Costs of clove marketing systems*

	Marketing regulations	
Marketing chain	1990	1994
Farmgate price	5,500.00	2,800.00
- Collectors' margin	2,404.85	1,200.00
KUD price	7,904.85	4,000.00
- participation for KUD	1,000.00	2,000.00
- fee to KUD	500.00	250.00
- fee to BCN	70.00	50.00
- fee to Sucofindo		5.50
- packaging cost		45.00
PUSKUD price	9,474.85	8,250.00
- marketing cost	50.00	45.50
- clove rehabilitation	500.00	
- rent fee to BPPC	500.00	
- buffer cost	0.08	
- depreciation	315.75	
- insurance	0.06	
BPPC price	10,840.74	8,300.00
BPPC selling price to *kretek* manufacturers	12,500.00	12,500.00
Gross profit margins for BPPC	1,959.00	3,700.00

Source: Calculations based on Decision No. 306/Kp/XII/1990 of the Trade Minister and Presidential Instruction No. 20/1992.

Conclusion

The economy of Eastern Indonesia strongly depends on agriculture, especially tree crops. So far, neither government development policies nor pricing policies on cloves, nutmegs and other commodities have been effective in accelerating economic growth in the region.

Farmers in Eastern Indonesia are mostly smallholders. They grow mainly tree crops for cash and food crops for basic needs. Like farmers elsewhere they are efficient and responsive to price changes and want a better living. Most live at or below subsistence levels. A small decline in copra or cloves prices affects their basic needs. Their ability to increase production and productivity is not supported by effective development, and is especially hindered by pricing policies. Farmgate prices for their crops are often far below the prices they need to survive. Dramatically low farmgate prices are not mainly caused by declines in demand but by the huge marketing margin.

Ironically, the government prefers to impose ceiling prices rather than floor prices in agricultural export commodities. Where the government has imposed a floor price, as in cloves marketing, the price has been set far below prevailing domestic prices. On the contrary, in the case of certain commodities like soya beans that are expensive to produce in Java, the government has imposed import tariffs which make domestic prices higher than c.i.f. prices.

Thus, there are relatively more poor people in Eastern Indonesia than in Western Indonesia and the former lags behind in development. People are poor and backward, not because they do not have resources and do not like working hard but because they have been trapped into a man-made poverty cycle cause by uncertainty in prices and by government policies.

In short, in Eastern Indonesia the provinces with abundant resources and reasonably dynamic people do not necessarily have better economic development. Agricultural growth in the region has not proceeded hand in hand with economic development. The main reason for the paradox is the double face of development policy: on the one hand, there are policies to increase productivity and production, but on the other hand there are pricing policies that squeeze the fruits of development and transfer gains to other regions and other sectors of the economy. Since 1990, however, the government would appear to have become aware of these shortcomings and has begun to deregulate the economy. This should increase the speed of development in Eastern Indonesia.

8

Fishing Resources and Marine Tenure: The Problems of Eastern Indonesian Fishermen

James J. Fox

Introduction

Marine fisheries in eastern Indonesia are a complex subject. It is neither impossible nor contradictory to point to a potential for development of fisheries in eastern Indonesia and at the same time to describe a decline in marine resources. While a still unexploited potential for increasing pelagic fish production may exist in areas of open sea in and around eastern Indonesia, there would appear to be a pending, if not already apparent, pressure on closer, inshore fisheries of the kind that have been the traditional focus of eastern Indonesian fishermen.

To exploit the potentials that do exist in eastern Indonesia requires capital investment in large, relatively well-mechanized boats with the capacity to store a catch until it can be delivered to an appropriate market. Indonesian development planning has allocated significant resources for the establishment of such a fleet and substantial progress is being made in this direction.

By constrast, the overwhelming majority of eastern Indonesian fishers are small boat (*perahu*) fishermen. Historically the ecological and social pattern to this fishing is centuries old and continues to the present. This fishing may be described as 'specialised niche fishing'. The particular niche relied upon by eastern Indonesian fishers consists predominantly of inshore and seabed areas along island coastlines and reefs. The products of this fishing-and-gathering have been utilised both for subsistence and for sale. Close-shore fish species have been taken for subsistence needs but also to be dried for trade (traditionally, for rice and other farm commodities) and now increasingly for sale to large markets. Other marine products from this same niche, of which *tripang* (sea cucumber or *bêche-de-mer*; Indonesian: *teripang*) is the most notable, have been gathered almost exclusively for sale.

Fishing for sharkfin — not necessarily for shark *per se* — is another specialised pursuit of some eastern Indonesian fishermen. Although this activity involves longline fishing in open waters, it is an activity that has developed from close-shore fishing and is still carried out, most successfully, at the deep margins of the inshore niche.

There is one historical feature of this fishing that must be seen in perspective. Throughout the islands of eastern Indonesia most local populations have utilised their immediate offshore resources. However, certain populations have specialized in exploiting this rich marine niche and developed a mobility that has allowed them to venture over wide areas. The chief population to do this are the Sama or Sama-Bajau, who can be found in clusters throughout eastern Indonesia. Movement of individuals and households among the many Bajau settlements in eastern Indonesia has given the Bajau enormous flexibility in exploiting their chosen marine niche, but the ever-shifting pattern to this exploitation has led to a situation where these nomadic Bajau can lay claim to no permanent landbase and must now maintain themselves, with increasing difficulties, on the periphery of other settled populations. Some of these other populations — most notably the Bugis, Butonese and Makassarese — have also developed considerable mobility and have moved to expoit, in varying degrees, this same marine niche throughout much of Eastern Indonesia.[1]

The point to be made is that historically there has always been competition among different populations in eastern Indonesia for the exploitation of close-shore marine resources. One of the first recorded 'arrests' of unauthorised Bajau boats entering Nusa Tenggara — specifically the area around Bernusa near Alor — to gather *tripang* dates from 1725 (Fox 1977). As a result, there has occurred over centuries a 'repositioning' of specific groups of populations specialized to exploit close-shore marine resource niches.

Populations from the north and west have shifted to the east and shouth. Just as the Sama Bajau moved into Sulawesi from the north and west (probably along the coast of Kalimantan) before the 15th or 16th century so too, since the 17th and 18th centuries, groups of the populations particularly from South Sulawesi and Central Sulawesi have been moving into Nusa

---

[1] For some indication of the seasonal sailing patterns of the fleet of *perahu* from just one village on Buton, see Michael Southon, *The Navel of the Perahu* (particularly Chapter 2). It is also useful to realise that a label such as 'Butonese' is of historical significance but in fact refers to a diverse collection of linguistically distinct fishing and sailing communities. For a brief historical discussion of this identification as 'Butonese', see Fox (1995).

Tenggara and Maluku and to the coastal areas of Irian Jaya. Many of these populations regard the whole of this area as part of their seasonal fishing grounds.

The current situation in eastern Indonesia represents a clear development of this historical trend. What has changed is the demography of this development. There are now larger numbers attempting to exploit the same set of niches and many of these fishers are using new methods — some of which are extremely destructive — to gain economic advantage in their competition. The consequence is that the close-shore marine niches on which earlier historic developments were based have come under increasing pressure. In some cases, they may be dangerously near to collapsing.

To draw conclusions about what is happening in the fisheries of eastern Indonesia requires detailed local *kabupaten* data from six provinces -- South Sulawesi, Central Sulawesi, West Nusa Tenggara and East Nusa Tenggara, Maluku, and Irian Jaya. Lacking this disaggregated data, one can only point to particular indications and general trends. Thus, for example, the *tripang* fishery in West Nusa Tenggara is reported to have suddenly collapsed: dropping from 17.7 tonnes of *tripang* in 1993 to 6.25 tonnes in 1994, much of which was of very low quality. The effect of this was to send NTB *tripang* fishermen into NTT in search of new sources.[2]

This occurred at the same time as a large fleet of supposed 'Sinjai' Bugis (made up in fact of Bugis and some Bajau from various locations in South Sulawesi) appeared in Kupang with diving equipment to gather *tripang* (and other reef-dwelling fish) at depths not exploited by local fishermen. Refused access to the waters around Kupang, many boats in this fleet sailed into the Australian fishing zone where a good number were arrested and their boats confiscated.[3]   According to recent reports from Bugis settled around Kupang, this 'Sinjai' fleet has since sailed on to Irian Jaya in search of *tripang* and other reef fish.

---

[2] The collapse of the *tripang* harvest in Sumbawa was first noted in an article in *Kompas* (9 July 1995). The gathering of *tripang* in this area is carried out largely by Bajau populations on the island of Bungin in *kecamatan* Alas, *kabupaten* Sumbawa. The effect of this collapse has been to put more pressure on one of the more vulnerable of eastern Indonesia's fishing populations, but one that is noted for its capacity to shift rapidly to other areas when particular modes of livelihood become threatened.

[3] It is worth noting that most of these arrests occurred in waters where Australia only claims rights to the seabed. The `Sinjai' were arrested because they were diving for tripang in these waters.

Such 'incidents' — the demise of one small fishery, the shifting of
fishing populations, the conflict over particular reefs and so on — are a
regular occurrence in eastern Indonesia. It is essential, however, to view
these many small 'incidents' involving fishing populations in eastern
Indonesia within a wider national context.

The general view of marine fisheries

In 1994, Indonesia embarked on its second 25-year period of development.
In its official formulation of *Repelita* VI (the sixth Five-year Development
Plan), a great deal of attention was given to taking stock of the past twenty-
five years and looking to the future. According to *Repelita* VI (Vol
2:330;344), Indonesia's marine fish production increased from 700,000
tonnes in 1968 to 2.6 million tonnes in 1991, and by the end of the current
five-year plan is projected to increase to 3.4 million tonnes. According to
Indonesian fisheries calculations, this 3.4 million annual yield would still
represent less than half of Indonesia's sustainable marine fisheries potential.
Since, however, there are no reliable figures on what foreign fishing vessels
currently take from Indonesian waters and no indication on how such figures
are to be factored into calculations of potential sustainable yields for
Indonesia's marine fisheries, one must consider the statements in *Repelita*
VI as an optimistic forecast of the future, indicating that current pressures
on resources will continue to mount and indeed increase.

Figures for total marine fishery production in the main fishing provinces
of eastern Indonesia provide a general picture of the relative exploitation in
each provincial fishery. These fisheries can be arranged in a clear rank order
based on recent official production figures for 1991 and 1993 (see Table
8.1).

Although these figures ought not to be read as absolutes, they do give an
idea of the relative size of the different provincial fishing industries in
Indonesia. South Sulawesi ranks second only to North Sumatra in marine
fish production, whereas Maluku is in the top five fishing provinces behind
Central and East Java, South Sulawesi and North Sumatra.

Included in Table 8.1 is the percentage of this total catch that is
marketed locally as fresh fish. Whereas for the two Sulawesi provinces a
high percentage of the total catch is evidently marketed and consumed
locally, for the other provinces, a more complex and varied pattern is
evident. Thus, for Irian Jaya, over 56,000 tonnes of marine fish (54 per cent
of the total catch) are frozen mainly for export; whereas for Maluku, almost
54,000 tonnes (approximately 29 per cent of the catch) are similarly frozen.

In the other provinces of eastern Indonesia, including South Sulawesi, freezing facilities for fish are limited. In both East and West Nusa Tenggara, traditional drying represents the principal method for preserving fish for sales which are primarily for local provincial consumption. West Nusa Tenggara dries 34 per cent of its catch; East Nusa Tenggara 30 per cent.

Table 8.1: *Marine fish production in the main fishing provinces of Eastern Indonesia*

Province	1991 (tonnes)	1993 (tonnes)	Fresh market (% in 1993)
West Nusa Tenggara	64,825	79,200	70
East Nusa Tenggara	56,604	62,189	58
South Sulawesi	233,396	241,059	70
South-East Sulawesi	105,795	141,617	70
Maluku	167,851	185,450	57
Irian Jaya	90,860	104,294	42

Source: *Statistik Perikanan Indonesia* 1991/No 21: Table 0.8 (1993); 1993/No 23: Tables 0.1 & 1.8 (1995), Jakarta: Departemen Pertanian, Direktorat Jenderal Perikan.

New methods of exploitation

Indonesia is now the world's largest supplier of live reef fish, providing approximately 50 per cent of the total catch. The markets for this catch are mainly in Hong Kong and Singapore. Indonesia's position in this market is relatively recent and has come about because of the massive depletion of target species in the Philippines.

It is the destructive methods of this fishing industry that present the greatest current danger to sustainable marine fishery development in Eastern Indonesia. The brief history of this industry has been one of spectacularly rapid depletion of resources with accompanying devastation of reef ecosystems. Already the reefs around the Riau Archipelago are no longer considered commercially viable as a source of live fish and the islands to the south of Sulawesi are reported to be similarly depleted. This depletion has produced a rapid expansion of the live reef fishing into the islands of Maluku province.

Live reef fish are now being targeted and caught by divers who use various methods. The most destructive are the methods employed by divers who spray cyanide onto reefs and then extract the stunned fish from their lodgings in the reef. Smaller and less mature fish are regularly destroyed in the process as is the rich invertebrate life that forms part of the reef. The living coral framework is also chopped away to obtain a good catch. The recovery of reefs from such fishing may take decades.

The major entrepreneurs in Hong Kong and Singapore expect that at the present rate of exploitation it will take no more than a few years to exhaust the important grouper fish stocks in Indonesia. This fishing will have long term effects because the reefs of Eastern Indonesia are one of the world's centres of marine biodiversity.[4]

Another technology that is transforming the fisheries of the eastern islands is *bagan*-fishing. *Bagan* are fishing platforms that are either permanently fixed or rely on a narrow *perahu*-like vessel that supports a large outrigger-like structure. These platforms, strategically positioned offshore in bays and inlets, are used at night as a light-trap to attract and net fish. As a technology, this raft-net fishing is of major importance in Eastern Indonesia. The largest number of *bagan* are located in South Sulawesi and are particularly associated with Bugis populations. *Bagan* technology has spread to other areas of Eastern Indonesia, often in close association with the spread of the Bugis population.[5] The last ten to fifteen years has seen the establishment of *bagan*-rafts throughout East and West Nusa Tenggara, Maluku and Irian Jaya. Table 8.2 provides information on the number of *bagan* platforms, both fixed and floating, in the main fishing provinces of Eastern Indonesia and the amount and percentage of total provincial catch derived from these platforms.

Even where other fishing populations have also adopted this technology, the spread of *bagan*-fishing has coincided with the establishment of Bugis settlements that engage both in fishing and in marketing pursuits. Many local fish markets have come to be dominated by Bugis trade, which in turn has more effectively linked these local centres to Indonesia's major marine emporium in Ujung Pandang. At the heart of these developments are Bugis mobility, migration and the astute recognition and manipulation of local possibilities.

---

[4] Information on the current state of the live reef fishing industry has been supplied to me by Dr R. E. Johannes, who is one of two authors who have prepared a detailed report on this industry in Asia and the West Pacific for The Nature Conservancy (1995).

[5] Lampung and South Sumatra are two other provinces where *bagan*-fishing, relying both on fixed and floating platforms, is becoming of considerable importance. It is also possible that in these two provinces it is the Bugis migrants who have been responsible for the spread of this technology.

Table 8.2: *Bagan-fishing in Eastern Indonesia*

Province	Bagan Platforms	Catch (tons)	% of Total Catch (1993)
West Nusa Tenggara	646	16,616	21
East Nusa Tenggara	645	9,351	15
South Sulawesi	3913	43,890	18
South East Sulawesi	1633	29,016	20
Maluku	1677	10,486	5.6
Irian Jaya	325	7,886	7.5

Source: *Statistik Perikanan Indonesia* 1993/No 23: Table 1.4.
Jakarta: Departemen Pertanian, Direktorat Jenderal Perikan.

Conservation and resource management

In the face of current efforts to develop and exploit the marine resources of Eastern Indonesia, there are also efforts to protect and conserve these marine resources. The goal of such conservation efforts is to preserve the biodiversity of the marine environment and to insure that its ecological potential is maintained for future generations. Two major environmental threats concern the increasing damage to coral reefs and the increasing loss of shore-line mangrove forests. The reefs and mangrove swamps provide the habitats, breeding grounds and nursery for a rich and diverse fauna that is critical to the current marine environment.

Coral reefs are threatened not only by destructive fishing methods but also by the mining of coral for construction purposes and by the spread of pollutants, wastes and effluents from the land. Mangroves have been seen as a valuable source of readily exploitable timber, and the areas they occupy have been cleared to create shrimp farms and other commercial aquaculture ventures.

The complexity of the management of the environment is reflected in the jurisdiction of the Indonesian government bureaucracies. Fisheries within the Ministry of Agriculture is responsible for the development of marine resources whereas Forest Protection and Nature Conservation in the Ministry of Forestry is directly responsible for marine conservation, including the conservation of coral reefs and mangrove swamps.

Officially the Indonesian government has committed itself to establish an area of 10 million hectares for marine conservation with a view to expanding this area to 30 million hectares. By 1992, there were already twenty-three marine areas designated as 'Strict Nature Reserves' covering some 2.6 million hectares. In Eastern Indonesia, however, as elsewhere in Indonesia, virtually every area that has been targeted for conservation has a resident fishing population or is regularly visited, and has been traditionally exploited by various fishing communities. This includes such areas as the Cenderawasih Bay Marine Conservation Area in Irian Jaya, the Aru Tenggara Marine Reserve in the Aru Archipelago in south Maluku, the Strict Nature Reserve of approximately 200,000 hectares in the Tukang Besi Islands of Central Sulawesi, and the conservation area of the Bay of Maumere on Flores in East Nusa Tenggara. The declaration of such areas as nature reserves, although seemingly well-intended, has not as yet preserved them from continuing exploitation nor is it possible to envisage the implementation of such decrees without recognizing the involvement of both local and more mobile fishing populations.[6]

Secure marine tenure

Secure marine tenure, it is argued, is essential for effective, sustainable local fisheries management. Such tenure creates a recognisable core of stakeholders whose legitimate interests lie in the continuing care and management of valuable resources. Nowhere in Eastern Indonesia, however, can it be said that local marine tenure exists in a secure enough fashion to sustain local resources.

Systems of traditional marine tenure[7] have been identified throughout Eastern Indonesia, particularly in Maluku where such systems are commonly referred to as *petuanan* and customary regulation of access to

---

[6] The World Wide Fund for Nature (WWF) in cooperation with the Ministry of Forestry and the Minister for Population and Environment (now The State Minister for the Living Environment), has been involved in the development of a National Strategy on Coral Reef Development and Management. I am grateful to Rili Djohani for information on the marine conservation projects of the WWF.

[7] The literature on customary marine tenure systems in Maluku and Irian Jaya is considerable and growing. A key paper is one by Charles Zerner, 'Community Management of Marine Resources in the Maluku Islands' prepared for the Indonesian Fisheries Centre (Puslitbang Perikan) in Jakarta. An entire issue of the *Kabar Dari Kampung* (August 1990:43[8]) produced by the Yayasan Pengembangan Masyarakat Irian Jaya (YPMD-IRJA) was devoted to local customary sea rights in Irian. Dedi Adhuri, a PhD student in the Department of Anthropology, RSPAS, is currently preparing for research on customary sea tenure systems in the Kei Islands.

marine resources within such systems as *sasi*. These systems vary from simple tenure of permanent fish traps (*sero*) to more complex systems of tenure over specific sea areas known as *labuhan* (Adhuri 1993). Tenure rights in such systems are generally vested by tradition in quasi-corporate bodies or *adat* groups (families, clans or residential groups) that are not recognized under the national legal system as having the right to such tenure.

Frequently attempts have been made to 'reassign' such traditional rights to the *desa* (village) as a recognised legal body but, nonetheless, the possibility of individual villages enforcing rights of sea tenure has generally not been upheld by national courts. Poaching of local resources by mobile fishing groups remains a serious problem. Pannell has vividly described the problems posed by such poaching of trochus and *tripang* from the offshore reefs of Damer by Butonese *perahu* trader-fishermen (Pannell 1991:546-556).

Some groups — such as the Bugis and Butonese — are in a better position to defend their rights against other intruders and have demonstrated a capacity to establish settlements on other islands in Eastern Indonesia, whereas for most Bajau populations, secure marine as well as secure terrestrial tenure remains elusive.

Ashmore Reef and the 1974 Memorandum of Understanding

The issue of marine tenure is also a factor in the problems posed by eastern Indonesian fishermen who sail into Australian waters. Under a Memorandum of Understanding signed in 1974, Australia allows traditional fishermen access to a limited area within the Australian Fishing Zone.[8]

The 1974 Memorandum of Understanding identifies five small points on the northwest Australian continental shelf to which traditional Indonesian fishermen are given access. These areas are (a) Ashmore Reef, (b) Cartier Islet, (c) Scott Reef, (d) Seringapatam Reef and (d) Browse Islet. The original Memorandum allowed fishing around these areas to include the taking of trochus, *tripang*, abalone, green snail, sponges and all molluscs on the seabed adjacent to these areas, but not turtles of any species. It permitted landings to obtain fresh water at two points on Ashmore Reef and allowed boats to shelf within the group without landing except at Ashmore.

---

[8] The brief discussion in this section is based on a more detailed examination of the problem in Fox 1992 and Reid 1992, which are based on interviews with fishermen detained in Darwin and Broome.

This Memorandum, which is a simple document of three pages plus a map, provides the basis for traditional Indonesian fishing in Australian waters. It came into effect on 1 February 1975.

Ashmore Reef is the largest and most important of the five tiny areas designated in the Memorandum. It is a raised platform reef near the edge of the Sahul Shelf approximately 120 kilometres directly south of the island of Roti. As many commentators have pointed out, Ashmore — or Pulau Pasir, as it is known in Indonesian — is far closer to the islands of Roti and Timor than it is to the Australian continent. Historical evidence makes it clear that traditional sailing vessels from the Indonesian islands, particularly the island of Roti, have been sailing to Pulau Pasir from well before the middle of the 18th century.

The Ashmore Reef was officially discovered and named by Captain Samuel Ashmore in the brig *Hibernia* in 1811. The Reef was heavily exploited for its guano by phosphate miners, many of whom were from the United States. In the attempt to control this mining, Britain annexed the Reef in 1878, although by 1891 all the Reef's guano was reported to have been removed. In 1923 the Western Australian State government complained to the Commonwealth government about illicit Indonesian fishing at Ashmore. The Commonwealth government referred the matter to the British government. In response, in 1931, the British government transferred authority over Ashmore Reef and the adjacent Cartier Islet to Australia. The *Act of Acceptance* was approved in 1934. In 1938, control of the two areas was vested in the administrator of the Northern Territory. When the Northern Territory gained self-government, authority over the Ashmore and Cartier Islands was retained by the Commonwealth government.[9]

Defining 'traditional' rights of access

The 1974 Memorandum of Understanding implicitly recognises some form of (residual) right of access to specific reefs between Indonesia and Australia. In the Memorandum, Australia has defined — and has since clarified — just what `access' is to consist of in terms of such matters as

---

[9] For historical and other information on Ashmore Reef, I rely on the excellent unpublished document entitled *Report on Traditional Indonesian Fishing Activities at Ashmore Reef Nature Reserve* (Russell and Vail 1988) of the Northern Territory Museum of Arts and Sciences in Darwin. The document which is remarkable for its thoroughness, detail and reliability, was prepared for the Australian National Parks and Wildlife Service Research and Surveys Program.

landings, the gathering of fresh water, and the definition of permitted and prohibited marine resources.

The 1974 Memorandum of Understanding is less evidently successful in defining who has such rights of access and the 1986 attempt to clarify this issue seems to have had the opposite, unintended effect of increasing possible access to these reefs. The 1974 Memorandum of Understanding is explicit:

> By 'traditional fishermen' is meant the fishermen who have traditionally taken fish and sedentary organisms in Australian waters by methods which have been the tradition over decades.

This definition has two effective clauses that are intended to be interpreted as cumulative. Both clauses define 'traditional fishermen' by repeating the word 'tradition'.

In the attempt to clarify this definition, the 1986 Advisory Note focuses on the second of these clauses which has to do with the methods of fishing:

> The Australian government understands that 'the methods which have been the tradition over decades of time' referred to in paragraph 1 of the Memorandum of Understanding do *not* include fishing from vessels powered by motors or engines, or any form of fishing utilising motors or engines. Such fishing will be regarded as falling outside the scope of the Memorandum of Understanding.

The practical effect of this clarification is to shift the emphasis on determining `access' to the area to what kind of boat is used to gain access. The issue, in effect, ceases to be a question of who may have traditional rights and, instead, becomes one of who has a traditional *perahu*. Those who are obliged to patrol and monitor the area are obliged to make judgments on *perahu* type: whether it is motorized or not.[10]

Rather than limiting access, however, this particular interpretation has had the opposite effect of opening access to thousands upon thousands of fishermen. According to Indonesian Fisheries statistics, in 1988 there were 28,465 non-motorized small *perahu* in the Eastern Indonesian waters. Since, however, the Memorandum refers to Indonesia as a whole, access might

---

[10] It is worth noting that this attempt to identify 'traditional rights' by the use of traditional methods is expressly contrary to the advice of the Law Reform Commission to Australian government agencies in its summary report on *The Recognition of Aboriginal Customary Laws* (1994:71). On this basis, this clarification of the 1974 Memorandum of Understanding becomes highly questionable.

conceivably cover an even larger number of small 'traditional' *perahu*. In 1993, Indonesian Fisheries recorded 69,934 boats that would meet the 'traditional type' criterion implied in the 1986 Advisory Note (*Statistik Perikanan Indonesia* 1993/ No 23: Table 1.1).

The alternative to this unintentionally created open access to *perahu* of a certain type would be to recognise the historical claims of the particular fishing communities and populations who, over a long period, have regularly utilised the area designated with the original Memorandum of Understanding and to grant these peoples licensed access provided they obey the rules and guidelines specified for such access.

This relatively small area from the Ashmore Reef to Scott Reef and Browse Islet is where Australia has an immediate 'interface' with Asia. For this reason, it is important for Australia to endeavour to work out a solution that recognises traditional rights within their appropriate social and historical context. Also, should Australia endeavour to do so, this effort might also contribute to the recognition and development of customary sea rights throughout Eastern Indonesia.

9

Health and Poverty: A Look at Eastern Indonesia

Nafsiah Mboi

Introduction

That there is a connection between poverty and health is well known. One finds in poor settings insidious interaction among a set of negative forces — low incomes, low education, isolation from new ideas and information, poor living environments, inadequate or inappropriate nutrition, limited health care and so on. In many communities in Eastern Indonesia there are also deeply rooted sociocultural patterns, some of which intensify health problems, especially infant and maternal health. These factors tend to reinforce each other and result in persistently high mortality and morbidity rates, high fertility rates and malnutrition. Tragically, the situation is self-perpetuating unless there are interventions which break the cycle.

The urban poor in the Third World, including the poor in the towns and cities of Eastern Indonesia, are at a particular disadvantage. They are subject to the conventional diseases of poverty like infectious diseases and malnutrition, but they are also victims of the negative side effects of modern life styles, overcrowding and industrialisation associated with urban areas and urban growth. They live with urban land, water and air pollution and new risks such as death in traffic accidents[1] and the erosion of traditional systems of social solidarity. In short, as was said by WHO (World Health Organisation) in 1991, 'the urban poor get the worst of both worlds'.

It is the purpose of this paper to examine the health status of the people of Eastern Indonesia today and observe the complex interplay of factors

---

[1] This is a real threat. The National Health Trend Assessment carried out by the Institute of Health Research and Development (1989: 57) found that by 1989 traffic accidents had become a 'major health problem' and were the cause of injury for 59 per cent of all hospitalised injury patients.

contributing, for good or ill, to the current situation in both rural and urban areas. This is a policy paper focused on health but is not a medical-technical exposé of the health problems of Eastern Indonesia. I observe the interaction between poverty and health but my concern is health, not economics.

Indonesia's approach to health service during the first 25 years of planned development (PJP I, 1969-94) emphasised the quantitative build-up of a system for delivery of health services and information on as equitable a basis as possible. The challenge was to achieve broad coverage of large numbers of people (total population 195,283,200 in 1995), thus making it possible to address critical problems experienced by vast numbers of people. The system which evolved came to be based on a combination of formal health delivery and community mobilisation. The formal health system moved out from the centre with a network of community health centres *(Puskesmas)*. In 1993 there were just around 7,000 throughout Indonesia, 21 per cent of them located in Eastern Indonesia.

Nationwide, the accomplishments of this period were significant in terms of both the systems put in place and improvements in the general health status of the people. Between 1972 and 1992 the infant mortality rate (IMR) dropped from 134 per thousand live births to 60. Life expectancy rose during the same period from 43 to 62. The fertility rate dropped from 5.5 (1972) to an estimated 2.9 live births per ever-married woman aged 15-49 (1990). The overall annual population growth rate had declined from 2.3 per cent per year (1970) to 1.98 per cent per year by 1990.[2]

The challenge of the next quarter century will be to build the capacity to identify and respond to a more diverse spectrum of needs resulting in large part from not only the uneven impact of past efforts but also the increasing variety in both the physical environments within which people find themselves and the ever-broadening socio-economic spectrum found in contemporary Indonesia. The overall strategy of development for this period emphasises strengthening the quality of Indonesia's human resources to serve in, build and enjoy modern Indonesia and compete successfully in an increasingly competitive and globalised economy.

---

[2] All data in this paper are taken from Indonesian sources, either the various publications of the Biro Pusat Statistik (Central Bureau of Statistics) or the Ministry of Health.

The setting

The term 'Eastern Indonesia'[3] refers to the nine provinces lying east of Bali: West Nusa Tenggara, East Nusa Tenggara, East Timor, North Sulawesi, Central Sulawesi, South Sulawesi, South East Sulawesi, Maluku and Irian Jaya. At the present time (1995) they make up about 13 per cent of the total population of Indonesia.

Some aspects of life within the region exhibit great variety in ecology, colonial experience, dominant religious affiliation, educational levels, experience since independence, infrastructure, economic development and potentials for development. Irian has a glacier. East Nusa Tenggara is the driest province in Indonesia. Maluku has two rainy seasons while most of Indonesia has only one. South Sulawesi and West Nusa Tenggara are strongly Muslim while the people of East Nusa Tenggara are 85 per cent Christian and some areas of Maluku and South Sulawesi have been Christian for several centuries. Almost all the provinces have a rich ethnic mixture, which is reflected in great sociocultural and linguistic variety.

On the other hand, there is much that these provinces share which is of relevance to people's health throughout the region (Table 9.1). The majority of the population is rural. Educational levels, particularly among rural women, tend to be low. Many people live in conditions of extreme isolation. All the provinces are far from the political and administrative centre of the country (Jakarta).

In 1992, seven of the nine provinces were among the ten provinces with lowest per-capita income in the country. While only 19 per cent of Indonesia's villages lie in Eastern Indonesia, 26 per cent of the villages classified as 'poor' are in the provinces of the eastern region.[4] The percentage of villages which are poor varies considerably. In four provinces, fewer than a quarter of the villages are classified as poor. On the other hand, in three provinces more than 50 per cent are poor (Irian Jaya 78 per cent,

---

[3] For purposes of the current Five Year Plan (*Repelita* VI) Eastern Indonesia has been defined to include the four provinces of Kalimantan as well as the nine provinces to the east of Bali.

[4] Recognising the uneven impact of development efforts during the first 25 years of planned development, the government initiated a national program in 1993 with the specific intent of helping the poor in those villages which had been 'left behind' (*desa tertinggal*). References to numbers of poor people and poor villages come from the work of that program. Criteria to determine status of a village were grouped under three headings: (a) isolation of the village and available infrastructure, (b) housing and physical environment, (c) birth and death rates.

Table 9.1: *Basic data on nine provinces in Eastern Indonesia*

	Population	Income Rp '000	% Urban	% Illiterate	Pop. density	% people	Area km^2
West Nusa Tenggara	3,547,600	539.0	18.2	28.7	174	20	20,177
East Nusa Tenggara	3,464,000	489.8	12.9	18.1	71	22	47,876
East Timor	808,300	494.5	8.8	52.7	53	37	14,874
North Sulawesi	2,584,300	707.9	24.9	2.0	4	12	19,023
Central Sulawesi	1,850,800	854.6	19.7	2.9	26	10	69,726
South Sulawesi	7,346,300	746.3	26.8	19.8	100	9	72,781
South East Sulawesi	1,497,600	1,022.5	20.3	13.3	53	11	27,686
Maluku	2,001,200	1,013.3	20.2	6.6	26	24	74,505
Irian Jaya	1,828,700	1,582.8	20.0	29.3	4	24	421,981
All Indonesia: 27 provinces	189,135,600	1,161.50	34.0	14.3	99	14	1,919,317

Sources:

Population : *Profil Kesehatan 1994.* Lamp. II.A.1.
Income (1992) : Calculated excluding oil. (Source : *Statistik Indonesia 1994.*).
Urbanisation : *Profil Kesehatan 1994.* Lamp. II.A.4.
Illiteracy : *Kesejahteraan Rakyat 1994.* p. 136 (ten years of age 10 and over).
Pop. Density : *Profil Kesehatan 1994* Lam II.A.4.
Poverty : *Profil Kesehatan 1994,* Tables II.B.3, II.B.3A, II.A.1.
Area : *Profil Kesehatan 1994,* Tables II.A.4.

East Timor 71 per cent and Maluku 54 per cent) (Table 9.2). Because villages in Indonesia vary in population, we cannot equate 'poor villages' with any specific number of people. Nonetheless, it provides useful information about the number of places in which people live in settings which are not conducive to good health.

Population, in general, is thinly scattered across the region, making the issue of isolation a major challenge both for those needing and those providing health services. Particularly difficult circumstances prevail in three provinces: Irian Jaya because of its vast size, mountainous topography, and limited infrastructure for transportation and communication; Maluku, a scattering of islands stretching nearly a thousand miles from north to south and effectively isolated from each other at least twice a year during the heaviest periods of the rainy season; East Nusa Tenggara, a second archipelago dominated by barren, rocky islands and vast reaches of open sea, frequently visited by such natural disasters as such earthquakes, landslides and tidal waves.

The connection between education (particularly women's education) and child survival and welfare has been demonstrated around the globe and in Indonesia.[5] In the field of education the picture in Eastern Indonesia is mixed. In 1993 the provinces with the three highest illiteracy rates in the country (aged 10 and over) were all in Eastern Indonesia (East Timor with 52.7 per cent, Irian Jaya with 29.3 per cent and West Nusa Tenggara with 28.7 per cent) (see also Table 5.5). Two more provinces also had higher levels of illiteracy than the national average. On the other hand, four provinces were better than the national average, including North Sulawesi, which, with a long-standing tradition of education, has the best provincial literacy rate in the country. Only 2.9 per cent of the population over the age of 10 remain illiterate. Another important factor, often overlooked in discussion of health and poverty in Eastern Indonesia, is that much of the area is disaster prone. The earth is young and unstable. Earthquakes and volcanic eruptions are not unusual. The weather cycle can be punishing, with floods and landslides following close on the heels of prolonged drought in some areas. These natural phenomena can threaten people, their dwellings, their food sources and their access to help. They create special

---

[5] In 1984 the infant mortality rate for mothers who had less than primary school education was 160 per thousand live births. For those who had completed primary education it was 127, and for those who had completed secondary school or higher it was only 63 (Indonesia/UNICEF, 1984:62).

Table 9.2: Distribution of poverty in Indonesia, 1993

	Villages				People		
	Total	Poor	Not poor	% Poor	Total	% Poor	Total poor
West Nusa Tenggara	583	125	458	21	3,493,000	19.52	6,818
East Nusa Tenggara	1,734	468	1266	27	3,464,000	21.84	7,565
East Timor	442	312	130	71	808,300	36.84	2,978
North Sulawesi	1,396	361	1035	26	2,584,300	11.79	3,047
Central Sulawesi	1,380	601	779	44	1,850,800	10.48	1,940
South Sulawesi	2,617	655	1962	25	7,346,300	89.70	65,896
South East Sulawesi	835	327	508	39	1,497,600	10.84	1,623
Maluku	1,505	812	693	54	2,001,200	23.93	4,789
Irian Jaya	2,242	1738	504	78	1,828,700	24.16	4,418
All Indonesia: 27 provinces	65,554	20,633	44,921	31	39,135,600	13.67	258,548
Eastern Indonesia	12,734 (19%)[a]	5,399 (26%)[a]	7,335 (16%)[a]	42	24,874,200 (13%)[a]	15.98	99,075 (38%)[a]

[a] Percentages applying to Eastern Indonesia.

Source: *Profil Kesehatan 1994*, Tables II.B.3, II.B.3A, II.A.1.

health problems and, at the same time, can cause appalling set-backs which are destructive to systems already in place and to the morale of people in the community, health care providers and civil administrators. The challenge is how to address this 'fact of life' in the region.

While it is not my purpose to write a sociology of Eastern Indonesia, a comment on the influence of culture is important. Throughout most of the region, particularly in rural areas, traditional cultures are very much alive and often decisive in controlling how people live, socialise and interact. The situation of women is a case in point. The role given to women is profoundly influential in family and community health status, particularly in poorer communities. Throughout much of poor, rural Eastern Indonesia there are sharp limits placed on a woman's personal mobility, her access to outside information or people, and her independence to control many aspects of her own and her family's life which influence health — for example, her reproductive life, nutrition during pregnancy and lactation and her children's food in-take.[6]

In Eastern Indonesia, however, gender is not the only crucial factor in determining a woman's opportunities. The setting, rural or urban, is also of profound importance. The point is clear if we look, for example, at literacy rates of people aged 10 or older in the region. In every case the gap between urban and rural women is larger than the gap between urban men and women. We find, also, that rural women suffer a double disadvantage. In general, the gap between the sexes increases dramatically in size as one moves from the urban to the rural setting (Table 9.3). This fact takes on special importance when one notes the speed of urban growth.

Six of the provinces are among the country's ten least urbanised. They include East Timor, which is the least urbanised province in the country with only 8.80 per cent of its people living in towns and cities.[7]

---

[6]For example, in some areas a mother's first breast milk containing colostrum must be thown away rather than given to the child. Research shows that colostrum, if given to the baby, can provide immunity to certain common childhood diseases. In some areas an expectant mother's diet is severely restricted by taboos. Almost universally, the well-bred traditional women will give first priority to her husband and any guests, second to her children, and only third to herself in allocating food. Regardless of whether the woman is sick, lactating and so on, she will follow the sequence.

[7] A community qualifies as 'urban' in Indonesian statistics if it has (a) a population density of more than 5,000 people to the sq km, (b) fewer than 25 per cent of the households engaged in agriculture as their primary source of income, and (c) eight or more facilities associated with urban life (including among others an indoor market, a movie theatre, a high school and a boarding house or hotel).

Table 9.3: *Illiteracy among women and men 10 years of age and over,*
1992
(in percentages)

Province	Urban		Rural	
	Women	Men	Women	Men
West Nusa Tenggara	23.98	14.04	40.31	26.24
East Nusa Tenggara	8.59	5.23	25.74	17.63
East Timor	30.00	14.34	68.54	52.99
North Sulawesi	1.76	1.71	4.00	2.88
Central Sulawesi	6.39	3.81	14.83	7.85
South Sulawesi	13.46	7.23	28.78	20.90
South East Sulawesi	10.35	53.96	23.98	12.84
Maluku	5.50	2.75	15.16	8.70
Irian Jaya	7.48	3.62	44.22	30.71
All Indonesia: 27 provinces	11.67	5.21	26.18	13.32

Source: *Indikator Sosial Wanita* (1993:80).

All nine provinces fall well below the national average of 34 per cent but the pace of urban growth is high. For example, in the decade between 1980 and 1990, three of the ten provinces with the fastest urban growth rates were in Eastern Indonesia (Central Sulawesi, South East Sulawesi and Maluku). Some continue to experience extremely rapid growth. For example, between 1980 and 1993, the proportion of the population which was urban in South East Sulawesi and Central Sulawesi went from 9 per cent to 20 per cent. Maluku went from 11 per cent to 20 per cent (*Profil Kesehatan 1994*, Lampiran. II.A.4).

In all provinces of Eastern Indonesia an important fraction of the population is distinguished by a lifestyle interacting with and dependent on the sea, just as farmers are dependent on the land. The fishing communities of Eastern Indonesia cluster along the sandy strips of land between the sea and upland fields and forests. The men almost universally lead precarious lives of high mobility. In certain communities the women and children sometimes sail with their men. In others, the men sail for many months at a time, trading and fishing as they go, and have no contact with the home community. While physically some clusters of fishing families are not distant from public transportation and public services, often cultural, social and economic problems and sometimes strained relations with the local communities surrounding them complicate development (including health development). The result is that child nutrition, family planning acceptance, immunisation levels and general family welfare frequently lag behind their neighbours' conditions.

The health situation

As we have seen in the foregoing section, the setting of the eastern region is far from uniform. It is true, however, that throughout much of the region conditions are difficult and the evidence of many non-health indicators (literacy, income per capita and urbanisation, for example) demonstrates that the majority of people in most provinces still lead difficult rural lives. We turn now to look specifically at the health situation.

People's health

We focus our attention on data for infant, child, and maternal health and nutrition as the most sensitive indicators of overall health status, especially the status of the poor.

Patterns of mortality — infants (IMR), children below the age of five (CMR), and mothers giving birth (MM) — tell a clear story about the difficult conditions of life for mothers and children and the start a child gets in life. Reductions in IMR and CMR have been significant in many parts of Eastern Indonesia (Table 9.4). Nonetheless, only North Sulawesi has been consistently above the national average in IMR since 1971. Five of the eight remaining provinces are worse than national averages for both infant and child mortality.

The trend in IMR, however, is good. In 1971 only three provinces were the same as or better than the national average; by 1993 four provinces had reached that level. Unfortunately the same is not true for CMR, which, although improving across the region, has lost ground compared to national levels. Maternal mortality rates in Indonesia are still relatively high, the estimate being 450 per 100,000 live births. Province-specific data are not available for Eastern Indonesia.

The presence or absence of diarrhoea, as a childhood disease, tells us something about the environment within which children live and general health knowledge among parents and the wider community. It also has direct influence on the nutritional status of the individual. Diarrhoea is one of the most universal (and easily managed) of the 'diseases of poverty', being in some cases the result of and other cases the cause of malnutrition, general weakness, and the inability to resist simple contagious diseases. It can even result in unnecessary death. In Indonesia three sorts of data exist on diarrhoea: reported morbidity, exceptional outbreaks, and the case fatality rate.

Table 9.4: *Eastern Indonesia: Infant and child mortality rates (1971 and 1993)*

Province	IMR[a]		CMR[a]	
	1971	1993	1971	1993
West Nusa Tenggara	221	110	327	162
East Nusa Tenggara	154	59	231	82
East Timor	n.a.	67	n.a.	99
North Sulawesi	114	54	170	76
Central Sulawesi	154	75	225	109
South Sulawesi	161	56	242	80
South East Sulawesi	162	62	251	89
Maluku	143	59	216	85
Irian Jaya	86	71	126	102
All Indonesia : 27 provinces	145	60	218	81

[a]IMR = Infant Mortality Rate; CMR = Child Mortality Rate
Source: IMR for 1971 and 1993, and CMR for 1993: *Profil Kesehatan 1994*, Lamp. III.A.1. CMR for 1971: *Kesejahteraan Rakyat,*

The reported incidence of diarrhoea has declined dramatically on a national scale from 27/1000 in 1984 to 12.17/1000 in 1993. In Eastern Indonesia, progress has been uneven. East Nusa Tenggara, for example, recorded great progress. At the same time, however, South Sulawesi and South East Sulawesi lost ground.

In 1993 eight of the nine provinces in Eastern Indonesia reported exceptional outbreaks of diarrhoea. The case fatality rate in the outbreaks was 2.3 per cent nationwide. Among the eastern provinces the case fatality rate was the same as or, in two cases (East and West Nusa Tenggara), better than that. In the six other provinces the case fatality rate ranged from 2.4 in South East Sulawesi to a high of 12.3 in Maluku (*Profil. Kesehatan 1994*. Lamp. III.B.6).

Nutrition of children under the age of 5 is a critical indicator of the prospects for healthy physical and mental development. While there have been impressive improvements (Table 9.5), problems of people's isolation from appropriate information and, in some cases, the persistence of traditional patterns or attitudes which may not be conducive, make it extremely difficult to take sustained and effective action against malnutrition in some areas.

Interestingly, disaggregation of child nutrition by sex shows girls doing better nutritionally than boys in six provinces of the region in 1992 (Table 9.5). Comparison with earlier data reveals this to be a marked change from only five years earlier. In 1987, exhibiting a pattern common to national figures, boys in Eastern Indonesia did better than girls nutritionally in seven of nine provinces. The research questions arise: why are the girls doing so well and why are the boys losing ground?

Table 9.5: *Percentage of well-nourished children by sex, 1987 and 1992*

Province	1987		1992	
	M	F	M	F
West Nusa Tenggara	45.0	39.9	78.6	82.5
East Nusa Tenggara	46.6	41.8	79.4	90.0
East Timor	43.1	44.9	75.1	83.5
North Sulawesi	70.5	59.6	90.4	91.0
Central Sulawesi	55.8	40.5	93.7	93.5
South Sulawesi	49.5	46.0	83.3	86.5
South East Sulawesi	44.0	38.2	85.5	91.3
Maluku	45.1	46.8	84.4	90.5
Irian Jaya	44.2	42.5	81.8	88.3
All Indonesia : 27 provinces	51.2	46.0	85.95	90.42

Sources: *Profil Kesehatan 1994*, Table. III.C.1; *Kesejaheteraan Rakyat* 1989.

A crucial nutrition issue for pregnant women is anaemia. It influences their energy and sense of well-being and their physical strength. It can reduce a woman's ability to carry a pregnancy to a successful conclusion. Thus, anaemia is of double concern. It is associated with the well-being of the woman in her own right as well as playing a critical role in getting a baby off to a healthy start. In 1992, five of the nine provinces had prevalence rates that were lower than the national average of 63.5 per cent while four had higher rates (Table 9.6).

Table 9.6: *Prevalence of anaemia in expectant mothers, 1992*
(percentages)

Province	Reported prevalance
West Nusa Tenggara	71.3
East Nusa Tenggara	59.7
East Timor	48.0
North Sulawesi	48.7
South Sulawesi	50.5
Central Sulawesi	45.5
South East Sulawesi	71.2
Maluku	69.8
Irian Jaya	71.4
All Indonesia: 27 provinces	63.5

Source: *Profil Kesehatan 1994*, Table 111.C.4.

Data on patterns of assistance to women in childbirth are interesting in their reflection of local patterns and education. If we compare data for 1985 and 1993, we find impressive improvements from untrained towards trained assistance in several provinces in the region (Table 9.7). North Sulawesi, with the highest level of literacy in the country and nearly a quarter of its population in cities, also has the highest level of delivery by doctors (18.39 per cent in 1993) in Eastern Indonesia and the second highest level in the country. However, in some parts of the region more traditional assistance is the norm: traditional birth attendants (TBA) who may or may not have been trained, and family members. It is not surprising perhaps that these are among the provinces with the highest levels of infant mortality; the nature of assistance to a mother in the prenatal period and at the time of delivery has an impact on both IMR and MM. Because of this and to accelerate improvements in the quality of maternal and child health care, a program was initiated to place trained midwives in all villages. Between 1991, when the program began, and 1994, 33,475 midwives had been placed throughout the country, including Eastern Indonesia.

Table 9.7: *Assistance during childbirth, 1985 and 1993*
(percentages)

Province	Professional[a]		TBA[b] or family	
	1985	1993	1985	1993
West Nusa Tenggara	8.00	15.62	92.00	84.38
East Nusa Tenggara	14.60	19.57	85.40	80.43
East Timor	17.70	16.20	82.30	83.80
North Sulawesi	40.20	56.93	59.80	43.07
Central Sulawesi	14.60	21.87	85.40	78.13
South Sulawesi	31.20	40.30	68.80	59.70
South East Sulawesi	8.60	21.87	91.40	78.13
Maluku	14.20	28.27	85.80	71.73
Irian Jaya	31.00	34.86	69.00	65.14
All Indonesia: 27 provinces	29.40	39.85	70.60	60.15

Notes: [a] Doctor, nurse, midwife, or other paramedic.

[b] TBA = traditional birth attendant.

Sources: *Indikator Kesejahteraan Rakyat* (1994: 111);*Indikator Kesejahteraan Rakyat* (1989:85).

It is important to mention one general health issue which is widely spread through the region and which affects men, women and children. Malaria reduces energy, productivity and pleasure in life. It can induce life-threatening high fever. In the case of pregnant women, a bout of malaria can contribute to foetal development problems and delivery of low birth weight babies with a much reduced likelihood of survival. Certain virulent kinds of malaria can lead to insanity and death.

Health infrastructure and efforts

When reviewing achievements in the field of community health in Eastern Indonesia, which are seemingly modest compared to what has happened in some other areas, it is easy to feel that 'commitment must be lacking', 'policies must be wrong' or the 'government must not be trying very hard'.

Table 9.8: *Health service infrastructure: government centres and posyandu, 1993*

Province	Population	Community health centres	Sub-centres	Mobile units[a]	Posyandu
West Nusa Tenggara	3,547,600	110	372	110	3,853
East Nusa Tenggara	3,464,000	231	768	204	5,942
East Timor	808,300	78	249	114	927
North Sulawesi	2,584,300	138	663	147	3,470
Central Sulawesi	1,850,800	124	593	113	2,569
South Sulawesi	7,346,300	328	991	285	8,317
South East Sulawesi.	1,497,600	124	455	113	2,271
Maluku	2,001,200	153	539	174	2,386
Irian Jaya	1,828,700	177	600	217	1,929
All Indonesia : 27 provinces	189,135,600	6,954	19,977	6,024	251,459

[a] Jeep, boat etc. providing regular service like a health centre.
Source : *Profil Kesehatan 1994*, LamP. V.C.1; *Posyandu*, LamP. V.C.1.2.

A closer examination of the facts, however, makes it clear that these views would be overly simplistic, and in fact inaccurate (see Table 9.8).

Trends in a number of critical fields are promising. Increases in government and community health infrastructure continue. Clearly infrastructure alone is not enough, and yet accessibility to community health centres, subcentres, mobile units and the like must be part of an overall approach to the problems of public health in the region.

Health's portion of Indonesia's overall national budget is not large. However, per-capita expenditures within the health budget are almost universally higher in the nine provinces of the east than many other parts of the country (see Table 9.9). This is in part a recognition of the difficult setting and in part an effort to ensure an acceptable minimum level of health infrastructure and programs, no matter how limited the financial strength of the province.[8]

Table 9.9: *National government health expenditure: Provincial allocation and per-capita equivalent, 1993-94*

Province	Total allocation (million rupiah)	Per capita health expend.
West Nusa Tenggara	13,900	3,918
East Nusa Tenggara	30,400	8,776
East Timor	22,900	28,331
North Sulawesi	31,400	12,150
Central Sulawesi	18,300	9,888
South Sulawesi	44,000	5,989
South-east Sulawesi	13,900	9,282
Maluku	21,400	10,694
Irian Jaya	39,900	21,819
All Indonesia : 27 provinces	1,027,500	5,433

Source : Total Allocation from *Profil Kesehatan 1994*, LamP V.B.6.

The reality of life is that health care professionals and others concerned with public health in Eastern Indonesia are faced today in many areas with 'ordinary problems' in an extraordinary setting. In meeting such a challenge, human resources become critical.

---

[8] Government expenditures for development activities in Indonesia are paid for from both national and local sources. In a province which is economically well-off, operational activity does not depend too heavily on national funding. In the poorer provinces, however, much depends on national budgets.

Community health centres are, in almost all cases, headed by a doctor. In an effort to assure adequate medical leadership for the centres, Indonesia in 1963 began a program of compulsory National Service for graduates of medical schools, both state and private. Before being allowed to continue with specialisation or other medical work, every graduate was obliged to serve a period of time in a community health centre. Those assigned to more difficult posts, for example, in Eastern Indonesia, served two to three years. People in more comfortable surroundings, most of Java and Bali, for example, served five years. This system has ensured a steady supply of new doctors for assignment to health centres. Starting in 1992, the policy was changed somewhat. All doctors serve three years but community health centres are classified into three categories — 'normal', 'isolated', and 'very isolated' — and compensation is graded according to the degree of isolation. The more isolated the assignment, the higher the compensation. Among the young doctors there are men and women of high dedication and creativity, young adults who see their service outside Jakarta as an opportunity to learn things they would never meet in medical school but which are part of Indonesia. However, there have also been those marking time, counting the days until they could return to a comfortable urban practice of their own. Good or bad, the doctors spend a considerable amount of their short time getting orientated, attending district and provincial meetings, and preparing to return to 'civilisation' after their period of work in the community centre.

At one time it was hoped that young doctors might like their situation and choose to stay on. In Eastern Indonesia that has been unusual. It even became difficult to get young doctors to accept assignments in the areas that were more difficult, such as East Nusa Tenggara, East Timor, Maluku and Irian Jaya. In 1993, when 91.52 per cent of all *Puskesmas* had a doctor, only three of the eastern provinces were as well-off: North Sulawesi with 100 per cent, South Sulawesi with 94.82 per cent, and West Nusa Tenggara, the province of Eastern Indonesia closest to Java, with 97.27 per cent (Table 9.10). The other six ranged from 58.44 per cent (East Nusa Tenggara) to 83.87 per cent (South East Sulawesi).A management challenge for the heads of many provincial health offices is the question of how effective community health centres can be without the leadership of a medical doctor. In many cases basic services and management have run equally smoothly with or without a doctor. However, when a good doctor is in place and he or she exercises good leadership, extraordinary things can be accomplished in mobilising the community and educating non-health colleagues in government about priority health issues and their importance.

Experience shows that there are three critical issues in mounting successful community health programs in settings such as those found in most of rural Eastern Indonesia: (a) reaching the people with appropriate service; (b) gaining acceptability for health-related action by community members and health care professionals as well as non-health government, community, and religious leaders; and (c) achieving the frame of mind and infrastructure to ensure sustainability and consistency of action. The latter means the reappearance of women and children if a series of injections is needed, uninterrupted practice of family planing, safe and consistent use of oral rehydration therapy for children by everyone if children are suffering from diarrhoea, regular participation in growth monitoring activities, adaptation of feeding practices as needed, and so on.

In addition, in many parts of Eastern Indonesia the complications of logistics are daunting. If not recognised and effectively addressed, they can easily become the cause of failure in otherwise well-conceived action. Fragile equipment, heat-sensitive vaccines, vehicles that run on scarce fuel, bridges that wash out, pack horses that get colic — any of these non-health issues can determine the health impact of a given effort if not properly addressed.

Finally, in our review of health development efforts, a word is in order about *Posyandu*, that is, the integrated village community health service post. Not a formal part of the government health service, nonetheless *Posyandu* has been the absolutely essential link in many locations between community health centres and the people they are to serve in the village. *Posyandu* originally evolved as a consolidation of a number of community-run maternal and child health and nutrition activities (growth monitoring, immunisation, family planning, nutrition training and the like).[9] Community health centre staff train village leaders and volunteers, mostly women active in the village family welfare movement (PKK), who then

[9] The objective of *Posyandu* is an acceleration of reductions in infant and child mortality as well as birth rates, understanding and acceptance of national norms of a happy and prosperous family (a small family with well-spaced children living a happy, dignified and self-reliant life), and growth in capacity of community people to develop health and related activities according to their local needs and potential.

Table 9.10: *Community health centres with/without doctors, 1993*

Province	Centres	Community Health Centres			
		With doctors	%	Without doctors	%
West Nusa Tenggara	110	107	97	3	3
East Nusa Tenggara	231	135	58	96	42
East Timor	78	61	78	17	22
North Sulawesi	138	138	100	0	0
Central Sulawesi	124	104	84	20	16
South Sulawesi	328	311	95	17	5
South East Sulawesi	124	79	64	45	36
Maluku	153	97	63	56	37
Irian Jaya	177	104	59	73	41
All Indonesia : 27 provinces.	6,954	6,364	92	590	8

Source : *Profil Kesehatan 1994*, Table V.A.2.A.

sustain and manage *Posyandu*. The villages of Eastern Indonesia are often large (sometimes as much as 30 kilometres from one side to the other and.sometimes divided by rivers or mountains); thus to assure women and children of easy access to the basic health activities of *Posyandu,* many villages have developed several of these posts

As with management of the community health centres, the question of human resources has been the key to the effectiveness and survival of *Posyandu*. The critical issues relate to the pool of trained volunteers. Can the pool be maintained? Is the turn-over rate so high as to reduce the effectiveness of *Posyandu*? After disappointments in the early years, PKK leaders and the Health Department have become considerably more sophisticated about the importance of *Posyandu* and the problems of volunteers. Training and supervision have grown stronger and, in some areas where there is good leadership, women have come to see participation in *Posyandu* as a way to have a larger role in the community, receive training in health and basic management skills and achieve respect in the community.

The annual data collected on *Posyandu* now include the number of *Posyandu* registered with the community health centre and the number of *Posyandu* which provide reports and number of active volunteers. In 1993, 74 per cent of all *Posyandu* reported nationwide. In Eastern Indonesia four out of nine provinces had no reports at all (Irian, Central Sulawesi, North Sulawesi, and West Nusa Tenggara). In all except one of the five remaining provinces reporting was above the national level (South East Sulawesi at the low end of the scale with 71 per cent of its *Posyandu* reporting, East Timor and East Nusa Tenggara at the high end with 91 per cent and 84 per cent respectively reporting). Combining reports from community health centres and the *Posyandu* themselves, Eastern Indonesia had a total of nearly 125 thousand active volunteers (*Profil Kesehatan, 1994*, Lamp IV.E.1).

Challenges: today and in the future

Having looked at data for Eastern Indonesia from various perspectives, we now turn to the question: what next? What are the priority issues for attention today and in the future?

Today's primary challenge is to find ways to accelerate the process that will lead to better health among the broad majority of people, men and women, urban and rural, in Eastern Indonesia. One key will be the quality of human resources both on the health side and in the community. Leaders are needed — politicians and administrators, planners and managers, men and women, public sector and private — who are convinced of the importance of health as a part of the overall approach to local development, leaders who are willing and competent to think creatively and sensitively about their people's specific health needs.

Given what we know of the close association between women's education and child and family health status and the low levels of female education in some rural areas, it would be easy to shrug and say, 'when the situation is better, health will get better, also'. It is a fact that for another ten years a substantial percentage of the mothers with whom health care providers will be working (including women of reproductive age) will have either very low or no levels of formal education, particularly in provinces such as Irian Jaya and East Timor. By the end of the century this particular situation will have eased, however; the vast majority of young adult women will be the generation that has received at least primary education.

Experience in provinces such as East Nusa Tenggara in the 1980s, where the infant mortality rate dropped dramatically from 124 to 78 in 1988 and even lower subsequently (Table 9.4) in spite of high illiteracy levels, a difficult, disaster-prone environment and major problems of transportation and communication, demonstrates that low educational levels do not automatically mean 'nothing can be done'. Integration of health and non-health concerns is critical as are people-oriented, gender-sensitive, locally appropriate approaches to mobilise people. Clear partnership and division of labour are needed between government and community if the two partners are to work effectively together. Finally, to hold the whole effort together and energise all partners in the campaign, there must be visible and articulate leadership at all levels.

A special challenge in the field of public health in Eastern Indonesia will be working to find new and more effective ways to reach, engage, and serve the people of the fishing communities throughout the region. Around the globe, fishing communities tend to be ingrown and highly committed to their independence and their own way of life. It is, however, a way of life which often does not provide their children with the improvements in the quality of their lives to which they are entitled. Eastern Indonesia is no exception and special efforts will be needed to ensure that they are not further marginalised as the world around them improves. Health will have an important role to play in such an overall effort.

In the current situation we find indications of the key health challenges of the future. Conventional health problems associated with poverty still persist but new issues will also arise as society goes through a transition from more rural to more urban, from less to more educated, from a less to a more money-based economy and from more to less agriculture-based employment. In most provinces of Eastern Indonesia one can already find examples of both situations.

Problems will arise from changing lifestyles and changing environments in urban areas. Problems of reproductive health, for example, will take in a rising incidence of sexually transmitted diseases including HIV/AIDS as traditional values and methods of social control loosen. There will be more industrial and traffic accidents involving both men and women, and ill health from indoor and outdoor urban pollution. Research in India and Indonesia has demonstrated conclusively that poor urban women are often particularly vulnerable to health problems from pollution as many live and work in highly polluted environments.[10]

On the human side, changing social values, the rising marriage age and other circumstance of urban life combine to put a whole generation of younger men and women (adolescent and young adults) in urban areas at risk in new ways. Many young people will have a period of eight to ten years when they are sexually mature and have the potential for sexual activity, regardless of their marital state.

Rising figures on teenage pregnancy outside of marriage indicate that much more needs to be done in the provision of sexual health education and training in sexual responsibility. In this era of HIV/AIDS this is not just a question of social mores; it is an issue of life and death. In Indonesia HIV testing is done on only a modest scale. Nonetheless infection has been reported in three of the nine provinces of the east (West Nusa Tenggara, Maluku and Irian Jaya). Irian Jaya, in fact, has the second highest number of reported cases in the country. Sadly, it can be assumed that the virus is spreading in more urban areas, transportation centres and port cities, and that with steadily improving systems of public transportation the virus will have little difficulty travelling to rural areas. Health care professionals need training in how to present and discuss issues of sex and sexuality with men and women in ways which are understandable and communicate information, not judgment, and which make it easy to ask questions and

---

[10] Research in India (Pachauri 1994) and Indonesia (Surjadi 1994) has demonstrated conclusively that indoor air pollution is often as bad as and sometimes worse than outdoor pollution and that the highest levels are found in poor squatter areas and informal settlements where houses are protected from mosquitoes by the burning of chemical mosquito coils, where women cook over fires fed with material giving off high levels of pollutants and where air circulation is poor or non-existent, thus retaining any pollutants from cigarette or cooking smoke and the like.

facilitate the growth of the skill and self-confidence needed to avoid high risk behaviour.

Unfortunately, it must be assumed that Eastern Indonesia will continue to experience more than its share of disasters. From the perspective of both economy and public morale, prevention and preparation are better than disaster relief and public grieving. It is important that the health systems and community welfare people include disaster preparedness and mitigation of the worst health impacts in their overall conception of community development and health planning.

At the policy level, approaches to urban and health development are needed which will help avoid the worst and most predictable negative impacts of urban growth. Creative policy will be needed to attract, reward and retain   dedicated health care providers who can become a new generation of locally knowledgeable managers and policy makers in the field of health.

Given the distinctive nature of Eastern Indonesia as contrasted with the rest of the country, local research into problems and alternative solutions will have an important role to play. Two approaches to research will be equally important throughout the region, the first focused on identification, new analysis and utilisation of existing research and the second concerned with formulation and implementation of new research. Universities throughout Eastern Indonesia have a special and important role to play in this regard and due attention must be given to strengthening their capacity to carry out locally appropriate research on health, poverty alleviation, and the nature of the health transition in Eastern Indonesia.

In connection with new research field studies, dialogue with community members and with potential 'consumers' of research (policy-makers, planners, community leaders and the like) should play a prominent role at the stage of design and selection of both research questions and methodologies. Research for the sake of research has little place in health development in Eastern Indonesia today. However, action research, longitudinal studies and parallel field studies in multiple locations, if well done, could all make a significant contribution to existing and future health development.

In summary, what can we conclude about health in Eastern Indonesia? First of all, we must recognise that diversity is the keynote for the region today — diversity in the setting, the range of health problems and the possible responses. Within the region we find a full spectrum of urban and rural challenges as people and communities represent a wider socio-economic spectrum with varied needs and demands. On the other hand, there is no question but that poverty is one of the decisive factors contributing to health problems in many parts of the region. The main issue is not poverty in the sense of money. Rather, we see poverty as a system of interlocking negative factors which tend to be self-perpetuating. But poverty is not the only significant factor in determining health status. The demographic and economic transitions underway in the region, the processes of environmental change and urbanisation and the spread of education are also profoundly important. On the ground we find government programs and activities of community groups in a broad range of health-related fields and much work in poverty alleviation. The challenge for those of us concerned with public health is to advocate, educate, and collaborate to help bring about synergistic interaction among people, institutions, and programs which will accelerate the process of health development and bring benefit to the people of Eastern Indonesia and thereby to the Indonesian family as a whole.

10

Human Resources Development in Eastern Indonesia

Riwanto Tirtosudarmo

Introduction

In the last five years, Eastern Indonesia has become the focus of regional development discussion in Indonesia. The development contrast between Eastern and Western Indonesia has replaced the classic dichotomy of 'Java' and the 'outer islands'. After 25 years of New Order development the relative lack of progress in Eastern Indonesia has now become a major concern of the central government. There is a common perception that underdevelopment in Eastern Indonesia is strongly associated with the poor quality of human resources endowment in this region.

While this paper supports the crucial role of the physical conditions of human resources as a major factor in social development, I argue that political and cultural factors also play very decisive roles. As correctly pointed out by a leading Malaysian scholar, the only dimension of intrinsic value in development is the human dimension in its totality. He argues that human resources should not be limited to aspects of the physical well-being of the people, such as life expectancy, infant mortality, rates of morbidity and levels of nutrition, but should also include sociocultural aspects, such as education and employment, social cohesion and stability, political expression, cultural diversity and even ecological harmony (Lim 1986:29).

Although this paper supports the argument that human resources should be considered as a totality, much of the discussion will be directed at the relationship to economic development, and the paper will therefore adopt a more narrow approach. Wherever possible, however, human resource development from a broader perspective will be discussed. The first part of the paper gives an overview of the situation of human resources in Eastern Indonesia as reflected in the various physical as well as social indicators, such as health, education and economic conditions.

The second part links human resource conditions to the wider development context both in Eastern Indonesia and in Indonesia as a whole. Finally, I will address the lessons that can be learned from the observation of human resource development in Eastern Indonesia.

Human resource development: the regional perspective

The sparse and unevenly distributed population in Eastern Indonesia (Table 1.6) reflects long human ecological processes and the development of a cultivation system suited to local soil and climatic conditions. The cultivation systems adopted by people in Eastern Indonesia vary from wet-rice cultivation, particularly in the southern part of Sulawesi and Lombok, to predominantly shifting cultivation in almost all islands to the east of Lombok as well as Maluku and Irian Jaya. The most densely populated settlements consistently correspond with the practice of wet-rice cultivation, whereas shifting cultivation is associated with scattered and less densely populated settlements. The most densely populated part of Eastern Indonesia is Central Lombok in West Nusa Tenggara where wet-rice cultivation has become the major agricultural activity of the population. In Eastern Indonesia, Lombok is perhaps the only place that replicates Java's human ecological pattern.

In Eastern Indonesia, while the development of wet-rice and shifting cultivation has mainly resulted from a long process of interaction between population and ecology, the spread of tree-crop agricultural systems only began when Western people occupied the territory in the 16th century. In North Sulawesi and Maluku the Dutch cultivated coconuts and cloves, while the Portuguese introduced coffee to Timor.

As happened almost everywhere in the colonised world, Western occupation not only introduced cash crop economy but also modern education systems and Christian religions. The Islamic religion is found mostly in South Sulawesi, West Lombok and the northern parts of the Maluku islands, such as Halmahera and its surroundings; Christianity is widely practised in most parts of North and Central Sulawesi, most parts of the Maluku islands, Irian Jaya, East Timor, East Nusa Tenggara and part of West Nusa Tenggara. The spread of Christianity came hand in hand with the introduction of modern education. Therefore, it is no surprise that in North Sulawesi, Maluku and East Nusa Tenggara populations generally have a better education level than those in other provinces.

After the early 1970s an expansion in education development programs in Eastern Indonesia, as in other provinces, was accelerated as the New

Order government began its First Five-Year Development Plan. In many development programs, Eastern Indonesia apparently received less attention relative to the western provinces. Part of the reason is that Eastern Indonesia is less populated, and access to communications and transportation is very limited. Western Indonesia's provinces, particularly Java, because of their large populations and accessibility to Jakarta, have been given higher priority by the central government.

From the regional perspective, the development of education in Eastern Indonesia during the period 1980-90, as shown in Table 10.1, testifies empirically to its significant achievement. In all provinces the percentage of population that has completed primary school increased by 15 to 20 per cent from 1980 to 1990. This increase indicates the success of the government in implementing its compulsory education policy at the primary school level, which was introduced in 1984. The achievement of Indonesia in the expansion of education led to President Soeharto being awarded UNESCO's Avicenna Medal in June 1993. In May 1994, the government extended compulsory education to junior high school level.

North Sulawesi and Maluku, where education is a legacy of the colonial era, show sustainable development in education. The increased percentages of people who have with completed primary education in Irian Jaya, West Nusa Tenggara, East Nusa Tenggara and East Timor are relatively less impressive than percentages for the provinces in Sulawesi. Perhaps this is due to the inadequacies in program delivery as transportation and communications are limited.

The 1980-90 changes in the participation rate at the junior and senior high school levels also proved that human resource conditions in Eastern Indonesia have significantly improved. Except for the high school level in Irian Jaya, all the provinces have experienced a remarkable increase in student-teacher ratios, at both primary and high school levels. In the case of Irian Jaya the slight decline in student-teacher ratio at high school level could be the result of the government's difficulties in recruiting teachers willing to be posted to Irian Jaya, particularly in places outside the major urban areas. The uneven distribution of teachers between districts is one of the problems in education development in Eastern Indonesia's provinces. Teachers are usually overrepresented in districts close to the provincial capital cities. Maluku, for example, shows a strong imbalance in the distribution of teachers between Ambon, the provincial capital, and the rest of the province.

Although education development in general shows an improvement, the cost of education in Eastern Indonesia is higher than in Java or Western

Table 10.1: *Human resource development: education indicators, 1980-90*

Province	% population completed primary school		Education participation rate %						Student/teacher ratio			
			Junior High		Senior High		Primary		Junior High		Senior High	
	1980	1990	1980	1990	1980	1990	1980	1990	1980	1990	1980	1990
West Nusa Tenggara	21.9	38.1	12.3	48.7	14.3	37.4	33.7	22.6	19.1	19.4	15.7	13.1
East Nusa Tenggara	28.7	42.1	29.5	44.7	19.6	26.7	24.9	21.7	15.9	12.9	15.3	11.2
East Timor	na	27.5	na	79.0	na	41.0	na	21.0	-	25.0	-	20.0
North Sulawesi	41.4	58.2	19.2	62.7	9.6	45.3	20.5	14.0	19.4	12.6	20.2	13.7
Central Sulawesi	37.8	56.1	na	41.8	na	26.4	35.0	21.0	18.0	12.0	15.0	10.0
South Sulawesi	28.4	49.0	na	na	na	na	na	na	na	na	na	na
South East Sulawesi	31.3	50.6	70.5	68.8	41.4	47.8	32.7	19.1	22.2	14.2	18.2	12.7
Maluku	41.1	59.2	na	na	na	na	na	24.0	na	17.0	na	20.0
Irian Jaya	25.0	40.9	na	78.7	na	52.2	24.8	23.0	16.6	27.0	25.2	26.0

Sources: BPS, Sensus Penduduk 1980, 1990.
Propinsi Dalam Angka (various provinces and years).
Statistik Pendidikan Propinsi (various provinces and years).

Indonesia. This is understandable as communications and transportation are expensive by comparison with Western Indonesia. For the majority of people, education at the secondary and tertiary levels, which are located mostly in urban areas, has become very expensive in a situation where they are also poor and cannot afford to send their children to schools in the cities.

In Eastern Indonesia, the problems of accessibility, which have increased costs, will likely influence the quality as well as the relevance of education. The government effort to provide better education facilities will always fall short of the actual needs of the population. In such a situation, the discrepancy between the capacity and the need to provide better education facilities will remain the underlying factor creating further problems for the quality and relevance of education in Eastern Indonesia.

The development of human resources in Eastern Indonesia can also be depicted through the change in health indicators. In Table 10.2, all the indicators show the significant improvement in health conditions that occurred between 1980 and 1990. The infant mortality rate declined by 30 to 55 per cent between 1980 and 1990. Central Sulawesi and East Nusa Tenggara in particular achieved a remarkable reduction in infant mortality. However, while all provinces have rates below 100, West Nusa Tenggara still has an infant mortality rate as high as 151.2 per thousand. Between 1980 and 1990 life expectancy at birth increased by around 6 to 10 years. Again, West Nusa Tenggara has the lowest and North Sulawesi the highest life expectancy at birth. Further details are given in Tables 9.4, 9.5, and 9.6.

Government programs to improve health conditions in Eastern Indonesia have been implemented vigorously, as can be seen from the significant increase in the number of doctors, nurses and health centres from 1980 to 1990. More background is given in Tables 1.7 and 9.8. The provision of fresh water and sanitation has also widely improved, although there are variations between provinces. Irian Jaya, for example, enjoys the highest degree of improvement, relative to the other provinces, in the provision of doctors and nurses as well as facilities such health centres, fresh water and sanitation. Although the statistics show improvement in human resource conditions, the distribution is still a problem particularly since most of the health facilities have been concentrated in urban centres, especially in provincial capital cities.

Although the improvement is not as remarkable as the increase in other human resource indicators, general economic conditions, as indicated by per-capita income, increased between 1980 and 1990 by between Rp80,000 and Rp175,000. Irian Jaya and Maluku have the highest, while West and East Nusa Tenggara as well as East Timor have the lowest per-capita

Table 10.2: *Human Resource Development: Health Indicators, 1980-1990*

Province	IMR		Live expectancy at birth (Yrs)		Population per doctor		Population per nurse		Population per health centre		Imunisation coverage		% Households with			
													Fresh Water		Sanitation	
	1980	1990	1980	1990	1980	1990	1980	1990	1980	1990	1980	1990	1980	1990	1980	1990
West Nusa Tenggara	193.1	151.2	38.6	44.9	27.236	30.678	8.278	3.202	37.829	7.445	-	52	71.4	79.9	6.5	46.9
East Nusa Tenggara	129.3	74.6	48.5	59.2	75.447	26.36	4.502	1.652	22.971	21.937	-	71.2	37.7	38.3	4.8	7.9
East Timor	na	92.1	na	55.5	na	14.376	na	4.296	na	11.051	-	62.1	na	39.7	na	8.4
North Sulawesi	97.1	67.3	54.5	61.0	14.835	6.497	3.897	889	19.735	19.49	-	102.8	70	79.2	14.08	10.9
Central Sulawesi	136.2	83.3	47.4	57.3	12.005	7.707	1.39	663	18.89	3.175	-	82.1	10.2	23.6	7.5	22.7
South Sulawesi	109.3	73.1	52.2	59.8	na	na	na	-	na	na	-	na	na	na	na	11.5
South East Sulawesi	108.5	75.2	52.3	59.0	19.251	10.069	2.783	1.396	22.459	14.498	-	85	64.3	71.4	4.5	na
Maluku	113.7	76.4	51.4	58.8	na	9.802	na	2.605	na	17.315	-	na	na	21.73	na	10.7
Irian Jaya	108	80.5	52.4	57.9	12.759	4.793	2.45	298	10.033		-	65	29.97	41.78	7.76	16.7

Sources: As for Table 13.175

income (Table 1.1). The income of the majority of the population in Eastern
Indonesia comes from the agricultural sector. The percentage of people
living in urban areas increased only slightly during the period 1980-90. This
change was most probably associated with the increase in the population
engaged in various kinds of non-agricultural employment in urban areas.

Significant differences in levels of human resource development, besides
occurring between provinces, are also evident between urban and rural areas
as well as between districts in the same province. Major urban centres
usually have more developed human resource conditions compared to the
rest of the province. In the case of Irian Jaya, districts in the northern part,
such as Jayapura, Biak and Sorong, tend to have better human resource
conditions than those inland or in the southern part, such as Merauke,
Jayawijaya, Paniai, Fak-Fak and Yapen Waropen (Rahardjo and Setiawan
1994: 23-4). In Sulawesi, districts comprised of islands, such as Sangir
Talaud in North Sulawesi and Buton and Muna in South Sulawesi, have
lower human resource development than others in the same province. The
poor natural resources of these islands have become a strong push factor for
people in Sangir Talaud to migrate, mostly to Manado, and from Buton and
Muna islands to Ambon.

Human resource development: the national perspective

The underdevelopment of human resource conditions in Eastern Indonesia
cannot be properly understood if it is isolated from the wider context of
national development. A comparison of human resource indicators for
Eastern Indonesia with those for Java-Bali, Sumatra, Kalimantan and
Indonesia as a whole shows clearly that Eastern Indonesia has slower
development in many respects. In terms of annual population growth
between 1971 and 1992 except for North and South Sulawesi and East Nusa
Tenggara which have a similar rate of growth to Java-Bali, all other
provinces in Eastern Indonesia have growth rates similar to Sumatra and
Kalimantan, which are above the national level (Table 1.6).

The rates of annual population growth during the period 1971-92
indicate a diversity of population dynamics in this area. Assuming that the
natural increase is evenly distributed, migration must therefore play the most
important role in affecting the dynamics of the population. The high annual
population growth in provinces such as Central and South East Sulawesi as
well as Maluku could be attributed to the high rate of in-migration,
particularly through the transmigration scheme, to these provinces. On the
other hand, substantial out-migration is most likely the reason for the low

rate of annual population growth in provinces such as South Sulawesi, North Sulawesi and East Nusa Tenggara.

The significant role of migration in determining population dynamics in Eastern Indonesia is confirmed by Mantra's (1992:43) estimates of migration rates grounded on the 1990 Population Census. Based on Mantra's estimates, Eastern Indonesia's provinces can be classified into two groups. The first group consists of provinces which have a negative net migration rate: West Nusa Tenggara (0.8 per cent), East Nusa Tenggara (1.5 per cent), North Sulawesi (2.6 per cent) and South Sulawesi (6.0 per cent). The second group consists of provinces which have a positive net migration rate: Irian Jaya (14.2 per cent), Maluku (5.0 per cent), South East Sulawesi (9.6 per cent), Central Sulawesi (14.1 per cent) and East Timor (4.5 per cent).

There is no doubt that migration is a principal indicator of human resource development in Eastern Indonesia. As noted by Hugo (1993a), migration both affects and is affected by regional variations in the match between human resources and labour market needs. If a region cannot provide adequate employment opportunities for its educated population, out-migration will probably take place. Since this outflow comprises a disproportionate number of educated persons, the result will be a drop in the quality of human resources in the province of origin. While the relatively high proportion of student enrolment at senior high school level reflects the better education conditions in North and South Sulawesi (Table 1.6), out-migration from these two provinces, mostly to major urban centres in Java, can be regarded as a loss of high quality human resources.

At the tertiary educational level, efforts to strengthen the human resource base in Eastern Indonesia through education and training have become the concern of various organisations outside the government. Many private institutions, mostly with a religious background, have long been involved in providing formal and non-formal education for the people. At present, besides the state universities, several private universities have been established in all provincial capital cities. In some cases such as those of the Universitas Timor Timur in Dili and Universitas Flores in Ende, local government subsidies play a crucial role in supporting the university and supplement strong patronage from Catholic foundations. It is no secret that the core of lecturers in private universities is mostly recruited from the state universities.

Foreign assistance to strengthen the human resource capacity of Eastern Indonesia's universities has existed for a long time. The Dutch have links with many state universities in Eastern Indonesia, particularly with the University of Cendrawasih in Jayapura. The establishment of the Summer

Institute of Languages in Jayapura, for example, has connected foreign researchers with local researchers based at the University of Cendrawasih. In more recent times, Australia's AusAID and Canada's CIDA are among aid bodies which are particularly involved in projects related to the improvement of tertiary as well as vocational education in Eastern Indonesia.[11]

Except for major urban areas, in most parts of Eastern Indonesia where the economic situation is relatively poor, education facilities and the availability of transportation are also generally limited. The problem is less felt, however, in areas close to urban centres. Tertiary education is accessible in all provincial capital cities, as well as in several district capitals. The problem of accessibility for most senior high school graduates who wish to enter tertiary education in their province is a result of the limited number of places available, and the lack of transportation for people who are living on different islands or in remote areas. For some high school graduates who come from better-off families, tertiary education outside their own province often becomes an ambition. They perceive that universities, particularly in Java, are more prestigious than those in their own provinces.

An education and employment survey conducted in Manadi, Mataram, Kupang and Dili among young people aged 15 to 29 years by the Centre for Population and Manpower Studies, LIPI in 1992-93, indicated that the number of educated unemployed persons is increasing. High school and university graduates in urban areas generally perceive that employment opportunities in the modern private sector are very limited, and that additional skills besides formal education are needed to obtain jobs in this sector. It is surprising that a majority of young people see employment as a government public servant (*pegawai negeri*) as the ideal job because it can offer security for their future life.

Human resource conditions are also reflected in the level of infant mortality and the availability of health facilities such as community health centres, hospitals and medical doctors. In the national context, North and South Sulawesi have a rate similar to Java-Bali, Sumatra and slightly lower than the national average (Table 10.3). The number of availability of health centres and other medical facilities in Eastern Indonesia are also lower better than in Java-Bali and Indonesia generally. In the regional context, North and South Sulawesi show the lowest infant mortality rate, which also

---

[11] For the complete list of AusAID and CIDA projects in Eastern Indonesia, see the Eastern Indonesia Population and Development Research Project Newsletter (Published by LIPI and ANU), Volume 1, Nos. 1 and 2.

Table 10.3: *Human Resource Development: Economic Indicators, 1980-90*

Province	Per-capita income (1000 rupiah)		Urban population %		Population in non-agriculture %		Households with electric lighting %		Ratio of population/ ashphalt road per km²	
	1980	1990	1980	1990	1980	1990	1980	1990	1980	1990
West Nusa Tenggara	143	234	14.1	17.3	45.5	44.8	7.3	40.8	5	1.883
East Nusa Tenggara	140	201	7.5	14.5	22.8	24.8	4.3	14.8	3.597	na
East Timor	na	181	na	na	na	na	na	16.6	na	1.748
North Sulawesi	249	353	16.77	22.8	44.7	44.2	22.27	56.2	2.771	1.911
Central Sulawesi	208	314	9	16.4	na	32.5	9	26.5	4.157	500
South Sulawesi	226	358	na	na	na	na	na	na	na	na
South East Sulawesi	233	367	9.3	17	29.9	29.9	6.4	19.4	2.799	821
Maluku	279	434	na	na	na	36.61	na	37.81	na	2.109
Irian Jaya	374	509	na	na	na	na	10.4	24	2.925	1.525

Sources: BPS, Sensus Penduduk 1980, 1990.
Propinsi Dalam Angka (various provinces and years).
Statistik Pendidikan Propinsi (various provinces and years).

coincides with the best health facilities. By contrast, West Nusa Tenggara has an extremely high rate of infant mortality, implying the worst physical human resources. In fact, the number of health facilities available in West Nusa Tenggara is not low compared with provinces such as East Timor or South East Sulawesi. However, the infant mortality rate in West Nusa Tenggara is remarkably high, being almost double the national rate as a whole. The level of outside interventions, from both the government and non-government organisations, to improve heath conditions in West Nusa Tenggara is in fact quite high. It is therefore no wonder that West Nusa Tenggara has become of interest to health development observers. West Nusa Tenggara represents a good example of the complicated and multifaceted linkages between internal cultural values and the various external interventions to increase the social well-being of the population. It seems that a great deal of outside intervention is not a guarantee of improvement in human resource conditions. In such a situation, the attitude of officials, people's habits and social norms have their own dynamics which can reverse the outcome of the interventions.

In terms of per-capita income, all provinces in Eastern Indonesia except for Irian Jaya are below Java-Bali, Sumatra and Kalimantan, as well as below the national average (Table 1.1). While all provinces in Sulawesi can be classified as being in the 'middle income group', West Nusa Tenggara, East Nusa Tenggara and East Timor are the poorest provinces, not only of the nine provinces in Eastern Indonesia but of all Indonesia's provinces.

From the human resource perspective, however, income per capita can be a misleading indicator as it does not depict the actual welfare conditions of the population. Irian Jaya and Maluku are good examples. The high income per capita in Irian Jaya and Maluku, even after oil revenue has been excluded, is still heavily influenced by the revenue from copper and gold mining (Freeport in Irian Jaya), timber exploitation and fisheries. With their relatively small populations it is no surprise that for Irian Jaya and Maluku have a high per-capita income.

In the case of West Nusa Tenggara, East Nusa Tenggara and East Timor, low per-capita incomes genuinely reflect the extent of human resource development. These three provinces, except for some parts of Lombok, are similarly affected by their poor natural resources. Poverty and economic hardship in West and East Nusa Tenggara have become a strong push factor encouraging people to migrate to other places to seek employment. The people who live on the small islands to the east of Flores are well known for their tradition of migrating to Johore in West Malaysia and Sabah in East Malaysia. The migration route from Flores to Johore is via Batam Island in

Riau, and to Sabah via Pare-pare in South Sulawesi (*Kompas*, 24 January 1995). Labour migration into Sabah is apparently an extension of a long-standing migration system based in Pare-Pare, by which the Buginese move to East Kalimantan (Hugo 1993b:47).

According to the Head of the Manpower Regional Office in Kupang, every year around 3,000 migrant workers from East Nusa Tenggara enter Malaysia illegally; he estimated that 70 per cent of the migrants are male and 30 per cent are female. In Malaysia they are employed in unskilled rural-based work especially on plantations and in forestry (*Pos Kupang*, 2 February 1995). In more recent times, however, this migration network has been adopted by people from Lombok. During the last ten years, with the increasing demand from the Middle East for housemaids, many women from Lombok have been attracted by labour-recruiting companies to meet the increase in international labour demand.

While West and East Nusa Tenggara have become sending areas, Maluku, Irian Jaya and East Timor, particularly their urban areas, have become the destination of migrants from other provinces in Indonesia. Migrants from the southern part of Sulawesi and Java mostly enter the informal sector, which is opening up in major urban centres such as Ambon, Jayapura and Dili. From my intermittent observations and interviews in Jayapura and Dili over the last three years, it is very clear that the local people generally perceive migrants as displacing local people in labour market competition. Such a perception can cause serious social resentments, which can easily trigger ethnic conflict. The riots in Dili in November 1994 originated from a personal quarrel between Buginese and East Timorese traders in Dili's market. The low level of economic competitiveness of the local people is essentially the reason why they are easily defeated in labour market competition by migrants who are more experienced in business.

In Indonesia, economic migration has increased remarkably in the last ten years. The increase has primarily stemmed from the increasing numbers of job-seekers on the one hand, and the opening up of job opportunities in major urban centres outside Java, such as Batam, Samarinda, Ambon, Jayapura and Dili, on the other hand. The 1990 Census, as the only recent source of migration data at the national level, clearly indicates that although the scale of the government sponsored transmigration program has been reduced drastically since the mid-1980s, the volume of non-sponsored migrants has significantly increased, particularly to urban areas (Mantra 1992). As argued elsewhere, a shift in the mode of population mobility occurred in Indonesia in the 1980s from 'sponsored transmigration' to 'human resource migration' (Tirtosudarmo 1994).

A broader perspective of human resources development

As stated at the beginning of this paper, human resource development should be viewed in its totality, that is, not only the physical aspects but also its social and political dimensions. Improvement in human resources will not be satisfactorily accomplished if it is tackled only as a matter of the education or the health of the people. Although the statistical indicators clearly indicate a significant improvement in education and health conditions, genuine development in human resources in Eastern Indonesia is still a problem. The strategic consequences of such a view will be an approach that places human resource development in a broader perspective of national development.

The strategy adopted by the New Order government has been based on the assumption that economic growth should be the prime mover of national development. The emphasis on economic growth has resulted in the high priority given to the improvement of infrastructure, at both national and regional levels. This, in turn, has resulted in the lower priority given to human resource development. As noted by Kano (1995:127), the financial allocation procedure in Indonesia is very centralistic in character, and is also strongly dominated by economic assumptions that have given education and social welfare development a relatively small proportion of the national budget.

Dhakidae (1995:1-2) argues that Eastern Indonesia's economy, which is dominated by a monocrop agricultural system and which has no industrial base, is vulnerable to external shocks. Since 1955, there have been two significant central government policies that have severely affected the local economy in Eastern Indonesia. The first, in 1955, was the government monetary policy which led to a drop in the value of coconuts as the major commodity. An important event in late 1950s was the transfer of the trading centre from Makassar (Ujung Pandang) to Surabaya due to the PRRI-PERMESTA rebellion, which also affected Eastern Indonesia's economy. The second shock occurred in the late 1980s, when the government introduced a trade regulation policy, which is practically a cloves monopoly; thus the viability of the local economy in Eastern Indonesia was further reduced.

Government recognition that Eastern Indonesia has been economically left behind by the western provinces was formally made by the President at a parliamentary meeting in January 1990. Although the presidential statement on Eastern Indonesia's development attracted wide academic debate, real action by the government to accelerate the pace of development in the eastern provinces has been very slow to emerge. Part of the problem is seemingly the incapacity of the central government to come to grips with the task, given the social and geographical complexity of Eastern Indonesia.

The slowness of the decision-making process in the central government has, among other things, been indicated by the clumsy creation of the National Advisory Council on the development of Eastern Indonesia in December 1993. The nature of both the organisational structure and the wide area designated as Eastern Indonesia clearly reflects the tendency to compromise within the central government in the management of the complex task of speeding up development in Eastern Indonesia. The Council also reflects the symbolic format in which the central government attempts to solve coordination problems between departments, provinces and local elites in Eastern Indonesia. It is very likely, therefore that the Council will face problems in the decision-making process. For example, it took more than a year after its formation for this organisation to hold its first plenary meeting in January 1995.

The government definition of Eastern Indonesia, which includes Kalimantan, also creates a problem in itself. The area consists of not only resource-rich provinces such as East Kalimantan and Irian Jaya but also very poor provinces, such as East Nusa Tenggara and East Timor. The centralistic character of national government which tends to standardise policy has resulted in similar treatment of rich and poor provinces. Greater flexibility and autonomy for provinces where strong regional potential is evident are needed. On the other hand, separate treatment is needed for poor provinces, such as East Nusa Tenggara and East Timor which perhaps require more central government subsidies to develop. The allocation of *Inpres* grants is an example which clearly shows the bias toward Western Indonesia and Java in particular; this is because the only significant variable taken into account is population size (Azis 1994:45). This aspect is discussed further in Chapter 5.

A great deal of public discussion is occurring at the moment with the beginning of the government pilot project on regional autonomy in 1995. The project will be tested in 26 districts in all provinces except Jakarta. As far as can be judged from press reports, many observers have expressed scepticism that the current plan will have any significant effect on the existing central and regional structure and relationships, particularly since the structure of central and regional financial arrangements, which is strongly centralistic in character and procedure is not likely to be altered in the near future.

Conclusion

The present condition of human resources in Eastern Indonesia is an outcome of a long process of social, economic and political development in the past, but it is also a key component for sustainable development in the future. The generally low level of human resources and the imbalances within and among provinces are major problems in Eastern Indonesia. From a national perspective, narrowing the human resource development gap between Eastern and Western Indonesia is crucial in sustaining national development.

The slowness of government interventions in reducing the imbalances in human resource capacities and economic development between regions, particularly between Eastern and Western Indonesia, naturally forms the basis for population mobility. The consequence for local populations, which generally have a low level of human resource endowment, is open competition with the bulk of opportunistic migrants who move to seek employment in Eastern Indonesia. In such a labour market, local people will most likely be defeated by the more aggressive and highly skilled in-migrants. In Eastern Indonesia potential conflicts between the local population and migrants will obviously affect social cohesion and in turn political stability in the region.

A strategy to prevent the build-up of potential conflict between local people and migrants in several places, such as Jayapura and Dili, is therefore urgently needed. In such a strategy, an employment creation policy has to be an integral element. A viable human resource development policy indeed has to be formulated, not mainly to serve economic development but also to convey the political and cultural aspirations of the population.

11

Community Development on Savu Island: Lessons Learned

Frans Radja Haba

The island and the community

Savu Island is a small island of 450 sq km in the outer arc of East Nusa Tenggara in Eastern Indonesia. It lies 160 kms west of Kupang, between the islands of Timor and Sumba in the midst of a seasonally dangerous sea (Figure 1.1). The sea is almost impassable during the west monsoon (December to March) and the passage is rough during the east monsoon, from June to August.

The rainfall is erratic, ranging from 375 mm to 2100 mm annually, with 14 to 100 rainy days. The land is barren, denuded and heavily eroded. These land conditions, compounded with erratic rainfall and unsuitable agricultural practices, give rise to harvest failure once every two or three years, on average.

Savu's small size and population, geographical isolation and poor natural resources have given the island low priority in the development efforts of the region. Its population of 60,000 is a homogenous community with a very small number of outsiders, who mainly come to the island for public service posts.

Traditional social organisation, culture and basic values

We Savu people can trace our patrilineal genealogy back to a common ancestor for about 71 generations. The genealogy tree then branches into *udus* (clans), which divide further into *kerogos* (subclans). Each *udu* was entitled to a certain area as clan land, which could be used by any member of the clan under the auspices of the clan head (*Bangu Udu*). The clans then grouped to form five traditional states, each with its own head of state. Each state has its own board of priests (*Mone Ama*) and each clan is entitled to a permanent post on the board. The clan member who is appointed to a post on the *Mone Ama* works not for his own clan but for the welfare of the whole community.

Besides the patrilineal lineage, each of us also belongs to a matrilineal lineage called *Hubis*, which is divided further into *Winis*. This lineage through marriage runs horizontally across clan and state borders, even island and country borders. The potential conflict among clans is reduced by the all-embracing *Mone Amas* and cross-clan matrilineal lineage. It is often said that the people of Savu are divided by men but united by the women and the *Mone Amas*.

Our traditional mode of subsistence is a variant of dryland farming which centres on a sugar-producing palm (*Borassus Sundaicus*) and dryland crops of sorghum, mungbean and rainfed paddy. We tend small animals (chickens, pigs, goats and sheep) but cattle, buffalo and horses are owned by only a few.Palm-tapping is an activity to obtain sweet juice from the *Borassus* palm; it can be drunk fresh, or cooked into a syrup called *gula Sabu* that can be stored for later consumption. Sorghum, mungbean and rainfed paddy, due to the climatic, land and social factors, are prone to low yields or total failure once in every two or three years.

The *Borassus* palm is the only crop that has never failed in Savu. This crop has become the pivot of the island's subsistence economy. Its juice and syrup form the staple diet. In times when the harvest is bad or when the foodstock is low, palm-tapping activities become more intensive to make up for the food storage. During such times we rely totally on the juice or the syrup. The juice and syrup are also fed to animals, especially pigs. The houses are made from parts of this palm: the frame and deck from the trunk, the roof from palm leaves bound to the frame by ropes made from strips of palm stalk and the walls from the woven leaves of the palm.

Socio-economic and cultural changes

The first early contacts with the Portuguese and Dutch in the 18th and 19th centuries took a serious toll in the form of smallpox and cholera epidemics, which reduced our population to less than half.

We are very suspicious of foreign ideas and values but in our culture there are mechanisms by which new ideas and values are appraised closely before adoption occurs. For example, Christianity, after 300 years, has managed to convert only about 60 per cent of our people. Education began to be accepted only 100 years after its first introduction. Despite this strong resistance to foreign ideas, once an idea is proven to be good, we will pursue it with great determination. For instance, in education we have been able to achieve the same level as our neighbours, the Rotinese, who had accepted education 100 years earlier. Conversion to Christianity has also created groups of non-participants in rituals, which reduces its total participative dramatic effects and compromises the whole culture and its values. Education and modern employment are associated with Christianity and many people have begun to condemn the traditional system. Although the traditional beliefs are formally acknowledged by the government as *aliran kepercayaan* or traditional beliefs, they are not infrequently stamped as obsolete and anti-development and are often pointed to as obstacles to the large-scale development process now flooding our country.

The government system has changed several times since colonial days. Under our present national system (the Acts of Regional Government and of Village Government), the five traditional states have been changed to three subdistricts and the *kampongs* have been changed to *desa*, which are not necessarily in accordance with the traditional system of clans, villages and states. Many clans and villages have become truncated, which has weakened the older system and also caused operational difficulties in the new system. In the present national system, as in colonial days, we still try to maintain our own system parallel with the government system.

The national development that has occurred in education, health services, roads and bridges, rainwater catchment dams, irrigation, electricity, television, harbours, airfields and transportation has brought about further change in the community. The present economy is changing to a cash economy, although the old mode of subsistence, palm-tapping, is still retained as a safeguard against the erratic climate. Now many of us have achieved higher degrees and advanced education, locally or abroad. But it is also this pursuit of higher education and better employment that started the brain drain, which has left our island with the less educated and less skilled.

We represent only 3 per cent of the population of East Nusa Tenggara or 0.06 per cent of the total population of Indonesia. Our island is only one small island among the 13,000 islands of our country. Due to our tiny size and isolation, economically and politically, we are insignificant. With this insignificant position in a vast nation, with the flood of development and tight competition, and in the midst of a rapidly changing world, we know that we have a precarious position and we scarcely know what we shall have to face in the future.

Community development: lessons learned

Our NGO, the Ie Rai Foundation, was formed by some concerned Savu people dedicated to the development of our island and community. Founded in 1981 with the long-term goal of creating prosperity and the medium-term goal of increasing income and food production, we developed a program called the Savu Island Community Development Program, which originally consisted of the four main subprograms of Food Production, Income Generation, Networking Development and Institutional Development.

Formulation of projects in each subprogram is done through dialogue with community groups and leaders to identify needs, problems, ways-out, resources and the like. External factors such as related government policies and programs, funding availability, supply systems and market access are considered before a project is decided on. A vast number of dynamics, problems and constraints inevitably determine the viability and sustainability of programs and projects. The organisation has to adjust continuously to external factors such as sociocultural issues, government policy and political, economic and funding policy changes as well as internal problems. The adjustment can be summarised as follows. From 1981 to 1984, we relied totally on foreign funds. Then between 1984 and 1991, we developed a company for the marketing of our group's products which enabled us to begin to develop our own funding, though some projects were still funded by foreign organisations. The government helped by providing various forms of assistance to expand our marketing network. Between 1991 and 1994, after the government banned Dutch aid, we gave up other foreign funding and tried to be totally self-sustaining. We had to reduce projects and retain only the income-generating projects. The government, however, continued to assist with marketing development.

Since 1994 our company has negotiated a soft loan from Pertamina (the State oil company) and PLN (the State electricity company), two government-owned companies which, by Presidential Instruction, have to use 5 per cent of their profit to develop small businesses and cooperative activities for developing income-generating projects. In the process of negotiation, the government directed us to cooperate with the government-sponsored village cooperative (KUD). The loan then had to be shared with the KUD, which is responsible for organising production while our company is responsible for marketing. The company also has to assist the KUD in institutional strengthening and management.

Understanding community priorities

Global and national issues are set by the elites, and every person or organisation breaks them down to suit their own needs, interests and aspirations. Many believe that they understand the problems and needs of the community and come up with preconceived ideas of how to solve community problems.

The NGOs and funders also have their own vision and mission regarding rural community development issues. We might glibly override the people's argument and they reluctantly have to agree with what we say, decide and plan. In the implementation of projects, we are often surprised that people do not seriously involve themselves in the activities and that later they do not utilise and maintain the project. Verbally they might admit that we are right, but we fail when we get messages like, 'we have more pressing priorities'.

This also happened to us on Savu island. Our people understand and agree with the importance of soil and water conservation, safe drinking water, health, nutrition and so on but the sustainability of these projects is always doubtful. On the other hand, the quick-yielding, income-generation and food-production projects are enthusiastically accepted, expanded and maintained by the people. This reflects the fact that their pressing needs are food and income, and that they cannot afford to waste their time and energy on less urgent requirements.

With this insight, we decided that longer-term goals should be achieved indirectly by incorporating them into efforts to fulfil the more pressing needs. Our soil and water conservation program had achieved very little success after five years of implementation. Most of the trees planted had been destroyed by free-roaming animals, and efforts to pen the animals were futile because the people were afraid that the animals might die from lack of fodder, a loss they could not afford. Then we changed the program to a goat husbandry project in which a family was credited with five goats after they had a certain amount of fodder trees or *Leucaena* rows. The acceptance was dramatic; last year hundreds of thousands of fodder trees were planted together with some 300 km of *Leucaena* rows to enrich a pasture area. This year three more pasture areas with about 700 km of contour lines are being worked on for enrichment with leguminous fodder trees. There are many more examples that lead to the same conclusion: we have to be aware of peoples' priorities.

Understanding the ecology

Geologically, West Timor and the other islands of East Nusa Tenggara (Figure 1.1) represent 'tectonic chaos' with scattered patches of arable land. Rainfall is very erratic, especially in small islands like Savu. The traditional mode of subsistence is an adaptation to these ecological conditions. As this area is an exception to the generally wet and tropical conditions of Indonesia, its specific ecology is not adequately understood by the decision-makers of the nation. Given the strong top-down and sectoralised planning of development programs, generally it can be said that agricultural development efforts in this area have been biased towards the wetland agriculture of Java. Dryland resources such as the vast savannah, dryland crops and trees and the long and strong sunlight and winds, as well as the local dryland culture should be seen as a sound ecological basis for further development. Futile cries that blame the dry climate and rocky land for underdevelopment should stop. Instead, we should begin to think of utilising the strong sunlight, winds, vast savannah and the little water we have, as assets for development of the area.

The *Borassus* palm is the only crop that has never failed. The tree starts to produce after six or eight years, and continues to do so for as long as 150 to 200 years. It produces juice throughout the year with the highest peak between September and November, the driest part of the year. Annually a single tree can produce 400 litres of juice with 15 per cent saccharose content, which means 60 kg of saccharose. A thousand trees can be planted on one hectare, which means that one hectare of Borassus palm can produce 60 tonnes of saccharose annually for 150 to 200 years! As far as I know, this is the highest carbohydrate-producing tree in the world. And this huge potential is not yet recognised by the world. With this knowledge we always encourage our people to plan more and more *Borassus* palms.

Dryland leguminous fodder trees like *Leucaena, Glyricideae* and *Sesbania grandiflora* never fail to produce fodder irrespective of the amount of rainfall. This means that animal husbandry is a more secure economic basis than food crops in this semi-arid island. Based on this conviction we launched our goat husbandry project.

Sunlight is the source of world energy. Red seaweed is a raw material for phycocolloid industries as agar and carrageen. The marine algae need seawater and strong sunlight, which are abundant in Savu. Since 1986, we have developed a seaweed culture project in which our people plant a carrageen-producing seaweed, *Echema cottonii*, which is now exported to Denmark and has become a reliable source of cash income for our people.

Ikat-weaving produces one of the more exotic traditional cloths. Weaving is a traditional skill mastered by almost every woman and is done during the dry months. Since 1984, we have organised women's groups to produce *ikat* cloths which are now marketed in the big cities of Indonesia and abroad and have also become a source of cash income for families.

There are many more traditional skills that can be developed in a market-oriented economy. Developing these skills for market purposes, however, will need modern technological, management and marketing inputs.

Empowerment, not hand-outs

Our *ikat* project would not have been able to enter the market without help from the government, funders (particularly Oxfam, UK), friends and business partners. Financial grants alone would not have brought the products to the market where the sustainable cash income comes from. Technical assistance from the Department of Industry has improved the quality of and diversified our *ikat* products. Networking assistance for marketing and promotion assistance from our NAFED (BPEN) helped to open the way to the market. Personnel training in business management, accounting, marketing and exporting, which was funded by Oxfam, helped us to run the business.

Without consultancy help from Oxfam, our seaweed project would not have been able to turn out an export quality product, and we could not have linked ourselves with the exporter and the factory in Denmark. Without proper training, our extension staff could not have assisted our people in group formation and management or trained our community in the various skills needed. Without the voluntary help of an English friend, our staff would not be able to operate and maintain hand tractors and without the voluntary help of an Australian mechanic our island would not have its present and only workshop. In the near future we will need a veterinarian and goat expert to help us to develop our goat husbandry project. We will need agronomists and various experts and technicians to develop our *Borassus* palm activities, and so on.

It seems that the key to rural development is to develop the knowledge and technical skills of the people as well as developing their organisational, management and networking capacity. Without this empowerment, financial grants alone are not of much help.

NGOs and the government

The frontal and challenging stance of transformist NGOs such as legal aid and human rights organisations, which usually receive wide publicity in the media, affects the general feeling of the government and its officials towards NGOs. It seems that the government does not fully understand the difference between NGOs, because developmentalist NGOs, which by nature are more cooperative, have also become suspect and are deliberately disregarded. In our own experience, there are many examples of this situation.

One of our villages was named the best village in East Nusa Tenggara for dam utilisation. In that village we organised a successful onion-farming project and the village has become well known for this product. The village was given an award but the NGO behind this success was never mentioned. The same happened in two other cases, where one of our school clients became the best school in regreening and one village became the best in women's programs.

One of our staff responsible for development of traditional *ikat*-weaving as a home industry for women was awarded an Upakarti, the presidential award for development of small industry, but there was no mention of the NGO that runs, organises and funds the whole project. All the credit for marketing was given to the company (our marketing arm), without any recognition of the NGO that actually organised the whole venture.

All the income-generating projects organised by our NGO, which received a soft loan from Pertamina and PLN (through the efforts of the NGO and its company), have to be transferred to the KUD without any regard for the pioneering NGO. Ironically, the company is accepted as part of the cooperative scheme but the NGO is disregarded even though the NGO leader was elected chairman of the KUD.

Yet despite all this deliberate disregard of our NGO, I must admit that we have never experienced any coercion. As individuals, many government officials acknowledge and encourage the good work of our own and other NGOs.

Community development and private business

Private businesses provide employment and markets for community products. Developing cooperatives and small businesses should be part of community development so as to link the community to the bigger and wider business world, to sustainable capital and to income sources for the community. Private business can become the nucleus of an agro-industry involving the community. Examples for this kind of scheme are our seaweed, goat husbandry and *ikat*-weaving projects.

In our seaweed project, the cooperatives provide capital for the farmers, who sells their products to the partner company which then sells to the agent who exports for the Danish factory. The company, in turn, helps strengthen the management of the cooperatives and provides extension services and quality control for the farmers. The former roles of our NGO in organising extension work and in the provision of capital have now been taken over by the cooperatives and the company.

Another example of a different scheme is our onion and garlic project. This project is also run by our NGO, which provides extension services and capital for farmers. The market is in towns in the bigger, surrounding islands of Timor, Sumba and Flores. We encourage farmers to sell their products either to middlemen or directly to buyers in the towns. This scheme has been running well for twelve years.

Local NGOs and funders

Funders provide financial support for projects and organisational costs, which brings a temporary feeling of security. Many NGOs seem to be quite happy with this false security, and are reluctant to develop their own means of funding which is quite contrary to the basic principle of community development, namely, self-reliance. This financial dependence puts local NGOs at the disadvantage of an unbalanced bargaining position. Funders often steer the project to suit their own ends, which not infrequently differ from the NGO's or the community's actual needs and priorities. Sometimes they antagonise government authorities, which then has a backlash on the NGOs. Many funders do not really understand the importance of institutional strengthening of NGOs, and many do not know when and how to phase out. The prolonged involvement of funders can hamper the institutional development of NGOs by causing dependency, while a hasty withdrawal without programmed phasing out can leave the NGO partner and the community high and dry in the midst of program implementation. Thus the strengthening of NGOs and community institutions should be the main phasing-out strategy of all funders if they wish to see sustainable development in their wake.

12

Strengthening Local Institutions, People and Community Participation: The Potential Role of Non-Government Implementing Agencies in Rural Development

Tonny Djogo

Introduction

Since the beginning of this century, non-government implementing agencies (NGOs) have been playing an important role in facilitating the process of social, economic and ecological change in East Nusa Tenggara and generally in Indonesia. Several development models, generally with a rural, agriculture-based approach, have been tested and developed by different implementing agencies with varying degrees of sustainability.

One of the most significant supports has been in human resource development implemented by non-government implementing agencies through the provision of education and health care programs in both villages and urban areas in Indonesia. Physical facilities or infrastructures were not the focus of these NGOs at the outset, since they considered people's development to be the foundation of any development endeavour. The impact of these development programs is still being felt today, in that socially and politically there are many potential leaders, professionals and resource persons who were educated in the past by non-government organisations. Economic and social changes also have to some extent been supported by these human resource development activities.

Over the last few decades the role of NGOs has diversified into different forms of advocacy or action such as human rights, the economy, rural development, education, natural resource management and physical facilities. Due to the strong voice of several NGOs working in advocacy, the role of organisations operating in rural areas with small-scale programs is often also suspected of being a form of political activity.

Several NGOs that work through advocacy in the area of human rights and environmental issues tend to be so overreactive that their activities are suspect. Nevertheless, the government of Indonesia actually provides opportunities for these organisations to work in social welfare, education, human rights and the economy so as to contribute to the development process and play a role as government partners. Although many are small-scale organisations that keep a low profile, they have produced reasonable approaches or models for rural development. Their experiences may be used to bring about significant change locally, and may even provide a sound model of approach for a people-centred or community-based development process for a wider area. They also do not hesitate to cooperate with government agencies in small-scale development programs and they do so without pretension to any claim of the success achieved as the result of their endeavours.

This type of organisation is believed to obtain more sustainable results than other development programs, which usually commence with substantial amounts of funds and expertise, are target-oriented, employ a top-down approach and are often more bureaucratically oriented and scientific in nature. Although the impact of NGO activities is usually not substantial in terms of biophysical performance or target-oriented areas of coverage, several have provided the foundation for a long-term significant impact which directly or indirectly has addressed the key issues in the rural community and ecosystem.

This paper will analyse issues, dynamics and processes of rural development programs from an NGO's perspective. It will describe examples of several development models in East Nusa Tenggara implemented by non-government implementing agencies, a term that the present writer sometimes uses rather than 'non-government organisation', which can be misinterpreted as a kind of instrument for non-government political movement.

The cornerstones of rural development are community participation, community organisation and local leadership, which allow the possibility for local people to reduce their dependency on external support, strengthen their own capability and resource utilisation and adopt technologies because they feel that they are relevant to local needs. This can ensure the continuity of any rural development program. The people, with their indigenous knowledge and community organisations, need to be understood as key actors in development.

Community participation and the participatory process have been widely discussed but very few examples can be observed and used as appropriate models for sustainable development either by government or NGO rural development programs. Collaboration between government and NGOs is in serious need of inter-agency collaboration in the future. Rural people often do not care who is the external institution to support an improvement in their lives.

There are a few key questions which need to be answered regarding rural development experiences in the past.

- Why is there continuous degradation of natural resources, and yet the rural economy does not grow significantly?
- Why were many development programs in the past not sustainable?
- What significant impact was achieved by NGOs in the past, making non-government implementing agencies necessary?
- How can NGOs view problems in such a way that they can enable local people to solve those problems with the assistance of government and other NGOs?
- What opportunities are there for NGOs and other implementing agencies to collaborate in solving these problems so that there will be a significant impact on wider areas?
- What development models can be used to improve the local economy gradually and to keep pace with human resource development and orientation in farming systems?

Key issues in rural development : lessons learned from past experiences in East Nusa Tenggara

On the basis of the process and dynamics of development programs undertaken by different implementing agencies over the last few decades, there are several key issues to be taken into account in rural and agricultural development and in natural resource management.

Various implementing agencies including policy-makers, NGOs and scientists have translated these issues into different programs. The priority of the programs not only depends upon the local condition and level of development but also is often determined by the priorities and policies of the implementing agency, which sometimes ignores local conditions and the basic needs of the community. Some of the programs remain sustainable, but most are terminated during initial activities or else cannot be continued by local people when external support is terminated.

The major issues relating to rural and agricultural development and environmental conservation are listed below. Those illustrated here are problems related to rural development which NGOs may have the capacity and opportunity to address. Government programs, of course, will be able to address these issues, considering their position, policy power and financial resources. The most important part is the approach, where to some extent NGOs play the major role in helping to cope with issues where government programs need support from external institutions.

1. The poor community approach, extension strategy and process of transfer and development of technology in rural development. Also included in this issue is the process of selection and development of appropriate technology relevant to the change in orientation from subsistence to market-oriented farming systems.
2. Limitations on farmers' technical skills and knowledge of improved farming techniques.
3. The limitations of local institutions or community organisations as well as of local leadership in facilitating the adoption of introduced technology or other development efforts.
4. The significant degradation of the carrying capacity of natural resources such as soil, water and forest areas. This condition has been made worse by unpredictable changes in climatic conditions and weather patterns.
5. Land tenure issues.
6. The marketing of agricultural products. There is need for the development of appropriate small-scale, farm-based economic development models. There is also a need also to bridge the gaps between agricultural production processes, marketing and industry in terms of institutional regulations, technology, human resources and physical infrastructure.
7. Institutional arrangement and collaboration amongst implementing agencies.

In order to cope with these issues, different implementing agencies have undertaken various programs. The results of these programs, however, have so far not significantly improved rural farming systems, ecosystems or economies. Farmers, for instance, cannot wait five to ten years for a research program to provide recommendations that they can adopt.

In order to improve the economy, the government has launched various programs, particularly in agricultural and rural development, since the 1960s. NGOs also started through various programs to work closely with rural communities. Since there was not enough experience, many programs were not sustainable. At the same time many research institutions have undertaken considerable study programs, but most of the research is still in the initial   stages and it is difficult for farmers to proceed with the application of findings.

Research and development agencies have introduced various types of new approaches and technologies to facilitate the process of rural economic development and environmental protection. Many shortcomings from these past endeavours can be noted. Most of the technologies were developed outside and then transferred, and thus were not appropriate. The process of transfer of technology did not create a situation in which the farmer would continue to work with the program when the service and extension provided had to be terminated. Unpredictable markets forced farmers to make difficult decisions in determining the selection of cash crops or cropping systems in general. The development and spread of many new pests and diseases associated with most hybrid species have slowed down the adoption of new crops and cropping systems. The poor cannot keep pace with rapid economic growth in places where the capacity of subsistence farming systems and their communities to respond to this change is very low. Unpredictable changes in global climate and weather have caused serious problems in dealing with the management of declining natural ecosystems and unproductive farming systems. Meanwhile, the evolution of new approaches, technologies and research models has neither encouraged nor reinforced the development process significantly. As a consequence, many programs continue for only a few years, then have to be terminated because farmers are not interested anymore.

These shortcomings in past development endeavours can be attributed to several causes. The first is the fact that needs assessments made for project planning and implementation were not necessarily related to local needs and capabilities. The problems and needs identified by the project programs were not the issues that local people considered to be a priority and solvable at their level. Secondly, many programs or projects did not consider the orientation of farming systems, while many tended to focus on physically and biophysically oriented technology and infrastructure to which local people could not adjust. Thirdly, the community approach and extension process provided by the programs tended to be top-down and did not create a situation where farmers would solve their problems and adopt the recommended technologies. Fourthly, technologies were designed and tested outside without preliminary trials with local people before they were widely promoted. Finally, many programs could not facilitate the participatory process because they were very formal and there were gaps in communication and approaches.

The potential support of non-government implementing agencies

Many programs have been implemented by NGOs with varying degree of impact. But there are some situations where NGOs have been recognised as having more flexibility and potential than the government implementing agencies in conducting programs. At the recent fourth annual general meeting of the Nusa Tenggara Upland Development Consortium in Kupang it was revealed by government agencies during a panel discussion that they realise how important NGOs are in rural development programs. NGOs usually have a better community approach and extension strategy, with more flexibility to prepare the community to accept government programs. NGOs usually provide a facilitation and motivation process which makes it easier for the government to work with rural communities. There is, however, a need for partnership, mutual understanding and continuous communication between both parties.

NGOs in East Nusa Tenggara, particularly church organisations and other religious groups, hold a strategic position, given their role in the community and their closer relationship with local people. NGOs are also recognised as having appropriate methods which can encourage community participation in rural development programs. They are expected to contribute to the support of government programs in terms of training, extension and information media on technical issues for rural development programs. Government programs usually have very few extension workers in terms of numbers and qualifications. Rural development programs are a continuous, never-ending process. Government extension workers tend to be limited by bureaucracy, budget and time as well as by centralised policy. In contrast, NGO extension workers can work over an unlimited time and can be very informal.

There have, however, been some problems where communication between NGOs and the government was often not good. Some successful models of NGOs were not recognised by the latter, while on the other hand the NGOs did not get enough information on government policy and programs. Sometimes there was an overlapping of programs, which were implemented in different ways and languages but with the same objectives.

Several local government programs currently involve NGOs in planning, implementation and evaluation. Planning meetings at the rural and urban level are gradually involving more NGOs and other implementing agencies, including the private sector. NGOs are expected to provide a contribution in the form of training and encouragement for extension workers and farmers.

Government programs such as poverty alleviation in rural areas might also obtain better results if the government collaborated with non-government organisations. NGO experiences with community approaches and extension strategies in rural development can be adopted in the poverty alleviation program.

But there are also weaknesses within some NGOs, which have been working with minimum impact, have created dependency on external support and have themselves adopted a top-down approach. Sometimes, because of the background of personnel, they could not communicate very well in the language understood by local people. They were not really practising participatory democracy within their own organisations.

One of the major differences between the government approach and that of NGOs is the time frame involved in the implementation of rural development programs. Government programs tend to be limited by fiscal years, while most NGOs have a more flexible budget. This is another factor which determines the impact of a program in the field, namely, its timeliness for local people to adopt or adjust to new ideas in their main activities in rural life.

NGOs can be various groups or organisation working in different areas not affiliated with the formal government structure. They can be scientific organisations, chambers of commerce, self-reliance organisations, religious groups, non-profit institutions, community bodies or local indigenous organisations. Although there are some NGOs which are viewed negatively, most NGOs actually avoid controversy (Singh 1995).

The professional and scientific organisations are generally concerned with promoting knowledge of the sciences and the interests of their members. With rare exceptions, they shun controversy and avoid entanglement with political and societal forces that impinge on forestry, for example (*ibid.* 1995). Singh has also pointed out that the political interaction between NGOs and forestry, for instance, is not simple or always negative. Some NGOs engage in formal lobbying at the national and international levels for responsible management, while others monitor the work of the transnationals in forest exploitation and degradation. Yet others help to increase public awareness. Most of these do not avoid controversy in furthering their causes. There are several organisations working at the lower level such as community bodies or indigenous people. They are able to mobilise for direct action, and are concerned with how natural resources and forestry or agricultural production systems affect them and their families directly.

Many NGOs have blossomed, and they have done a great deal to create awareness of issues, organise communities and increase the diversity of views that influence land use, forestry and agricultural policy. Some have played an invaluable role in developing and testing new systems and approaches to better, more sustainable practices. Others, however, have fuelled controversy, sometimes making negotiation, compromise and consensus difficult to achieve. On balance, NGOs have probably done more to move environmental and social issues up the political and international ladder than the efforts of scientists. There are lessons to be learnt from the NGO experience: professional and scientific bodies could benefit by working more closely with them, since they are so effective (Bennett 1995).

Whatever happened in the past, the major point in this matter is that the relationship between government and NGOs should be facilitated. Collaboration should be underscored as a wide range of interactions and sharing as well as mutual understanding. The difference between the two kinds of organisations should be minimised by positive thinking that the ultimate goal of development is for the benefit of rural communities and the implementing agencies themselves (the stakeholders). The strengths and weaknesses of both sides together will form a stronger potential to facilitate the development process.

Although several NGOs have had significant impacts on rural development, there are key questions that need to be addressed with respect to collaboration. Can the impact of NGO programs and experiences be taken into account by the government or other implementing agencies in formulating policies.? How best can NGOs create a mechanism for collaboration with other institutions, such as government, research institutions, or educational institutions, for the sharing of ideas, experience, technology and information? How can research institutions collaborate with NGOs to implement farmer or people-centred research programs to enable rural people to understand the needs and objectives of research and translate it into action for improving rural livelihoods? How can all NGOs have the same strategies and approaches in strengthening community participation and providing a basis for the long-term sustainability of any introduced programs so that they can adjusted to different regions, communities and biophysical ecosystems? How can rural development and issues, as viewed by different implementing agencies, be formulated into similar languages and programs without sacrificing the local community as the object of development experiences. How can NGOs establish collaboration with the private sector to develop the rural economy on the basis of social problems rather than on the basis of biophysical potentials and constraints only?

The major problem in current rural and other development programs is again the question of sustainability. Many programs started with a substantial amount of money and with large areas and a large number of farmers as the target group to be covered. Many of these programs terminated, and local people could not continue them. Moreover, many programs tended to improve the local economy rapidly by providing various kinds of support, but farmers' acceptance and their capabilities were not strong enough.

Several rural development models

There are several rural and agricultural development models in East Nusa Tenggara from whose experiences lessons can be learned.
1. The process of change from shifting cultivation toward *Leucaena*-based farming systems with fattening livestock production systems as the basis of the local economy in Timor (the Amarasi Model) (Metzner, 1983).
2. The process of change from traditional dryland farming systems towards stable or permanent agricultural production systems with cash crops as the economic base of the local people (the Sikka Approach) (Metzner, 1976).
3. Community development in a participatory farmer-based soil conservation program (Yayasan Tana Nua) (Djogo, 1994b).
4. The process of change from traditional farming systems towards permanent farming systems with soil conservation, using live hedgerows of diversified multipurpose tree and shrub species and family forestry, an agroforestry model in Flores (Yayasan Geo Meno).
5. The process of motivation by providing training for motivators and extension workers who will then be working in the village with rural communities (for example, Yayasan Alpha Omega).
6. The provision and development of physical facilities for rural communities such as water supplies, roads, schools and markets (Yayasan Dian Desa, Plan International, Yayasan Alpha Omega, Delsos).
7. The provision of support and facilitation processes for human resource development such as schools, health care and training through religious organisations (Delsos, YAO, GMIT etc).

Many NGOs work in different parts of East Nusa Tenggara in various ways, and with varying degrees of impact. Most of the programs tend to take a long time to show a significant effect. Other programs have been analysed by Fox (1977 and 1988).

These are a few models of rural development programs adopting different community approaches and extension methods for community development. These models involve different degrees of participation that are determined by their approach and extension strategy. They are also impressive in their approach to developing community participation, encouraging equitability and providing the baseline for sustainable development in the long-term process.

Some of these models, such as the Sikka and Amarasi Models, have shown an impact twenty to thirty years after the initial activities. In these two models there was impressive collaboration between government and non-government or local community institutions in the use of local knowledge. *Leucaena leucocephala* as a single species for live hedgerow establishment was used as an entry point in the transfer of technology which provided profound changes (see Metzner 1976 and Fox 1988, Djogo, 1994a). These two models were quite sustainable until there was a disturbance of some magnitude when the *Leucaena* was destroyed temporarily due to the Psyllid infestation in 1985.

The sustainability of these systems was questioned for some time, and it remains to be seen whether *Leucaena* will still be the major species to support these systems or whether there is a need to reorient the model to include other alternative species and introduced cropping patterns and systems such as agroforestry or other sustainable models (Djogo 1992).

These two models have, however, shown how gradually during a long-term process remarkable changes in local farming systems and the rural economy were generated. The key question to be addressed now is how the two models can be sustained in the current context of rapid economic and social change. What more commercially-oriented component may be incorporated in case all farmers have to move to market-oriented farming systems?

Yayasan Tana Nua (1992), another non-government organisation, used *Leucaena leucocephala* in the beginning but then diversified with other species. This NGO has a very impressive approach which focuses on community development by providing the opportunity for local people to develop themselves. Community participation is the major feature of this NGO. There are significant changes biophysically and on peoples' behaviour in the areas where the organisation is working.

There is, however, the question of how this approach can be maintained or adjusted to the shift of local people to market-oriented farming systems.

Many farmers now seek more opportunity to get the products of their farm marketed. Another issue is the relationship with government programs which in some places have overlapped. Whatever the result, this will determine local peoples' perceptions of introduced technologies. Significant changes in cropping patterns should be accompanied by the encouragement of a farmer-based management of farming systems and should allow for the possibility of incorporating cash crops. Interaction with other implementing agencies working in the same areas may reduce the rural people's level of participation. How can this interaction be strengthened to produce more constructive and productive development programs?

Yayasan Geo Meno is another very small NGO in whose establishment in 1988 the present writer was closely involved. Although it is a young institution, some remarkable changes have been made in several rural areas where it is working. Yayasan Geo Meno began its program in 1988 in Desa Gerodhere, Ngada, Flores (Djogo 1990). After the Psyllid infestation in *Leucaena leucocephala,* Yayasan Geo Meno worked with village communities, establishing live hedgerows of various types of shrub legumes such as *Gliricidia sepium, Calliandra calothyrsus, Calliandra tetragona, Flemengia congesta, Desmodium renzonii, Cassia siamea* and *Leucaena leucocephala.* This NGO learned from the experiences of other NGOs, particularly Yayasan Tana Nua, in terms of community-based extension strategy. A more detailed illustration of its work will be provided in the next section.

Many other NGOs exist in East Nusa Tenggara and certainly in the eastern part of Indonesia. Some focus on education and health care, others on training or providing physical facilities. The sustainability of these different NGOs also varies, depending upon their approach and strategy.

The participatory development process : a new trend in the development approach

Many programs in developing countries need to keep pace with the new trends in rural development strategies where a participatory approach is adopted. Although technologies in farming systems have been significantly improved, problems related to the involvement of local people remain major issues.

Rural farming systems development models in most developing countries are currently shifting from a technology-centred orientation to a more people-centred orientation. People in rural areas are in a difficult position where their dependency on natural resources is very high. Their positions economically and ecologically are crucial, considering the rapid degradation in natural resources and the fast growth of the economy.

Many agricultural development and natural resource management programs in the past were very specific, either in terms of their disciplinary approach and commodity orientation or farming-system orientation. Different programs were under way, each with its own orientation that often ignored the necessity of helping the development process of the others. The exploitation of natural resources such as logging, shifting cultivation and hunting and the development of commercial farms tend to deplete natural resources significantly, which results in non-sustainable production systems. In order to cope with this problem, the programs mostly focused only on the ecosystem or on biophysical issues. Rural communities, farmers and their farming systems were usually not included in the process.

The major problem is that once again most of the programs were not sustainable. Almost constantly a new program, technology or approach was introduced to replace previously introduced technology, approaches or species and varieties of crops. Farmers and the community then felt that they had been exploited for trial-and-error programs. This evolution sometimes created a situation where farmers and extension workers at the field level felt they were part of an experiment. Before an old model had shown its impact, implementing agencies were employing a new one.

There is, however, a trend for many programs to move towards a new perspective with certain characteristics   such as   an integrated and interdisciplinary approach, a participatory and people-centred orientation, ecologically sound agriculture and sustainable orientation.

Several new trends in agricultural development and natural resources management are under way in fields such as soil conservation, integrated pest management, agroforestry, social forestry, permaculture, ecofarming, ecologically sound agriculture, farming systems research and development, sustainable agriculture, natural resources management, watershed management, biodiversity, integrated agriculture and so on. These actually all have the same objective to improve productivity by minimising environmental destruction or otherwise improve the quality of the environment.

Many new programs have adopted a systems or integrated approach and participatory process in order to improve productivity with a sufficient degree of stability and sustainability. Many tend to be more integrated and diversified to achieve a balance between economic and ecological considerations. How can this approach be   translated into agricultural development and natural resource management models that can be understood by extension workers and adopted by farmers?

In order to establish a participatory process, many institutions have developed several models of extension strategy. The evolution of extension model development will certainly provide a significant contribution to any sustainable development efforts. The extension process has now become more participatory oriented, and many organisations are beginning to use a farmer-based extension strategy in a people-centred development process.

The diagnostic process of problem identification is also very important. Over the last two decades there has been increasing attention to the implementation of agricultural research and development by employing a systems analysis and interdisciplinary approach. Diagnostic studies have now become more participatory from the early stage where farmers are involved. A variety of research and development models has been developed, including pure anthropological research, ethnogeographic research, farming systems research, agroecosystem analysis, rapid rural appraisal, diagnostic and design study and participatory rural appraisal. The development and evolution of these methods and techniques reflect an interesting, gradual process from very scientific and complex models through to more application-oriented and simpler models. Interdisciplinary research is conducted by individuals (scientists, extension agents, planners and so on) with expertise in different disciplines, each developing lines of inquiry with local people. This type of approach allows interaction with local people and planners and can be a useful way of approaching complex multidimensional problems (Lai 1993).

Considering this experience and lessons learned from past development programs, there is considerable information and a significant foundation which can be utilised to develop a model of applied research. This applied research should   lead to better attempts to provide a constructive contribution to help future research and development programs. A baseline of information will be required, however, in order to formulate appropriate applied research and development programs in rural and farming systems schemes.

Considerations related to initiating rural development: the experiences of NGOs in East Nusa Tenggara

Yayasan Tana Nua (YTN) and World Neighbors (WN)

Yayasan Tana Nua (the Tana Nua Foundation) is a leading NGO and possibly one of the best in Indonesia in terms of a people/farmer-centred development process. The Foundation was established in 1981 with the help of World Neighbors, and was inspired by World Neighbors' method of using a farmer-to-farmer based extension strategy. Its strategy of working with farmers has influenced many other NGOs, including Yayasan Geo Meno, in community approach, extension strategy and the process of transferring technology to farmers. Extension workers usually come to the villages without any promises, nor do they start with any technology. Field staff always commence the program with a community approach and an orientation program, while at the same time they perform an assessment or appraisal to understand the basic needs of the local people. Then a small field trial is conducted with selected farmers. YTN always starts with a very small program involving very committed farmers.

The organisation usually introduces soil conservation techniques with live hedgerows as the beginning of the program (entry point). Before 1985 when the Psyllid infestation occurred, most of the program involved *Leucaena leucocephala* (locally named *Lamtoro*). Together with farmers, the Foundation has experimented with several types of multipurpose tree and shrub species since 1985. Farmers are involved in planning, designing and planting as well as the measurement of growth and production.

YTN and WN always respond very quickly to any new issues that influence agricultural production systems. Their response also strongly influences not only their own program and their farmers but also other programs from either government or non-government organisations. YTN always works on the premise that the program should be started on the farmers' own land. The assessment of needs should be based on the farmers' basic needs, not the Foundation's objectives. Therefore YTN never starts with a demonstration plot or model to be replicated by farmers; rather, the model is established on farmers' plots, and is developed, designed and implemented together with farmers. Methods employed in the farmer-to-farmer extension strategy are farm planning, cross-visits, farmers participation in the needs assessment, regular farmers' meetings, farmer leaders acting as YTN's main people rather than YTN staff in any discussion, meeting or visits, and farmers acting as researchers.

Yayasan Geo Meno (YGM)

Yayasan Geo Meno (the Geo Meno Foundation) was started in 1988, entirely by people from an academic background. Some preliminary activities took place three years before that in the form of research, field trials, group discussions and intensive visits to many villages in West Timor during 1985. From 1985 through 1988 a group of students from the Faculty of Agriculture, organised and directed by the present writer, conducted a series of research case studies and simple experiments involving local and introduced multipurpose tree and shrub species.

These activities were carried out for various reasons. Many villages in West Timor and Flores are located in dry zones and have a very marginal, harsh environment which results in low and unstable productivity, low on-farm incomes and a fragile environment. We were keen to form a group of people who were interested in the philosophy, concepts, programs and technologies for dryland farming systems management. At that time there was increasing activity in the application of systems-oriented research in rural farming development activities, and farming systems research and agroecosystem analysis were being tested. The group found that these approaches in agroecosystem analysis were appropriate and pragmatic.

The group also realised that they should find a method to help local farmers, since for a long time people from universities and research institutes in this province had never made any significant contribution to help local people improve their farming systems by using the findings of their research. The group tried to merge the approaches employed by NGOs, research institutes and government programs to help local people. The group was particularly interested in agroforestry and social forestry as approaches, methods, techniques and systems that seemed appropriate to help small-scale farming systems in the rural areas at a very low cost at the outset. At that time *Leucaena leucocephala* had been seriously damaged, but most of the dryland farming systems were *Leucaena*-based. Many farmers found that their farming systems needed serious action to cope with the problems, so the group tried to find alternative or supplementary species that could be utilised and developed.

The major activities carried out at that time were case studies involving agroecosystem analysis in several villages; inventory, collection and pre-selection of local multipurpose species that could be utilised as an alternative to *Leucaena leucocephala*; inventory and analysis of traditional agroforestry systems, nursery experiments with local and introduced multipurpose tree and shrub species for agroforestry; and social forestry. The group, however, realised that its activities had so far been very informal but too academic. It was a loose organisation that had difficulty in being recognised as a formal organisation able to communicate and share ideas and experiences with other formal organisations.

In 1988 two members of YGM went to Flores with sacks of seeds of several types of multipurpose trees and shrubs for the establishment of nurseries. At that time Yayasan Geo Meno was formally established. As the key field staff, these two members wanted to work closely with farmers and to help them as much as they could. They tried to cooperate with farmers and influence or attract as many as possible. The way in which they worked with farmers, however, did not involve farmers actively as initiators, nor did the farmers feel that they should do the job. Rather, they waited until the Foundation provided something for them, such as seedlings and seeds as well as other contributions. The staff did too much while farmers waited for the results and anything that they could obtain from YGM. The Foundation also tried to encourage farmers through a classical extension strategy where farmers were collected in the village office or meeting hall, or in fields. They tried to create a good model of a nursery and to produce seedlings of many species. Since the Foundation staff had previous experience in collecting local seeds and had successfully tested those species in a good nursery in on-station experiments, it was expected similar results would also be obtained in the village situation. What actually happened in the field fell far short of their expectations.

Yayasan Geo Meno then visited Yayasan Tana Nua's program in Sumba, and received several visits by YTN's field staff, farmers and World Neighbors as well as a CUSO consultant. Most of those people made very strong criticisms about the community approach, the extension strategy and particularly participatory process, which was thought to be very weak.

YGM then had to slow down its ambitions, limit its technological orientation and slowly build up its field staff capabilities in the area of needs assessment, community approach, extension strategy, promotion of leadership in the program and the participatory development process. The staff gradually changed from a 'motivator oriented' role towards one that was 'facilitator oriented'. Farmer-based experiments were also promoted.

However, some modifications based on ideas generated and on the locality are also being encouraged. Since staff mostly have an academic background, significant analysis of every stage of the implementation of a program can be performed effectively. Farmers should be given important roles, the staff think, in analysing the program's relevance to a wider area and trying to correlate with any other programs (run by the government and other NGOs). YGM has established very good relationships with almost all government programs, and also with the university and with research institutes working on dryland farming systems and agroforestry programs.

YGM also tries to formulate needs assessment and impact analysis criteria and assessment tools. This will help it to build a good bridge linking it with any parties concerned with dryland farming systems, particularly at the village level. Even before YGM was formally established, its staff had always focused on the driest areas in the province, which certainly are very difficult to manage. YGM assumes that if we are able to cope with the problems of small-scale dryland farming systems in this region, it will be easy to work in areas where rainfall or humidity are much better. The Foundation employs agroforestry and social forestry to help improve local farming systems. These two approaches are expected to provide solutions to basic problems. If farmers can solve their basic problems, the improvement of farming systems will be much easier.

Since the introduction of agroforestry, farmers' initiatives are expanding. There are opportunities for farmers to plant horticultural crops and tree cash crops and to incorporate beans and other secondary crops since the soil has improved gradually. When YGM commenced the program in the village of Gerodhere on the island of Flores in 1988, many types of species were introduced. Although the process was wrong, whereby species were introduced without a previous needs assessment, farmers were attracted and wanted to be involved in the selection process.

Together with farmers, YGM experimented with the establishment of hedgerows using several species such as *Gliricidia sepium, Calliandra calothyrsus, Calliandra tetragona, Cassia siamea, Flamengia congesta* and *Acacia villosa* and others. At the same time staff tested several species in the nursery such as *Swietenia* mahogany, *Tectona grandis, Albizia saman, Pterocarpus indicus, Cassia fistula, Tamarindus indica* and other local species. From the Oxford Forestry Institution, the Foundation received several Central American drought-resistant species such as *Calliandra calothyrsus, Leucaena diversifolia, Prosopis juliflora, Guazuma umifolia* and *Leucaena shanoni*. Most of these local and introduced species grew very well in the nursery. Farmers then selected the seedlings which they liked, based on the information given by field staff about the function and characteristics of the species. Since there were so many species, not all could be planted. Over the next year farmers were still waiting for the seedlings from the YGM's nursery. The fact that it established its own nursery while farmers waited for the seedlings, proved to be a big mistake.

Since then the Foundation has focused its activities on the community approach and extension strategy. Every half year, selected farmers are sent to other NGO programs, government projects and the Kupang Agricultural Polytechnic farm and workshops.

Farmers' meetings, where farmers are the leaders while field staff just act as facilitators as much as possible, have also been increased. YGM has also had visits from both farmers and field staff from other NGOs, particularly YTN where the latter usually make very strong criticisms of the programs under way at YGM's site locations.

These interactions and relationships have considerably changed the orientation of both staff and farmers. Farmers' leadership and discussions and the sharing of ideas have been dynamic and progressive. Now farmers even criticise and modify the program, and create new ideas to be implemented. Farmers have also carried out their own farm experiments with the assistance of field staff. They have often held their own meetings in their working group, teaching each other and even encouraging the Foundation in new ideas.

The morale and spirit of YGM field staff has increased greatly. Several villages nearby have sent their farmers or their leaders to learn what progress is under way in YGM's area of work. They have asked YGM to help their villages, but since the Foundation's capacity is not very strong, it has limited its areas of work while giving people from other areas opportunties to become involved in farmers' meetings and extension activities.

Since then farmers, either by themselves or through their own original working groups have established individual and group nurseries. Farmers have also shared seeds, seedlings, information and experiences and collected their own seeds of locally available species. Farmers have even carried out their own small-scale experiments, which of course may not be scientifically valid, but practically are useful and can be interpreted by the farmers themselves.

YGM has also created a very good relationship with the Agricultural Polytechnic, the Forestry Department, government agricultural development programs, other NGOs and Hutan Tanaman Industri or the Industrial Timber Estate Program. Staff have learned many new technologies in silviculture, agroforestry, dryland farming systems, and have also tried to create their own new strategy of community approach and participatory development (see YGM 1991 and 1992).

Experience over the last four years reveals the following. The creativity, initiative and spirit of farmers have considerably increased. Since farmers have been made the centre of the program. YGM therefore strengthens local farmers' leadership, so that they can act as initiators while the staff of YGM stand beside them as facilitators. In the future structure of YGM, farmers should be placed at the top as the persons given the mandate to influence policies, planning, needs assessment, design and implementation of the program. YGM's staff should be very open to criticisms and comments from farmers and visitors, and should always invite comments for the improvement of the program so that it can achieve its goal and objectives. Farmers' participation in all aspects of the program can be slowly improved by continuous encouragement, discussions, cross-visits and activities that provide the opportunity for farmers to interact with each other and with the Foundation staff (coordinators, supervisors, extensionists and other field workers). In working with farmers, the organisation of the YGM should be kept as informal as possible, since informal relationships will help staff to communicate better and obtain realistic information and facts. The design of the program should not come from outside. We try not to focus too much on improved technologies which were designed elsewhere. We help with the basic principles.

Community approach and extension strategy

There are certain guidelines to be considered in a farmer-based extension strategy. These consist of key activities related to a community approach that is founded on experience in Indonesia. Basically, implementing agencies should start with small and participatory programs at the outset. The basic principles in this process are outlined below:

1. Use a community approach, establishing an informal or personal relationship between field or extension workers and the local community and its leaders.
2. Identify the basic problems which will become the foundation of the development process.
3. Perform a participatory needs assessment and devise possible solutions to local problems.
4. Involve farmers in program planning and specifically in farm planning.
5. Identify and design basic technology that can be developed together with farmers in the context of their capability and local resources.
6. Identify key local farmers and encourage local leadership.
7. Carry out a farmer-based extension strategy to facilitate the process of self-motivation.
8. Develop institutional collaboration for the exchange of experiences and information, and facilitate exchange visits among extension workers and farmers.
9. Carry out farmer-based farm trials when introducing technology.
10. Allow farmers to modify the program to suit their farm conditions.
11. Begin with what they have.
12. Start with small programs.

This is indeed a gradual and somewhat tedious process, and it needs a lot of patience on the part of field extensionists and technicians. The training and orientation of extension workers and field technicians is crucial to the community-based development process. It is essential to obtain appropriate field-level facilitators for community-based agroforestry development programs. Key farmers and local leaders also should be involved in the orientation process of the program to encourage similar understanding and encourage local leadership.

Implications and recommendations for Eastern Indonesian rural development

Eastern Indonesia has been considered a special region for further development. Generally, the region is lacking in many things compared to other more developed regions in the country. Considering the rural community in Eastern Indonesia and the ability of the government to provide physical facilities, more programs involving the participation of NGOs should be focused on activities that promote the strengthening of social infrastructure rather than physical infrastructure.

There are many NGOs working in the eastern part of Indonesia. However, they have different approaches and strategies, which have various impacts on local people's livelihood and environment. Training and sharing of information, experiences and technologies amongst organisations is required. They may have the same approach and strategies although they are working in different regions and with different priorities, each organisation will be strengthened in various aspects of its institution. More focus should be given to small-scale rural development programs that have the opportunity to strengthen local institutions and to encourage community participation. Large-scale development programs have never proven sustainable so far.

Whatever the results or strengths of NGOs, the relationship with the government is very important. Collaboration with government programs will result in a more pronounced impact, both socially and politically. In this case economic development and ecologically oriented programs will be easier to carry out.

There is a need to provide more training for personnel at the different levels of implementing agencies, whether those concerned be policy-makers, planners, scientists, engineers, extension workers or farmers. The different levels need to be given the opportunity to understand and have similar perceptions and perspectives of the community approach and participatory process in rural community development programs. NGOs must react to any discrepancies or limitations in the development process by offering alternatives, and they need to have a clear perception of both internal and external policy support.

NGOs and government organisations as well as other institutions need to have similar perceptions, which can be obtained through inter-institutional collaboration. This may involve government agencies (either at policy-maker level or at the operational level), research and educational institutions, non-government bodies and the private sector.

How can an NGO working with the private sector help strengthen the rural economy? This is very difficult due to the different orientation of an NGO and the private sector. So far, there is no significant example of how an NGO can work closely with the private sector or companies. NGOs tend to focus on social and ecological issues, while the private sector tends to focus on economic issues. Farmers' needs depend and focus on both areas of concern.

The important factors determining the productivity and sustainability of any introduced rural development program may be social and economic as well as biophysical, institutional and policy-related. The major constraint in the development process involving the rural community in socially oriented programs is that the sustainability of programs depends on community participation and social issues rather than on economic and biophysical considerations. Many programs in the past tended to focus on physical or technical and biophysical considerations. Externally aided projects often lack compatibility with the conditions and needs of the local community. Many projects have failed because they ignored local institutions and tried to establish new institutions and external design models. Local people tended not to benefit from the sophisticated design and introduced technology.

Community participation is only possible when the local people, their community organisation and their leadership are strengthened. Strengthening these three elements is usually a time-consuming and long-term process. This, however, is the foundation for any program involving rural communities.

13

Rural Community Development in Irian Jaya: In Search of An Appropriate Model

Cliff Marlessy

Introduction

Irian Jaya is the easternmost province of Indonesia (Figure 1.1). Its 410,600 sq km are inhabited by 252 ethnic subgroups who live in 2,216 villages. Of the total population of 1,706 million, the majority live in the mountains and interior. The population growth rate is 3.46 per cent.

Since Irian Jaya has specific conditions due to its geographical, cultural, and political isolation, the development approach to this area should be special. Problems with policies concerning Irian Jaya's development are closely related to the general problems of Indonesian development, because in the current system, the province follows the policies decided by the central government.

The problem of rural development is closely related to the problem of overall development in Irian Jaya. These two issues cannot be separated, because problems in rural areas are actually the results of provincial policy on development. For this reason, this paper will focus more on the problems of development policy in Irian Jaya, their impact on rural communities and the contribution of NGOs to rural development.

Indonesia's first 25-year development program (PJP I) focused on the development of the western part of the country (which some depict as the region from Sumatra to Bali). This focus has resulted in the decrease of natural resources in this region, and a widening gap between the western part and the eastern part of Indonesia (West Nusa Tenggara to Irian Jaya) in terms of infrastructure such as roads, telecommunications, transportation and public facilities.

To reduce the gap between Western and Eastern Indonesia, the Indonesian government launched the 'Go East Policy' in 1990. This policy primarily aims at inviting industry and investment to the region to boost its economic growth. The policy has resulted in the opening up of remote and isolated areas and the creation of employment. Looking at the policy closely, however, one can see a number of flaws. The policy has brought about fast and crucial changes in the area, for communities are forced to support development programs carried out by various parties, and community rights to access and use natural resources have been eliminated and transferred from communities to outsiders. This is clearly seen in the forestry, marine, tourism and agricultural sectors.

At the same time, this development policy, which is geared towards the exploitation of natural resources, does not benefit the regional government either, let alone rural communities, because of the unfair distribution system. Taxes obtained from the three major commodities of the province (forest, marine and mining products) provide more income for the central government. In this situation, what can the government and non-government organisations (NGOs) do?

Development policy in Indonesia

The 25-year development program carried out by the New Order focused on economic growth. This policy was adopted because Indonesian planners, among whom economists dominated, were of the opinion that economic growth is the best solution to increase people's incomes, and thus promote better standards of living among the community. This approach has certainly increased the GNP of the country. The World Bank has noted this progress, and has stated that Indonesia is one of the 'South' countries that have achieved a considerable measure of success. Poverty has fallen to 17 per cent by 1992 and the economy has averaged a growth rate above 5 per cent per annum for the past three years.

One of the main reasons for the above achievements has been the political stability of the country, which has been based on what is known as the security approach. The implication of such an approach is that the government has attempted to control all facets of democratic life through various regulations. For example, there is only one labour union, the government-controlled Serikat Pekerja Seluruh Indonesia (SPSI), and the mass media are controlled very closely. The freedom to organise is very limited in all aspects of community life. Where there is freedom to organise, it is usually controlled by government-sanctioned bodies. As a consequence of this approach, the wider community has become economically and politically dependent on the government.

In such a situation, democratisation efforts are hampered. The main barrier is the growth of strong government institutions which cannot be counterbalanced by community-based institutions due to their inability to organise freely. Moreover, in recent years there has been growing collusion between the government and the private sector which has a strictly economic or business agenda. In such a situation, the relationship between state and society is no longer balanced. The community's ability to voice its opinion is severely constrained, especially in the case of demands for clean government and good governance.

A second aspect is the one-way flow of information from the government to the community. This is the result of centralised control by the bureaucracies of the media. No other opinions, except the government's views, are acceptable. A third aspect of constraints on the democratisation process is the fact that traditional grassroots institutions are very weak due to the introduction of new institutions and structures by the government. A fourth is the role of political parties other than Golkar. Although other parties have been established, they are now dominated by government to such an extent that their room to manoeuvre is very restricted. Input from the community is so limited that they are controlled by the government. Finally, education is still limited outside of government circles. This includes the business sector, and also limits efforts towards democratisation.

The implication of a development policy that centres on economic growth is that a country ought to have enough capital to make its development programs run smoothly. In a situation where a country does not have enough cash and public saving is limited, the solution that is often adopted, as Indonesia has done, is to obtain loans from a multilateral development bank and/or other countries. To pay back the loan and the interest, Indonesia needs foreign exchange, and this is obtained by selling natural resources. One Indonesian province that is very rich in natural resources is Irian Jaya.

Development policy in Irian Jaya

The national policy of development also applies to Irian Jaya because structurally development in Irian Jaya cannot be separated from national policy, and also because funds for Irian Jaya's regional development come from the National Development Budget (APBN). This can be seen from the provincial policy that focuses on large-scale development, moves at a speedy rate, needs a lot of funds and skilled labour and at the same time eliminates the community's rights to natural resources. Natural resources are located in rural areas and are traditionally owned by the communities. What follows, after the shift in ownership of natural resources, is overexploitation of those resources, especially forest, marine and mining assets, without including any local communities in the process or sharing any of the benefits with them. This means that the exploitation of resources in rural areas creates a very striking difference in per-capita income between urban people (generally people from outside Irian Jaya) and rural people (generally indigenous people).

Research carried out by Lavalin International, Inc. (1987:27) shows that one of the main weaknesses of development policy in the province is the imbalance in growth rates between rural and urban areas. The growth rate in urban areas is 65 per cent while rural areas have only a 9 per cent growth rate. To illustrate the exploitation of natural resources in rural areas, some cases collected by Irian NGOs are presented below.

The first concerns the forestry sector. The total forest area in Irian Jaya is 40 million ha, and use of forests can be divided into two types: those intended to preserve the environment (national parks) and those allocated to forest concession companies. YPMD-IrJa (a Jayapura-based NGO) notes that at present there are 42 companies whose concessions range from 300,000 to 600,000 ha, or a total of 10,715,200 ha, that is, 25 per cent of the total forest in Irian Jaya.

Forest concessions, it has turned out, do not increase the foreign exchange of the region, let alone the income of the communities. As noted in a study by the Indonesian Environmental Forum (WALHI), economic rent from this sector is only 17 per cent, meaning that the benefit obtained by the government from this sector is only 17 per cent. In addition, the concession companies do not implement reforestation programs, even though this is a requirement. As a result, Irian Jaya will gradually suffer from severe deforestation like Kalimantan and Maluku.

A similar thing has happened in the marine sector. The government issues permits to fishing companies to catch fish in the sea without taking into account customary sea rights or boundaries set by local communities. This not only creates benefits that flow out of the province but also increases the destruction of marine resources and limits the access of coastal fishermen, especially in operating in the fishing areas and in marketing.

Studies carried out by the Environmental Study Centre, Pattimura University, Ambon, and YPMD-IrJa (1989) in Bintuni have shown that the operations of trawlers have damaged marine resources because the fishing gear that they use destroys coral reefs. What is more ironic is the fact that they throw 80 per cent of their catch back into the sea as a by-catch.

In the tourism sector, the government has attempted to develop a people's tourism program, but implementation still faces a number of obstacles. The result is that communities have had to sacrifice their assets for the program. This can be seen from the issue of land use in the tourism program. Land which is supposed to be their asset in the program has created disputes between clans. The land rights issue in the construction of the five-star Marau Hotel in Biak is a good example of this problem.

The above-mentioned issues have led YPMD-IrJa (1992) to carry out an economic study which among other things concludes that there are three factors causing impoverishment in Irian Jaya: net cash outflow, net natural resource outflow and net human resource inflow.

In search of a rural community development model for Irian Jaya

Since ten years ago the Irian Jaya government has been trying to develop a rural community development model for the province. The government has, for example, hired a Canadian consultant who produced thick reports that were never implemented. In addition, the government has also designed development packages to increase the standard of living in rural areas. There are at least two such programs: Gersatera (*Gerakan Desa Sejahtera* or Prosperous Rural Movement) in 1990, and IDT (*Inpres Desa Tertinggal* or the Presidential Instruction on Poor Villages) since 1994. On top of this, the government still distributes routine funds to villages totalling Rp6,000,000 (US$3,000), of which Rp900,000 (US$450) is allocated for PKK activities and R5,100,000 (US$2,500) for village programs. Unfortunately, so far there have been no concrete results from the programs. Why?

First of all, the rural development program implemented in Irian Jaya is a program designed by the central government and implemented nationally. Therefore the program fails to see the problems faced by specific communities and does not respond to the needs of the people. It can be said that the program is not rooted culturally or ecologically in the province.

Secondly, in this program communities are still regarded as the object of development. They are not regarded as the 'actors' of development, because they are regarded as being incapable of developing a work plan. Even if they did manage to develop a plan, there is no guarantee that it would be approved or financed by the village budget distributed annually.

Thirdly, in all rural development programs, even when they are implemented on a big scale, the orientation is still sectoral and there is no integration between sectors. For example, in the agricultural sector, the

introduction of agricultural technology is not supplemented with a program
to market agricultural products; furthermore, the communities do not have
the freedom to choose which agricultural commodity is appropriate in view
of local market conditions.

Fourthly, the program has neglected community-based local institutions.
This poses a question: who will take care of the program after the project is
completed?

Fifthly, a rural development program which is based on the *desa* or
village concept may not be the best approach, because the *desa* is more an
administrative and geographical concept than a cultural one.

Sixthly, no thought has ever been given to the development of rural areas
through investment in local human resources. What always happens is that
skilled rural communities are attracted to become urban.

The above examples show that there are many inconsistencies in rural
development programs, especially those introduced by the government.

The role of NGOs in rural development

The approach to development described above clearly excludes the
participation of local communities, and does not strengthen the position of
the people; thus communities in general remain weak. On the other hand,
the rights of indigenous people to the land and their access to natural
resources is diminishing.

In such a context, hopes of empowering the people come from NGOs,
which in Irian Jaya started in the early 1980s. These hopes stem from the
characteristics of NGOs, which have strong community bases, have a micro
perspective in their programs and emphasise the process rather than the
target.

The latter is apparent from various community development programs
carried out by NGOs that involve community participation in the planning
stage, the implementation stage and the evaluation stage. Besides
community development, NGOs also carry out a number of advocacy
programs to influence policy changes in order to create more space for
participation of the people.

The role of NGOs in community development in Irian Jaya can be said to
have started in 1981/82 with the establishment of IRJA-DISC (now known
as YPMD-IrJa), which takes the three roles of 'articulator' (that is,
facilitating the expression by the community of problems that they
encounter, channelling the information to decision-makers in order to

influence policy changes), 'motivator' (that is, encouraging the community to plan and develop realistic programs) and 'facilitator'.

In designing its community development programs, YPMD has tried to implement a participatory development planning model called the Community-based Development Planning Program. This model places the community as the development actor. This model functioned quite well in Kemtuk Gresi District, where a number of cadres who were chosen by the people to participate in a five-year development plan in the district have now been elected as village heads. This program has been successful in terms of human resource development, but implementation of the plan faced many obstacles due to rigid regulations from the government on budget allocation and the time frame.

A similar approach has been carried out by other NGOs, such as Yasanto in Merauke and Yayasan Rumsram in Biak. Yasanto developed a concept called *Pondok Bangun Diri* (Huts for Self-awareness Building), which is a place where people can express their problems and develop solutions to those problems. Yayasan Rumsram in Biak has meanwhile strengthened the community through the development of a community-based economy involving cooperatives and savings.

Meanwhile, advocacy to influence policy changes has been undertaken by a number of NGOs with different strategies. For example, YPMD has carried out research on the impacts of development and raised the resulting issues in seminars; it has also approached the decision-makers, the regional government and the Regional Planning Body (BAPPEDA). The Legal Aid Foundation has created public opinion by constantly making statements and bringing forward the cases that they handle, while YKPHM has focused on training about customary rights.

Unfortunately, the model adopted by these NGOs cannot be easily replicated in other areas due to a number of factors that include the following. The models are local and casuistic and improvisation is needed to develop the model in other areas. The process needs time. The government and funding agencies are not attracted to the financing of process activities or programs that seek to identify appropriate development approaches. Finally, when communities become critical, they are often accused of attempting subversive activities.

The relationship between NGOs and funding agencies

At present, there are several funding agencies that support NGO activities, even though most of these agencies prefer to finance the development of physical infrastructure. If there are funding agencies who are interested in supporting the community development process, their number is very few and their knowledge of strategies and the institutional development process is limited.

So far, the funding agencies that work mostly in Irian Jaya are development organisations from Europe and the USA. The relationship with Australian development agencies is limited (especially in Eastern Indonesia), and includes Indonesian government control over the selection of NGOs to be funded by AusAID.

The major obstacle faced by NGOs in working with funding and development agencies is that they have different interests and agendas. Often, foreign organisations have their own topics of interest, and will only support local NGOs if the latter agree to work on those themes. This practice does not allow the real problems from the field to be properly articulated.

This is also true of the relationship between Irian Jaya NGOs and AusAID. AusAID supports a number of NGOs in Irian Jaya (YPMD-IrJa, Yasanto and Yapsel), but limits its interests to issues that are non-political. Advocacy and people's rights to the land nearly always fail to attract AusAID attention. On the other hand, AusAID is very interested in rural water drinking supplies, agriculture and animal breeding, which are all very important but are not the basic problems of the community.

Meanwhile, the nature of the relationship between Irian Jaya NGOs and Australian NGOs is usually on a personal basis. Several Australian NGOs channel funds to a number of individuals, in the expectation that these people will then channel the funds to the community or the financing of the program. This approach makes the local NGO's position difficult, especially if the individuals concerned are not open about the support.

Conclusion

From the description above, it is clear that NGOs have a major role in strengthening the position of local communities. NGOs can function as both the partner of the government and the local controller of the government's policy and approach.

What is needed is more trust on the part of the government towards NGOs and more faith in the NGOs' objective of fighting against poverty, backwardness and ignorance. Prejudice against the role and activities of NGOs, especially those that work in strategic areas like Irian Jaya, can be counterproductive.

PART III: CONCLUSIONS

14

Conclusions

Colin Barlow

The chapters preceding this form a rich collection, much enhancing our understanding of Indonesia. This concluding chapter attempts to tie together key themes regarding Eastern Indonesian development, and also to highlight major policy issues.

There is at first glance little connection between Soesastro's and Gaffar's perceptive views from the centre (Part I) and the regional concerns of most contributions about Eastern Indonesia (Part II). But Azis in Chapter 5 usefully bridges the centre-periphery gap, looking explicitly from a Jakarta standpoint at patterns and problems of Eastern Indonesian development.

Yet at a deeper level Soesastro and Gaffar set out views and contexts clearly connecting with those expressed by the regionalists. Hence Soesastro's support of 'transparency' and dislike of 'non-market arrangements' (p.40) matches the advocacy in Eastern Indonesian chapters of measures to reduce pervasive market failure. His favouring of deregulation (p.36) coincides with regionalists' wishes for moves towards decentralisation. Again, Gaffar characterises the existence under the New Order of tight control and restriction of human rights (p.44), hence emphasising the centralist and authoritarian nature of government which regionalists see as obstructing much development. Gaffar's citing of the 'pro-democratic movement' including NGO's and intellectuals (p.44) covers parties similar to the 'transformist' elements reported by Radja Haba (p.220), and also dealt with by Djogo (p.229) and Marlessy (p.248).

These issues of market failure, deregulation and moves towards more regional autonomy are indeed crucial for Eastern Indonesia, and are taken up in different sections below.

Eastern Indonesia

The various chapters on Eastern Indonesia spell out in much more depth broad scenarios presented by Barlow in Chapter 1. The region is hugely diverse in geography, ethnography and economy, comprising several distinct regional political groupings having their own focus but no sense of common identity for the region as a whole (B. Mboi, p.136). The only mutual connection of all groupings and provinces, indeed, is to the political centre in Jakarta. Quite similar circumstances also existed historically, in a period whose regional strife and attempts to secede from the Republic (Chauvel, p.71) explain current desires to maintain a centralist emphasis within the political and government structure. Yet while Eastern Indonesian problems were not really addressed by the centre once it had gained control, this changed after the landmark speech of President Soeharto in January 1990 (Chauvel, p.). There have since been attempts to address the region's difficulties more effectively, and signs that some policies are working quite well (Azis, p.92).

Agriculture's dominance in the region has been emphasised in many chapters, with its prime importance of small farms (Azis, p.79) often working on a shifting cultivation or swidden system partly preoccupied with producing food for subsistence (Sondakh, p.147). The distribution of economic activity in terms of four rather distinct economic zones (Barlow, p.13) has been shown as well justified by local configurations of climate, land, labour and other natural resources, while the vigour of many economies has been demonstrated by high rates of real growth (Tables 1.1 and 5.3). The existence of economic enclaves around certain resource exploitation and urban centres has also been indicated, where these might be thought to exercise important spread effects on surrounding communities. But Azis (p. 117) has pointed out that large industries have failed to generate spill-overs to local populations, while Tirtosudarmo (p.208) and Marlessy (p.246) indicate that high per-capita incomes in Irian Jaya and Maluku do not depict the actual welfare of most local people. Although substantial efforts by government to enhance physical infrastructures are broadly confirmed (N. Mboi, p.187, Tirtosudarmo, p.202), the persisting inferiority of facilities and even more of human resource development centred around them (Azis, p.84) is also highlighted. The association of poverty with poor facilities and the persistence of many communities at low living levels, including especially those in remoter locations (Radja Haba, p.215) or involved with reef fisheries (Fox, p.164), is frequently emphasised. Ocean transportation across the eastern archipelago is barely mentioned, but despite considerable government help through providing motorised *Nusantara* vessels running on regular schedules still leaves much to be desired. *Perahu* shipping in the region during the 1970s was fully investigated by Dick (1975a and b).

The deleterious effects on the environment of some activities are stressed (Sondakh, p.147), where shifting cultivation begins to cause degradation once swiddens are reduced below reasonable lengths by increased population pressures (Hardjono 1994). Such effects are more marked in the drier eastern islands of the region, where long fallows of 20-25 years are needed but not usually observed. Indeed, Sondakh (p.147) indicates the shift to more intensively cultivated tree crops as one very sound and generally applicable reaction already undertaken to a great extent in Sulawesi. In fact, widespread environmental damage already existed in Timor half a century ago, being recorded by Ormeling (1957) in his classic geographical study of the island. Fox (p.169) describes the current undermining of long-run marine resources through devastation of reef systems accompanying more fishing and more intensive technologies. Widespread deforestation under commercial clear-cutting can also have deleterious effects, although such consequences in Maluku, Central Sulawesi and Irian Jaya are not taken up in the chapters.

The complex social structures of the region are stressed in Chapters 11, 12 and 13, where the need for effective improvement programs to properly match these is emphasised. Such structures are in many ways great strengths, and if properly harnessed can command vigorous community spirit and enterprise. But they are also regarded by some government and other outside agents with different agendas as obstacles to progress (Marlessy, p.247). The big influences of migration on regional societies are set out by B. Mboi (p.127), who stresses how recent population movements have been facilitated by better transportation. Yet while migration can advantageously transfer ideas and skills, Mboi also sees problems from its role in rapid urbanisation, including social conflicts and severe disintegration within previously homogeneous groups. This is notably exemplified in Dili, where migrants from elsewhere in Indonesia have caused widespread disruption and resentment. The key role of migration in recent Eastern Indonesian population dynamics is well sketched by Tirtosudarmo (p.205), and further issues have been covered by Manning et al (1989).

Government is generally seen as crucial in helping to develop the region, where this springs both from its Indonesia-wide macro policies (Azis, p.111) and huge apparatus of services, including those enhancing local infrastructures and encouraging human resource development (N. Mboi, p.189; Tirtosudarmo, p.200). Business too is seen as having vital part, especially through smaller scale industrial activities of chiefly local industries which have grown faster than larger concerns and had better spill-overs (Azis, p.118). But big business and notably resource-based ventures have generated large economic products despite their lack of surrounding benefit. Business of course also importantly includes small traders and others who supply vital market linkages to the myriad of little agricultural and other producers. NGOs in grass-roots groups are further viewed as having effectively promoted community level development (Radja Haba, Djogo, and Marlessy), notably in situations where government extension services are scarce and attention cannot be paid to local needs. Again, 'transformist' NGOs discussed by Marlessy (p.248) are seen as able to act politically through highlighting social injustices and promoting policy changes better suiting local peoples. The wider developmental and transformist roles of NGOs in Indonesian society are canvassed by Eldridge (1995).

Eastern Indonesia broadly appears as a poor and remote region suffering many difficulties, but nonetheless embracing substantial economic developments that entailed rational responses to market forces and comparative advantage. Some parts of the region are at early development stages, comprising subsistence agriculture, shifting cultivation and sometimes *perahu* fishing. Other parts and peoples, however, exhibit more advanced growth based on tree crops, livestock and *sawah*, using relatively less land but rather more labour and capital in their overall resource combinations. Yet further parts and peoples have moved to the next growth stage of employing more capital-intensive methods for activities, usually involving high-yielding crops and animals and greater external inputs. These are the more intensive forms of cultivation indicated as desirable by Sondakh (p.149). There is likewise some domestic processing of product, although that is limited. There are, too, the few very capital and management intensive enterprises of minerals and forestry, operated by big companies which introduced these as completely new package ventures from scratch.

Fundamentally Eastern Indonesia is only beginning its economic growth projectory. While it faces major constraints addressed below, it also has good potentials which are now examined.

Potentials

Exploiting these should build on the region's comparative advantages, as already manifested in the economic zones defined by Barlow (p.13) and explored in other chapters. Fulfilling the potentials entails progressive movement towards higher stages of development, along lines just described.

A suitable initial approach is attempting to base much effort around small farm agriculture, as the chief sector of the Eastern Indonesian economy with good prospects for generating higher incomes and living standards (Azis, p.79). Such an approach for agriculture and other sectors can usefully build around perceived growth nodes and enterprising undertakings within these nodes, relying on information spreading from such undertakings to extend growth in widening circles around first adoption points. This is a well recognised mode of advance in Indonesian and wider development (Boeky, 1991), and aims at the same time to better establish linkages with other local initiatives and outside markets. Farmers of the region have already demonstrated good ability to undertake such growth, notably in vigorous expansions of cattle from the 1930s (Ormeling, 1957), coconut from the 1950s to the 1970s (Rondonuwu, 1983), and cocoa in the 1970s and 1980s (Jamal and Pomp, 1993). These advances helped establish the current economic zones, and denote that cultivators may be expected to respond to further profitable opportunities.

One key potential for agricultural improvement lies in the subsistence stage, and entails enhancing the yield of subsistence crops including rice, maize and cassava (Table 1.5). Most farm households in Eastern Indonesia, as in other comparable situations, require production of minimal home-grown foods to support their consumption and act as insurances in cash-scarce circumstances. Once this top priority is met, however, families are more open to undertaking market-oriented activities. Thus raising subsistence productivity reduces the area of land needed for purely subsistence crops, while at the same time releasing labour and environmental pressures and allowing moves towards more advanced cultivation and higher incomes.

Rice as a main subsistence crop has good potentials for productivity improvement, where this can be achieved by earlier planting of quicker maturing varieties that avoid water stress characteristically encountered in the late growing season (Pellokila et al, 1991). Similar opportunities exist for enhancing maize yields, and there are also promising new types of cassava and sweet potatoes. All these introductions may give yield increases over those of Table 1.3, albeit employing method and variety changes *without* recourse to high cost purchased inputs including fertiliser. Although far more additional output may be secured through using the latter, most farmers at subsistence stage do not have cash to buy it. But even such 'low external input' approaches to improvement entail passing on new skills and information to cultivators, meaning that extension with its own substantial costs is also an integral part of the process. There are likewise numerous smaller possibilities of subsistence crop improvement, including for example the sugar producing palm *Borassus sundaicus* (Radja Haba, p.214) which is the staple of certain dry area populations.

The major cash product of cattle also has big improvement potentials, not so much through better breeding stock as through introducing new fodder trees and other forages which have exhibited superiority under low external input conditions (Piggin, 1991). But realising these potentials once more depends on appropriate extension and encouragement which are not usually available. Yet an excellent local example of such improvement put through from the 1930s to the 1970s under a traditional ruler is given by the case of Amarasi in West Timor (Metzner, 1983). There, however, success in new forage use depended on rigorously zoning different agricultural activities, in a manner hard to enforce without the ruler's strict authority. Today such authority rarely exists, and has to be substituted by willing community cooperation. Goat production too can be greatly improved, albeit again through more complex management systems.

There are moreover big improvement possibilities with tree crops, where current yields of largely unimproved coconut palms can be doubled under small farm conditions by planting with high-yielding hybrid stock accompanied by fertiliser and other inputs (Rondonuwu, 1983). But it has to be recognised that these and similar possibilities for coffee, cloves and cocoa differ from those just described for annual crops and animals, where low external input routes to improvements are available. With trees substantial input costs are incurred, and farmers must also wait five years or more for newly planted stock to start production. Both latter aspects are economic disincentives in low income situations, meaning that considerable credit support must accompany necessary skills imparted by outside extension.

Again, Fox (p.168) has described how the new technology of *bagan* platforms is transforming the coastline and reef 'niche' fishing of the eastern islands, although this once more involves considerable initial expenditure on materials and equipment. There are as well good low cost possibilities of producers raising revenue through quality improvements to most cash crops and fish, as demonstrated by the case of smallholder cloves from Maluku (Godoy and Bennett, 1990). There farmers were encouraged to raise their output quality through the well designed provision of information and incentives by cigarette companies buying the crop. Potentials finally exist to add value through downstream processing, including notably fish, cattle, coconuts, and coffee. Except in fisheries, however, such activities remain small (Azis, p.118).

Outside agriculture and fisheries, tourism is a small but promising sector in many parts of the region, which especially given the near saturation of Bali has definite potentials for the future. More importantly, Irian Jaya, Maluku and South East Sulawesi hold significant potentials for further productive investment based around minerals, oil and forestry. There are in particular large possibilities of expansion around the huge Freeport mine, producing copper, gold and silver in the Sudirman ranges of Irian Jaya and dwarfing all similar enterprises in the region. There are big remaining forestry reserves which can be profitably exploited in both Maluku and Irian Jaya.

It should lastly be noted in discussing potentials that much depends on 'outside agents' to accomplish envisaged changes. Exploiting the agricultural possibilities outlined above, for instance, entails substantial extension, training and credit from outside, where this may be provided by government, business or NGOs. Again, the giant mining ventures just alluded to require huge external investments of capital, technical expertise, and management. The roles as outside agents of government and the other two parties are addressed in more detail below.

First, however, attention is turned to constraints also attending the realisation of potentials, and helping to explain why Eastern Indonesia remains so underdeveloped.

Constraints and difficulties

These flow primarily from pervasive market failure (Barlow, p.16), emanating from poor infrastructures including communications and meaning that local peoples do not have information to appreciate market opportunities open to them. The difficulties of outside agents in adjusting to the intricate social situations of local groups exacerbate such constraints, meaning that most communities tend to be left in relative isolation, cut off to a large extent from new developments and openings. The lack of developed local capital markets which people can access to help in exploiting opportunities (Sondakh, p.152) is both a further barrier to development and consequence of isolation. But even given access to capital, both outsiders and locals tend to view proposed economic and social projects as having high risks which consequently discourage positive involvement.

These conditions tend to mean that economic activity promoted from outside is frequently in comprehensive 'packages', including all necessary inputs of capital, skill and management. Hence such packages characterise many government initiatives in Eastern Indonesia, including for instance the coconut improvement schemes described by Sondakh (p.150). But because the society surrounding such schemes cannot command such resource endowments on their own, spread effects and linkages are often very minor. That situation is seen at an extreme in the Irian Jaya mining projects. It is interesting to note similar features on the part of agricultural development schemes in the Philippines, where Balisacan (1993) ascribes to these a lack of linkages and more widespread economic growth.

The problems of outside agents in mediating with local social structures also mean there can be negative externalities when projects go ahead. That is illustrated in cases quoted by Fox (p.171), where traditional marine tenure rights vested in *adat* or *desa* groups were flouted by mobile fishing operators leading to destruction and non-sustainability of resources. But similar circumstances apply to many forestry and minerals ventures, including indeed the Freeport mines.

Yet even given rectification of the many constraints posed by market failure, there are other difficulties that need to be recognised. A major item are high transport charges, which add significantly to total costs of exported items. Such costs appear to be one factor preventing the development of meat processing in the region (Azis, p.119). Another difficulty affecting downstream processing are the large scale economies already achieved by big existing plants in Java and Sumatra that undercut new entrants. This is probably an aspect repressing local vegetable oil processing, and explaining the lack of development noted by Azis (p.118). A further big drawback explored by Djogo (p.181) is that notwithstanding undoubted potentials, many new technologies must still be properly tailored to variable local conditions of the region. As one example, most improved livestock forages coming from overseas remain to be tested rigorously and perhaps bred and developed further for suitability for particular locals. A similar comment applies to most new varieties underlying suggested crop production advances, and indeed to new technologies presently proposed for health and other improvements (N. Mboi, p.196). All such tailoring imposes substantial further costs that have to be taken into account.

Another large constraint perceived by many parties is the nature of government itself as an agent of change. Despite the latter's vital maintenance of stability and huge development contributions detailed in preceding chapters, it is also seen as making improvements hard to effect owing to its centralist nature. While tight central control was certainly justified in earlier years both for reasons mentioned and due to weak regional administrative and absorptive capacities, the latter are now much better and greater devolution is possible (Hill, 1995; p.217). Such devolution should provide more flexibility in the varied Eastern Indonesian situation, with its need for improvement programs adapted to local requirements (B. Mboi, p.137). Devolution should entailing decentralisation to local government levels, and a readiness to respond to experience-in-progress of socio-development programs (p.131). Yet currently the strong centralised apparatus remains notwithstanding plans to the contrary, and traditional 'government culture' ... 'has not changed very much since the departure of the Dutch' (B. Mboi, p.130). There is a 'one-way flow of information from the government to the community', where opinions from sources outside the official structure are not accepted (Marlessy, p.245), and 'mental attitudes' of certain local government officials have not shifted from earlier times (Azis, p.121).

One feature presently associated with central control is the centrally regulated trading environment, which despite recent relaxations still seems to slow possible expansions of exports from Eastern Indonesia. Thus Azis (p.89) points both to maximum quotas on inter-island livestock exports preventing increased production of live animals and the numerous remaining non-tariff barriers. As well Sondakh (p.162) criticises 'the double face of development policy', where measures to increase coconut and other production on the one hand are offset on the other hand by substantial siphoning to the centre of taxes which much reduce local producers' returns. Again, the cloves monopoly introduced from the late 1980s (Sondakh, p160) severely reduces returns of farmers from this crop, slowing what could otherwise be a greater and more profitable expansion.

Then with the top-down *aparatur* extending in its rigid hierarchy from the centre to *desa* and *dusun* levels and imposing centrally devised ideas, there is the difficulty of official activities not being well targeted and performing indifferently owing to lack of community interaction. Such development activities are hard enough, anyhow, and rigidity poses extra constraints on success. Hence Sondakh (1983b) has shown how the Small-farm Coconut Development Project package of credit, fertiliser and hybrid trees, introduced by government and the World Bank without local consultation to raise incomes of selected smallholders from the late 1970s, was basically unsuccessful. It failed owing to farmers' hesitancy over adopting the project package, as well as much higher than expected costs including peoples' losses of income during replanting. It also did not have much spill-over in surrounding non-project areas, while the big burden on limited extension officers in operating the scheme meant that services to these areas were largely withdrawn. Fortunately, officials have often proved adaptable in practical situations, but there are still numerous problems avoidable through more flexible systems. It is pertinent to note that Marlessy comments in similar vein to these criticisms of government on the penchant of the foreign funding agencies financing Indonesian development (p.250) to have rigidities of their own. These agencies frequently insist on their own agendas, where this is at the expense of solving 'real problems' at field level.

It must finally be added that contrary to the views of contributors to this book, influential political forces still wish to maintain strong central control although they may support decentralisation in a token manner. Such forces are indeed working vigorously against any relaxation from the present position.

Soesastro (1990) has pointed out that constraints to development are easier to identify than solutions, and this is undoubtedly valid. Yet while it is crucially important to proceed to solutions, constraints must still be carefully addressed in devising programs for the future. The roles of government, business and NGOs in such improvement programs are now considered.

Government

Here attention must be drawn to gains from deregulation already undertaken by the central government, where these offer strong support for extending that process. Thus Azis (p.111) suggests that recent exchange rate adjustments under the export-oriented strategy have probably improved the position of the many Eastern Indonesian small holders producing tree crops. Most other trade and investment liberalisation measures modelled by Azis also appear beneficial (p.115), although investment deregulation has so far had little perceived effect due to persisting non-tariff barriers which need to be removed. There is no doubt that measures supporting the cloves monopoly (Sondakh, p.160) should be withdrawn.

Central government also has a key role through its financial transfers to Eastern Indonesia and other provinces. Azis (p.96-110) shows in this sphere how *Inpres* grants with their greater regional orientation are superior in effects to DIP sectoral provisions. Azis also asserts that augmented Inpres transfers to Eastern Indonesia would improve that region's relative position. It accordingly seems that changes in these directions for *Inpres* should be given serious attention. A further central measure that can be endorsed is the *Inpres Desa Tertinggal* program (Azis, p.108), which with its chief focus on poor villages and despite Marlessy's (p.247) comments appears to have comparatively good linkages with constituent communities. A connected issue not addressed by contributors but directly impinging on effective decentralisation are routes other than central disbursements for raising the present miserably low provincial government revenues. Thus in 1990, only 11.5 and 7.8 per cent respectively of official *Tingkat I and II* total revenues came from local sources with the balance from the centre (Hill, 1995, p.237). One possibility in mineral and oil rich provinces to allow local governments to retain bigger shares of resource exploitation taxes now flowing mainly to Jakarta.

Regarding decentralisation of government, this should involve the important goals set out by Ben Mboi (pp.131-136), with purposive changes directed towards meeting local needs in a far more autonomous situation. It should certainly not comprise the kind of autonomy described by Mitchell (1970) for the *kabupaten* of 'Utawino', the fictitious name of an actual remote district in Eastern Indonesia (see also Arndt, p.xxix). There autonomy involved a self-sustaining government system maximising its own revenue, but providing little benefit to local populations. Decentralisation containing the devolved responsibilities and greater community interactions outlined by Mboi appears able to much enhance government effectiveness, but must be engineered carefully with key objectives kept well in mind. Unfortunately, the trial decentralisation to *Tingkat II* in nine *kabupaten* of Eastern Indonesia (and 18 elsewhere) does not seem to be going well (Azis, p.120), having been poorly planned and exhibiting inbuilt inclination towards retaining functions at *Tingkat I*. Manifestly, attention should be given to improving this initiative.

Several policy emphases have been suggested by contributors, and can be seen as usefully paralleling and benefiting from both macro-measures of deregulation and moves towards more decentralised administration. Hence there is major need to continue programs of upgrading physical infrastructures, and even more to invest in improved human resource endowments in health and education (N. Mboi, p197, Tirtosudarmo, p.212). Again, research to address the tailoring of new technologies to varying local conditions needs to be actively continued, building on what is a good network of research stations distributed around the region. Once more as part of the human resource development drive, the quality of education and of agricultural, health and other social extension needs to be much further improved, with benefits springing from changes that reduce the rigid top-down hierarchy and allow more interaction with local communities (N. Mboi, p.197   ). NGOs can helpfully assist with agricultural extension in particular, and cooperation with them seems a desirable move from present aloof and suspicious official attitudes. Lastly, government which to some extent has weakened local institutions and *adat* laws (Marlessy, p.245) has one sphere where it needs to intervene and impose its will more strongly. This is in clarifying and enforcing appropriate laws, including for example, those in the marine tenure situations quoted by Fox (p.171).

It is finally appropriate to draw attention to the absence of any significant government or other forum for the Eastern Indonesian region *per se*, hence continuing the historical situation described by Chauvel (p.73). Remedying this was not proposed by any contributors, but is nonetheless important to establishing a cohesive regional identity.

Business

The various constituents of private business, including traders making linkages, small scale industries and giant mineral extraction enclaves (p.256) are vital to economic growth and welfare improvement in Eastern Indonesia. Thus the penetration of trading channels from outside through to local villages is crucial to reducing market failure, and commonly entails a hierarchy of agents handling marketed items at successive levels. Hence with local crops offered for sale, 'collectors' at village level pass them to 'second-level buyers' who transport them to processing factories in Surabaya, Ujung Pandang or elsewhere; they are then distributed to consumers through a further network of retailers. Clearly, trading channels are assisted by better roads, ocean freight and other communications infrastructures, which both reduce costs directly and encourage entry of more agents and greater competition. Yet sometimes in remoter areas especially, 'middlemen' with protected positions in the market do indeed earn excess profits, thereby paralysing local producers and reducing further trade expansion. That situation is also encouraged by regulatory and other activities of local officials, such as the KUDs acting as 'agents of surplus appropriation' in the manner described by Sondakh (p.159). These circumstances support arguments for better infrastructures and more deregulation.

Similar strictures on improved infrastructures and deregulation also apply to the further network of small industries underpinning much economic activity in the Eastern Indonesian region, and providing transportation, processing, retailing and other services including tourism. For resource extraction enclaves the concern is once more with bettering infrastructures, but beyond this a main goal should be securing enhanced spill-overs to local communities, both through tax transfers and other more directly engineered efforts.

It is significant as well to note that while private investment rates in Eastern Indonesia as a whole have recently exceeded the national average (Azis, p.89), this trend needs to be further encouraged while obstacles to investment are removed. Investment is again often deterred by insufficient infrastructures, while those looking from the centre or overseas at business opportunities face circumstances with little information and accordingly high costs of exploring them with big perceived risks. Under such conditions envisaged returns from possible packages may not even good enough to encourage further investigation of interesting potentials already mentioned. There may too be a tendency because of these difficulties to restrict actual investment to existing growth centres, where infrastructures are more easily available and uncertainty less. Clearly there are good reasons for providing more comprehensive data on possibilities, where this is at least partly a function of government.

Non-government organisations

These groups other than private business have marked promise in helping small improvement projects at village level, especially in places where government services are restricted or hamstrung by top-down characteristics. Such projects notably include introduction of new technologies, being well exemplified by small ventures like the seaweed and goat enterprises described by Radja Haba (p.218) and forage improvements outlined by Djogo (p.231). But they further comprise minor social infrastructures like wells, toilets and other facilities, as well as provision of training in relevant spheres (p.230).

A major characteristic of most NGO projects is the heavy involvement of local people, meaning that community needs are usually well targeted and villagers' contributions in terms of labour, materials and other resources are large. Because of the latter, dependence on external support is characteristically lower than in government projects, with consequently lesser outside costs (Djogo, p.223) and high benefit-cost ratios to external investments. Yet even given such cash advantages of NGOs their task in development remains hard, as illustrated by Vel's (1994) fascinating account of adjustments made by the Propelmas NGO in working effectively with an 'indigenous economy' in Sumba.

NGOs with their long previous history in Eastern Indonesia (Djogo, p.222) range in size from small localised groups entailing a leader and several staff serving a few villages to big national organisations like Dian Desa and Bina Swadaya; the latter are centred in Java, but have branches in most Eastern Indonesian provinces and a number of projects in each. In between there are medium-sized NGOs of 20-40 staff such as Ie Rai with its coverage of problems throughout the island of Savu (Radja Haba, p.216) and Yayasan Tana Nua operating in a broader sphere (Djogo, p. 235). While small local NGOs are usually characterised by good interaction with local groups, they tend to suffer from lack of information and low technical expertise, as well as great vulnerability to shocks stemming from low asset bases. Their technical problems are exacerbated by characteristic independence, and accompanying reluctance to seek advice from other NGOs or government sources.

The larger NGOs may be seen to exhibit economies of scale, as where Ie Rai in its seaweed project was able to retain outside technical advisers (Radja Haba, p.219) and use a marketing arm to sell the new product. They also have greater willingness for cooperation, as again shown by Ie Rai in its collaboration with government to develop goats (Radja Haba, p.220) and by Yayasan Tana Nua in its cooperation with World Neighbours (Djogo, p.234). The big national NGOs can additionally benefit from central marketing and technical specialists, who apply their expertise at local levels as needed. It should be added, however, that these economics of medium and big NGOs are to some extent offset by a lesser effectiveness in liaising with local communities.

It seems that the performance of small NGOs in particular could be much improved by more cooperation, both with other non-government groups and with government (Djogo, p.229). Thus cooperation between NGOs could usefully include more assistance in training and marketing, partly under the auspices of umbrella groups like YPMD-Irja in Irian Jaya

(Marlessy, p.248). Official cooperation could involve more active inclusion of NGOs in government development programs, as well as help with transfers of technology from the network of central and provincial research institutes. Government in doing this would have itself to adjust to better accommodate developmental NGOs, which certainly do not pose the threat sometimes perceived. Yet cooperation with government is a tricky sphere, which can lead at its worst to undue official influence over activities and the undermining of NGOs' special virtues in securing community cooperation. That has been well illustrated by Lee (1995), in a study embracing the activities of NGOs in Sumba.

Main policy needs

What, then, are the main policy and development needs in the economic and social improvement of Eastern Indonesia? These are now summarised in light of prior discussions.

Manifestly a basic step is to further eliminate market failure through enhancing infrastructures and human resources, where this is clearly a role for government (p.263). Another key thrust is further deregulation of the macro-trading and investment environments (p.262), with concomitant elimination of non-tariff business and other constraints at local levels.

Again, it is crucial to target and turn to account the promising regional potentials for improvement, ranging from upgrading subsistence agriculture (p.257) to raising cash crop performance (p.258) and further undertaking resource exploitation in minerals, oil, and forestry (p.259). Tackling agricultural potentials largely involves government agencies, small business and NGOs, all of which should be encouraged to collaborate more in this important task. Resource exploitation mainly entails big business, which should be motivated towards better local spill-overs through both direct and tax measures (p.265). All business investments should be aided through provision of better information about opportunities available.

Much more decentralisation of government will help in achieving these objectives, with devolution from the centre to the provinces and from *Tingkat I* to *Tingkat II* being systematically pursued (p.263). Effective decentralisation also entails greater government collaboration with other development parties (above), and the firmer local establishment and policing of laws regarding resource use (p.264). There should further be attempts to set up a vehicle embodying Eastern Indonesia regional identity, bringing provincial and other separate groupings together.

In the end the chief thrust for improvement must come from regional peoples themselves, where these have already shown high abilities in adapting to a difficult environment and undertaking economic and social changes. Given adjustments of the nature described, further positive advances can be anticipated. It is hoped that this book provides guidance in this vital process.

References

Agung, Ide Anak Agung Gde, 1985. *Dari Negara Indonesia Timur ke Republik Indonesia Serikat* [From the Nation of Eastern Indonesia to the United Republic of Indonesia]. Yogyakarta Gadjah Mada University Press, .

Anata, Aris and Evi Nurvidya Arifin, 1991. 'Projections of the Indonesian Population: 1990-2020', Demographic Institute of University of Indonesia, Jakarta.

Anderson, Benedict, and Audrey Kahin, (eds.), 1992. *Interpreting Indonesian Politics: Thirteen Contributions to the Debate*. Ithaca: Cornell University Modern Indonesia Project.

Australia, Law Reform Commission, 1994. *The Recognition of Aboriginal Customary Laws*, Report No.31. Canberra: Australian Government Publishing Service.

Azis, I.J., 1994. 'Survey of Recent Developments (Part II)', *Bulletin of Indonesian Economic Studies*, 30(2), 28-37.

―――, 1995. Data secured from the Interregional Social Accounting Matrix, 1990.

Balisacan, A. M., 1993. 'Agricultural growth, Landlessness Off-Farm Employment, and Rural Poverty in the Philippines", *Economic Development and Cultural Change*, 41:587-602.

Bank Indonesia, 1995. *Indonesian Financial Statistics, January.*

BAPPENAS and Ministry of Home Affairs, 1993. *Guidelines for the Program of Poverty alleviation in Desa Tertinggal*, Jakarta.

BAPPENAS, 1992. *Tinjauan Umum Anggaran Pendapatan dan Belanja Daerah (APBD) seluruh Daerah Tkt.I; 1990/1991* [Analysis of Total

Receipts and in Expenditures for all Level I Districts, 1990-91].
Jakarta: BAPPENAS.

Barlow, C., A. Bellis, and K. Andrews, 1991. (eds) *Nusa Tenggara Timur:
The Challenges of Development,* Monograph 12. Canberra:
Department of Political and Social Change, Australian National
University.

Bennett, A.J, 1995. 'Sustainable Land Use', Paper presented to the IUFRO
XX World Congress, Tampere, Finland, July.

Boeky, G., 1991. 'Regional policy in NTT', in Barlow et al (1991), 63-72.

Bidani, B. and M. Ravallion, 1993. 'A regional poverty profile for
Indonesia'. *Bulletin of Indonesian Economic Studies.* 29(3): 37-68.

Biro Pusat Statistik (BPS) 1989-94. *Produk Domestik Regional Bruto
Propinsi Propinsi di Indonesia Menurut Lapangan Usaha* [Gross
Regional Domestic Product of Provinces in Indonesia by Industrial
Origin, 1988-93]. 1988-93 Survei Industri, Jakarta.

———, 1990. *The Census, 1990.* Jakarta.

———, 1991. *Results of the 1990 Population Census - Series SNo.2.*
Jakarta.

———, 1992a. *Nilai Tukar Petani Seluruh Propinsi Luar Jawa, 1987- 1990
[Value of Farmers Trade for All Provinces outside Java, 1987-90].*
Jakarta.

———, 1992b. *Survei Perkebunan Rakyat 1991* [Survey of Small estates,
1991]. Jakarta.

———, 1993a. *Statistical Pocketbook 1993.* Jakarta.

———, 1993b. *Statistik Lingkungan Hidup Indonesia, 1992.* [Statistics on
Indonesian Living Standards]. Jakarta.

———, 1993c. *Womens' Indicators, 1991 and 1993.* Jakarta.

———, 1994. *Labour Force Situations in Indonesia, 1994.* Jakarta.

———, 1995a. *1993 Agricultural Census: Land Holding Farmers' Sample
Census.* Jakarta.

———, 1995b. *Buletin Ringkas* [Circular Bulletin], February, Jakarta.

————, 1995c. *Indikator Kesejahteraan Rakyat, 1994* [Indicators of Peoples' Welfare, 1995], Jakarta

————, 1995d. *Statistical Year Book of Indonesia.* 1994. Jakarta.

————, 1995e. Miscelaneous Data from *Susenas (Survei Sosio-ekonomi Nasional)*, Jakarta.

Budiman, Arif, (ed.), 1990. *State and Civil Society in Indonesia,* Monash Papers on Southeast Asia. Melbourne: Monash University.

Chauvel, Richard, 1990. *Nationalists, Solidiers and Separatists,* Leiden: KITLV Press.

Dhakidae, Daniel, 1995. *'Pendekatan Historis Terhadap Pembangunan Di Ngada Flores',* [An Historical Approach to Development of Ngada, Flores], Paper presented at the *Strategi Optimasi Pembangunan Pertanian Menunjang Pengembangan Kawasan Terpadu di Kabupaten Ngada-NTT*, Mbay, Flores.

Dick, H. W. 1975a. *'Prahu* shipping in Eastern Indonesia, Part I', *Bulletin of Indonesian Economic Studies*, XI, 2, 69-107.

————, 1975b. 'Prahu shipping in Eastern Indonesia, Part II, *Bulletin of Indonesian Ecomic Studies,* XI, 3, 81-103.

Djamin, A. (ed.), 1991. *Prosiding Seminar Ekonomi Perkalapcaan* [Proceedings of the Seminar about Personal Economy], Batam.

Djiwandono, J. Soedradjad, 1995. *'Meningkatkan Daya Saing dan Efisiensi Ekonomi Indonesia'* [Enhancing the Competitiveness and Efficiency of the Indonesian Economy]. Paper delivered to the 8th Plenary Meeting of the Indonesian Economists Association, Manado, July.

Djogo, A.P.Y., 1990. 'Yayasan Geo Meno and Its Work in the Village of Gerodhere, Flores, Indonesia', Network Paper 10e, Social Forestry Network, London: Overseas Development Institute.

————, 1992. *The Possibilities of Using Local Drought Resistant and Multipurpose Trees and Shrubs Species as an Alternative to Lamtoro (Leucaena leucocephala)*, Working Paper No. 32. Honolulu: East-West Center.

————, 1994a. 'Asian and Indonesian Experiences of Sustainable Development: Working with the Participation of The Poor Population in Small Scale Farming Systems Improvement Program'. Paper presented to the International Meeting on Poverty and Environment Alternatives Against Destruction. POEMA-UFPA. Belem, Brazil.

————, 1994b. 'Management of Mountain Watershed and Forest Resources: Agroforestry in Mountain Development'. Paper presented to the Regional Conference on Sustainable Development of Fragile Mountain Areas of Asia. ICIMOD, Kathmandu, Nepal.

Economic and Social Commission for Asia and the Pacific (ESCAP), 1994. *Resources Development in Asia and the Pacific: Its Social Dimension*, Bangkok.

Eldridge, P. J., 1995. *Non-government Organisations and Democratic Participation in Indonesia*, Kuala Lumpur: Oxford University Press.

Esbruck, D. and N.L. Kana, 1990. Development Program of Four Dioceses, Irian Jaya.

Esbruck, D. and N.L. Kana, 1990. Integrated Development Program, Irian Jaya: Evangelical Christian Church of Irian Jaya.

Fane, G. and T. Coudon, 1995. 'Trade Reforms in Indonesia, 1987-94'. Paper presented to the Conference on *Building on Success: Maximizing the Gains from Deregulation*, Jakarta, April.

Fox, J.J., 1977. *Harvest of the Palm*, Cambridge: Harvard University Press.

————, 1988. 'The Historical Consequences of Changing Patterns of Livelihood on Timor', in D. Wade-Marshall and P. Loveday, *Contemporary Issues in Development*. Darwin: North Australia Research Unit.

————, 1992. 'Report on Eastern Indonesian Fishermen in Darwin', in Occasional Paper Series No.1 (*Illegal Entry*), Centre for Southeast Asian Studies, Darwin: Northern Territory University.

————, 1995. 'Australia's Relations with Indonesia: The Case of the Eastern Indonesian Fishermen', in A.C. Milner (ed.), *Australia in Asia*. Kuala Lumpur: Oxford University Press.

Furnivall, J. S., 1976. *Netherlands India: A Study of Plural Economy*. Amsterdam: B.M. Israel BV.

Gaffar, Afan, 1992a. '*Politik Akomodasi: Islam dan Negara di Indonesia*' [Political Accommodation: Islam and the State in Indonesia], *Prospektif*, 4(1), 8-6.

Gaffar, Afan, 1992b. *Javaenese Voters: A Study of Election Under a Hegemonic Party System in Indonesia.* Yogyakarta: Gadjah Mada University Press.

Gaffar, Afan, 1994. *'Lembaga Kepresiden Indonesia'* [The Institution of the Presidency in Indonesia]. Paper presented at a seminar conducted by Gadjah Mada Student Council, Yogyakarta, April.

Geertz, C., 1963. *Agricultural Involution : The Process of Ecological Change in Indonesia,* Berkeley: University of California Press.

Glassburner, B., 1985. 'Macroeconomics and The Agricultural Sector', *Bulletin of Indonesian Economic Studies* 21(2):51-73.

Hardjono, J., 1994. 'Resource Utilisation and the Environment', in Hal Hill (ed.), *Indonesia's New Order. The Dynamics of Socio-economic Transformation.* Sydney: Allen and Unwin, pp.26-50.

Hardjono, Suhardi and H, Kasim 1993. *Data Penting Tanaman Pangan* [Important Data about Cash Crops], Pusat Penelitian dan Pengembangan Tanaman Pangan, Badan Litbang, Jakarta: Departamen Pertanian.

Hill, H. and C.Williams, 1989. 'The Economic and Social Dimensions of Regional Development in Indonesia', *Ekonomi dan Keuangan Indonesia*, 37(2):191-218.

Hill, Hal, (ed.), 1989. *Unity and Diversity: Regional Economic Development in Indonesia Since 1970.* Singapore: Oxford University Press.

Hill, H. (ed.), 1994. *Indonesia's New Order. The Dynamics of Socio-economic Transformation,* Sydney: Allen and Unwin.

Hill, H., 1995. *Southeast Asia's Emerging Giant: Indonesian Ecomomic Policy and Development since 1966.* Cambridge: Cambridge University Press.

Hugo, Graeme, 1993a. 'Population Mobility Issues'. Paper presented to the Seminar on Development Implications of Population Trends in Asia, Canberra: Australian National University.

————, 1993b. 'Indonesian Labour Migration to Malaysia: Trends and Policy Implications', *Southeast Asian Journal of Social Science*, 21(1):36-70.

Indonesia 1993. *Garis-garis Besar Haluan Negara (GBHN) Republik Indonesia* [Broad Outline of State Policy]. Surabaya: Bina Pustaka Tama.

Indrawati, Sri Mulyani and Muhkamad Ichsan, Budi Hikmat, Arief T. Mahmud, Sahminan, 1995. *'Model Inflasi Sebagai Dasar Kebijaksanaan di Sektor Riel and Moneter'* [An Inflation Model as a Basis for Policies in the Real and Monetary Sectors]. Jakarta: Lembaga Penyelidikan Ekonomi dan Masyarakat.

Jamal, S. and Pomp, M., 1993. 'Smallholder Adoption of Tree Crops in Sulawesi', *Bulletin of Indonesian Economic Studies*, 29(3): 69-94.

James, William E, 1995. 'Indonesia: Non-oil and Non-gas Export Performance in 1994', a report of the TIP Project, Jakarta: Ministry of Trade, Republic of Indonesia.

Jones, G. W. and Y. Rahardjo, 1995.(eds). *People, Land and Sea. Development Challenges in Eastern Indonesia.* Jakarta: PPT-LIPI and ANU Demography Program.

Kano, Hiroyoshi, 1995. *Sentralisme Keuangan dan Prospek Pembangunan Daerah Otonom di Indonesia,* [Financial Centralism and Prospects for Autonomous Regional Development in Indonesia], in Rachbini, D. (ed.), *Negara dan Kemiskinan di Daerah* [The State and Regional Poverty], Jakarta.

Lai, C.K, 1993. 'Overview of Participatory Methods and Techniques for Agroforestry Training and Research'. Paper presented to the Regional Training Workshop for Technical and Extension Level Agroforestry Trainers in the Asia Pacific. Khonkaen, Thailand.

Lavalin International Inc. & PT. *Hasfarm Dian Konsultan, 1987. Regional Development Planning for Irian Jaya.* Jakarta: United Nations Development Program.

Lee, J. 1995. Participation and Pressure in the Mist kingdom of Sumba. A local NGO's Approach to Tree Planting, Canberra.

Liddle, A. W., 1992. 'Regime In Crisis: Presidential Succession, The East Timor Massacre, and Prospects for Democratisation in Indonesia'. Paper presented to the 44th Annual Meeting of the Association of Asian Studies, Washington D.C., April.

Lim, T. G., 1986. 'Policies and Priorities in Human Resources Development for Asia and the Pacific'. Paper presented to the seminar on Human Resources Development in Asia and the Pacific: its Social Dimension, Bangkok: ESCAP.

Manning, C., A. Mende, and D. Rudd, 1989. *Outer Eastern Indonesia: an Exploratory Survey of Population Dynamics and Regional Development*, Discussion paper No.22. Adelaide: Flinders University: Centre for Development Studies.

Mantra, I.B., 1992. 'Patterns and Trends of Population Mobility in Indonesia, 1990'. *Populasi*, 2 (3):40-59.

Mauldon, R., 1994. 'Price Policy', in Williams, D.B. (ed.), *Agriculture in the Australian Economy*, Sydney: Sydney University Press. pp,.87-102.

Mboi, Nafsiah, 1989. 'Capacity Building in Indonesia: The Case of PKK, the Village Family Welfare Movement, in the Province of Nusa Tenggara Timur, Indonesia'. Paper presented to the UNICEP Symposium on National Capacity Building for Child Survival and Development in Africa, Nairobi.

————, 1993. 'Urban Women in Indonesia: Some Issues of Work and Health'. Paper presented to the Seminar on Women in Urban Areas organised by the UN Division for the Advancement of Women, Santa Domingo.

————, 1993. *'Wanita dan Persoalan Gender dalam Pembangunan Kawasan Timur Indonesia'* [Women and Gender in the Development of Eastern Indonesia]. Paper presented to the seminar on Women, Science, and Technology in the Development of Eastern Indonesia, Manado: Sam Ratulangi University.

————, 1994. 'Gender and Women's Health in Urban Indonesia: New Priorities for the 21st Century'. Paper prepared for the Takemi Program in International Health, Cambridge: Harvard School of Public Health.

————, 1995. 'Immunisation and the War Against the Child Killers of Nusa Tenggara Timur (NTT), Indonesia'. Paper prepared for discussion, Ankara.

Metzner, J.K., 1976. *Agriculture and Population Pressure in Sikka, Isle of Flores,* Development Studies Centre, Monograph No. 28. Canberra: The Australian National University.

————, 1983a. 'The Old in the New. Autochtonous Approach Towards Stabilizing An Agroecosystem , The Case of Amarasi, Timor', *GEO Abstract D* [Social and Historical Geography)].

————, 1983b. 'Innovations in Agriculture Incorporating Traditional Production Methods: the Case of Amarasi (Timor)', *Bulletin of Indonesian Economic Studies,* 19(3): 94-105.

Meyer, P.A. and M. Hardjodimedjo, 1989. 'Maluku: The Modernization of the Spice Islands', in Hal Hill (ed.), *Southeast Asia's Emerging Giant: Indonesian Ecomomic Policy and Development since 1966.* Cambridge: Cambridge University Press, pp.549-565.

Milner, A. C., (ed), 1995. *Australia in Asia,* Kuala Lumpur: Oxford University Press.

Ministry of Finance, 1995. Miscellaneous data, Jakarta.

Ministry of Health, 1995. *Data informasi Kependudukan Menurut Sensus Tahun 1971, 1980, 1990 dan Proyeksi* [Population information from the Censuses of 1971, 1980, 1990 and Projections], Jakarta.

————, 1992. *'Masalah Kesehatan di Indonesia Bagian Timur'* [Health Problems of Eastern Indonesia], Jakarta.

————, 1993. 'The Trend Assessment of Health Development in Indonesia: A Study for Providing Basic Inputs to the Second Long Term Health Development Plan', Jakarta: National Institute of Health Research and Development.

Mitchell, D., 1970. 'Wanokalada: A Case Study in Local Administration', *Bulletin of Indonesian Economic Studies,* 6(2): 76-93.

Morgan, Stanley, 1995. Indonesia: Building on a Firm Foundation, Jakarta.

Nasution, A and W. E. James 1995. 'Future Directions for Economic Policy Reform: Where Are We and Where Do We Go From Here'. Paper presented to the Seminar On *Building on Success: Maximizing the Gains from Deregulation,* Jakarta: The Indonesia Economists' Association and The World Bank, April.

Nasution, Anwar, 1995a. '*Lalu Lintas Modal dan Kebijaksanaan Moneter dalam Era Keterbukaan*' [Capital Movements and Monetary Policy in an Era of Openness]. Conferral Address at the Acceptance of a Professorship at the Faculty of Economics, University of Indonesia, August.

————, 1995b. 'Survey of Recent Developments', *Bulletin of Indonesian Economic Studies,* 31(2): 3-40.

Nazaruddin, L., 1991. 'Perkelapaan di Indonesia Bagian Timur [The Personal Economy in Eastern Indonesia], in A. Djamin (ed.), *Prosiding Seminar Ekonomi Perkalapcaan* [Proceedings of the Seminar about Personal Economy], Batam, pp.102-146.

Ormeling, F. J., 1957. *The Timor problem. A Geographical Interpretation of an Underdeveloped Island.* S Gravenhage: J. B. Woltens, Groningen and Martinus Nijboff.

Pachauri, R.K., 1994. 'The Risks of Exposure: The Challenges of Urban Air Pollution - The Impact of Houshold Energy'. Paper presented to the Second Annual World Bank Conference on Environmentally Sustainable Development, Washington, DC.

Pannell, S. N., 1991. 'Narrative Boundaries, National Horizons: The Politics of Identity in Amaya, Maluku Tenggara, Indonesia. Unpublished PhD thesis, Adelaide: University of Adelaide.

Pellokila, C., S. Field, and E. D. Momuat, 1991. 'Food crops developments in NTT', in Barlow et al (eds), *Nusa Tenggara Timur: The Challenges of Development,* Monograph 12. Canberra: Department of Political and Social Change, Australian National University, pp. 121-144.

Piggin, C., 1991. 'New forage technologies', in Barlow et al, *Nusa Tenggara Timur: The Challenges of Development,* Monograph 12. Canberra: Department of Political and Social Change, Australian National University, pp.105-120.

Rachbini, D., 1995a. *Negara dan Masyarakat dan Dampaknya Terhadap Pembangunan Daerah* [Nation and Peoples and Measures for Regional Development], Jakarta: Sinar Harapan.

Rachbini, D.,(ed.), 1995b. *Negara dan Kemiskinan di Daerah* [The State and Regional Poverty], Jakarta.

Rahardjo, Yulfita and Bayu Setiawan, 1994. '*Indeks Perkembangan Manusia: Irian Jaya*' [An Index of Living Standards, Irian Jaya], *Buletin Pengkajian Masalah Kependudukan dan Pembangunan*, (1-2):1-26.

Rais, Amien, 1995a. '*Suksesi Kepemimpinan Nasional*' [The Succession in National Leadership]. Paper presented to the discussions on The Dynamics of Contemporary Indonesian Democracy, Yogyakarta, June.

Reid, A., 1992. 'Indonesian Fishermen detained in Broome: a Report on the Social and Economic Background', in Occasional Paper Series No.1 (*Illegal Entry*), Centre for Southeast Asian Studies, Darwin: Northern Territory University.

Rondonuwu, O., 1983. 'Economic analysis of intercropping coconut smallholder farms in Minahasa district, Indonesia'. Unpublished Masters thesis, Adelaide: University of Adelaide.

Rumansara, A, 1990. Political Space for NGOs to Promote an Alternative Development Strategy: a Case Study from Indonesia with Special Reference to Irian Jaya, The Hague: Institute of Social Studies.

Russell, Barry C., and Lylah Vail, 1988. *Report on Traditional Indonesian Fishing Activities at Ashmore Key Nature Reserve*, Darwin: Northern Territory Museum of Arts and Sciences.

Schwartz, Adam, 1994. *A Nation in Waiting: Indonesia in the 1990s*. Sydney: Allen and Unwin.

Singh, G.K.S., 1995. 'NGO and Forestry: Dynamic Interactions', Paper presented to the IUFRO XX World Congress, Tampere, Finland.

Soemarwoto, O., 1993. '*Konsepsi Pembangunan Ekonomi Berwawasan Lingkungan dan Penanggulangan Kemiskinan. Makalah pada Konpernas XI*' [Concepts of Economic Development and the Connexion with Poverty Alleviation, An Essay on Konpernas XI]. Paper presented to PERHEPI, August, Jakarta.

Soesastro, Hadi and Mari Pangestu, 1995. '*Deregulasi Paket Mei 1995: Tinjauan dan Arah ke Depan*' [The May Deregulation Package: An Assessment and the Direction Ahead]. Paper presented to a CSIS Seminar, June.

Soesastro, Hadi and Peter Drysdale, 1990. 'Survey of Recent Developments', *Bulletin of Indonesian Economic Studies,* 26(3): 3-44.

Soesastro, Hadi, 1990. 'East Indonesia's Economy: A Challenge Towards the Year 2000', *The Indonesian Quarterly,* 18(3):197.

Sondakh, L. and G. Jones, 1989. 'North Sulawesi : Unexploited Potentials', in Hal Hill, *Southeast Asia's Emerging Giant: Indonesian Ecomomic Policy and Development Ssince 1966.* Cambridge: Cambridge University Press, pp.365-384.

Sondakh, L, 1983a. 'Growth and equity aspects of credit programs for small farm coconut development programs in Sulawesi Utara, Indonesia'. Unpublished Ph.D thesis, Armidale: University of New England.

————, 1983b. *Problems and prospects of the Small-farm Coconut Development Project (SCDP) in North Sulawesi',* Manado: University of Sam Ratulangi Research Centre.

————, 1993. *Disparitas dalam Pembangunan Perekonomian Rakyat* [Disparities in the Development of Peoples' Economy]. Paper presented to the International NGO Forum on Indonesia, Cimacan, September.

————, 1995. 'Deregulation and Its Potential Impacts on Agriculture and Regional Disparity in Indonesia'. Paper presented to the Seminar on *Building On Success: Maximizing the Gains from Deregulation,* ISEI and World Bank, 24 - April, Jakarta.

Strachan, L.W; J.C. Stickings and P.G. Prins, 1990. *Proyek Pengembangan Wilayah Sulawesi* [Project for Development in the Region of Sulawesi]. Direktorat Jendral pembangunan Daerah dengan CIDA, Jakarta.

Sulistyo, H., 1993. *Negara dan Masyarakat Lokal* [The Nation and Local People]. Paper delivered to the International NGO Forum on Indonesian Development, Jakarta.

Sumodiningrat, L., 1995. Private communication, Manado.

Surjadi, Charles, 1994. 'Environmental Problems at Household Levels in Jakarta: Some Selected Findings'. Paper presented to the Second Annual World Bank Conference on Environmentally Sustainable Development, Washington, DC.

Tanter, Richard, 1990. 'The Totalitarian Ambition: Intelligence Organisations in the Indonesian Case', in Arif Budiman, (ed.), *State and Civil Society in Indonesia*, Monash Papers on Southeast Asia. Melbourne: Monash University.

Tirtosudarmo, Riwanto, 1994. *Indonesia: From Transmigration to Human Resources Migration. A Paradigm Shift?*, Jakarta.

UNICED, 1984. *Situation Analyses. Jakarta*, Singapore.

Vel, J., 1994. 'The Uma-economy. Indigenous economies and development work in Lawonda, Sumba (Eastern Indonesia)'. Unpublished Ph.D thesis, University of Wageningen, Wageningen.

Wade-Marshall, D. And P. Loveday, 1988. *Contemporary Issues in Development*, Darwin: North Australia Research Unit.

Wallace, Alfred Russel, 1962. *The Malay Archipelago*. New York: Dover Publications.

Williams, D. B., (ed), 1994. *Agriculture in the Australian Economy*, Sydney: Sydney University Press.

World Bank, 1995. *Indonesia: Improving Efficiency and Equity. Changes in the Public Sector Policy,* Washington, D.C.:World Bank.

————, 1995. *World Development Report,* New York: Oxford University Press.

————, 1993. *Indonesia: Sustaining Development,* Washington, D.C.: World Bank.

————, 1993. *Targeting the poor,* Development Brief No.9, Washington, D.C.: World Bank.

Yayasan Geo Meno, 1991. *Laporan Tahunan. Tahun Anggaran 1990/1992* [Annual Report, 1990/1992 Budget Year], Kupang.

————, 1992. *Laporan Tahunan. Tahun Anggaran 1991/1992* [Annual Report, 1991/1992 Budget Year], Kupang.

Yayasan Tana Nua, 1992. *Laporan Tahunan. Tahun Anggaran 1991/1992* [Annual Report, 1991/1992 Budget Year], Kupang.

Yotopoulos, P.A. and J.B. Nugent, 1976. *The Economics of Development: An Empirical Investigation.* New York: Harper.

INDEX